AN ALETHEA IN HEART PUBLICATION
IN THE SERIES OF

THE LIFE AND WORKS OF ASA MAHAN.

VOLUME XII.

OUT OF DARKNESS INTO LIGHT

REPUBLISHED BY THE EDITOR
RICHARD M. FRIEDRICH
ALETHEA IN HEART
PO BOX 8516
Naples, FL 34101
TruthinHeart.com

2005

THE ASA MAHAN PROJECT.
BY ALETHEA IN HEART MINISTRIES.
THE LIFE AND WORKS OF ASA MAHAN.

Volume
1. Doctrine of the Will. 1847.
2. The System of Mental Philosophy. 1882.
3. A System of Intellectual Philosophy. 1854.
4. The Science of Logic; or an Analysis of the Laws of Thought. 1857.
5. Science of Moral Philosophy. 1848.
6, 7. A Critical History of Philosophy in two Volumes. 1883.
8. The Science of Natural Theology. 1867.
9. Autobiography: Intellectual, Moral, and Spiritual. 1882.
10. The True Believer. 1847.
11. Scripture Doctrine of Christian Perfection. 1837, 1875.
12. Out of Darkness Into Light. 1877.
13. Baptism of the Holy Ghost. 1875.
14. Misunderstood Texts of Scripture. 1876.
15. Life Thoughts on the Rest of Faith. 1872.
16. Lectures on the Ninth of Romans. 1859.
17. The Phenomena of Spiritism; and, Spiritualism a Discussion. 1875.
18. Modern Mysteries Examined and Exposed. 1855.
19. A Critical History of the Late American War. 1877.
20. Miscellaneous Articles, Letters, and Index of the Complete Works.
    Physical and Moral Law Obligatory. 1839.
    The Relation of Christianity in the Freedom of Human Thought and Action. 1849.
    Dr. Mahan's Speech on the Crisis in the Protestant Episcopal Church in America. 1862.
    The Natural and the Supernatural in the Christian Life and Experience. 1878.

Numerous additional articles and literary notices in the following published periodicals:
    OE   The Oberlin Evangelist, 1839-1862
    OQR The Oberlin Quarterly Review, 1845-1848
    BH   Banner of Holiness, 1872-1883
    DL   Divine Life and International Expositor of Scriptural Holiness, 1877-1889

    Reproduction of the complete published writings in hard and soft covers, with detailed indexes. To be available in print individually and in a complete series; as well as on CD with full searching capabilities; also recorded on tapes, CDs, and DVDs. Each sermon and lecture to be made available as individual booklets. Mahan's contributions to *The Oberlin Evangelist*, *Oberlin Quarterly Review*, *Banner of Holiness*, and *Divine Life* included in this.

    Work books and multimedia helps to be created to assist in the private or classroom study of these volumes. A presentation of the influence of Mahan upon the church and world to be given through the *American Reformation Project*.

OUT OF DARKNESS INTO LIGHT;

OR,

THE HIDDEN LIFE MADE MANIFEST

THROUGH FACTS OF OBSERVATION AND EXPERIENCE:
FACTS ELUCIDATED BY THE WORD OF GOD.

BY

REV. ASA MAHAN, D.D.

AUTHOR OF "THE BAPTISM OF THE HOLY GHOST," "THE PROMISE OF
THE SPIRIT," "CHRISTIAN PERFECTION," ETC.

London:
PUBLISHED FOR THE AUTHOR AT THE
WESLEYAN CONFERENCE OFFICE,
2 CASTLE STREET, CITY ROAD, AND 66 PATERNOSTER ROW.

1877.

[*All rights reserved.*]

Ballantyne Press
BALLANTYNE, HANSON AND CO.
EDINBURGH AND LONDON

Mahan, Asa, 1799-1889.

Out of Darkness Into Light: Or, The Hidden Life made manifest through Facts of Observation and Experience: Facts Elucidated by the Word of God.

(The Life and Works of Asa Mahan Volume XII.)

Republication of the 1877 ed. published by the Wesleyan Conference Office.

London.

1. Mahan, Asa, 1799-1889; Spiritual Biography.
2. Christian Character—Experience—Doctrine.
3. Sanctification—Holiness—Evangelism.

Library of Congress Control Number: 2005900074

ISBN 1-932370-73-0   Softcover edition.
ISBN 1-932370-44-7   (Volume XII of *The Life and Works of Asa Mahan*.)

Second Alethea In Heart edition published in 2005. Republished from the edition of 1877, London, without altering anything but page numbers.

Copyright © 2005
Richard M. Friedrich
All Rights Reserved.

To order more copies visit our web site: TruthInHeart.com

EDITOR'S NOTE

This new edition of Out of Darkness Into Light was transcribed from a personal copy of the original 1877 London edition published by the Wesleyan Conference Office. All the punctuation and English spelling has been retained. No changes have been made to the text other than changing the size of the book and therefore the page numbers. This is the second Alethea In Heart publication of this title; and is number XII of the twenty volume series titled, *The Life and Works of Asa Mahan*. When completed, each volume will be available in both hard and soft covers. There will therefore be two identical series with different covers. A similar series publication called, *The Life and Works of Charles G. Finney*, is also being produced by Alethea In Heart (see the last page of this volume for details). These two series compliment each other. Other series and individual works by contemporaries of Mahan, such as the sixteen volume bible commentaries by fellow Oberlin professor Henry Cowles, are also being reproduced. All these reproductions are part of a massive historical project that will help scholars and people know the religious, philosophical, social and political influences on nineteenth century English and American people. This volume is one of the original holiness classics; which not only explains the historic experience of the sanctification of president Mahan and other members of the Oberlin Collegiate Institute, but also describes Mahan's difficult progression from, and abandonment of, the strongholds of fatalistic Calvinistic philosophy. Several other volumes in this series focus on these two themes in different ways. Namely, *Doctrine of the Will; Autobiography: Intellectual, Moral, and Spiritual; Lectures on the Ninth of Romans; Scripture Doctrine of Christian Perfection; Baptism of the Holy Ghost;* and, *Misunderstood Texts of Scripture*.

OUT OF DARKNESS

PREFACE.

BELIEVERS in Jesus, as we read in the Scriptures, are "all children of the light, and children of the day," and are privileged to "walk in the light, as God is the light," God Himself being "their everlasting light, and their God their glory." Thus "walking in the light," they "have fellowship one with another;" and more than this, "with the Father, and with His Son Jesus Christ." Abiding in this light and in this fellowship, their "joy is full," "out of weakness they are made strong," in all conditions of existence they find perfect content, and are "more than conquerors through Him that hath loved us," and "having all sufficiency for all things, are abundantly furnished for every good work." If all this is not true of any believer, it is because he is living below his revealed privileges, and is thus living because he does not "know the things which are freely given us of God." It contradicts every true idea of Christian character, to suppose that a true believer in Christ will "walk in darkness," knowing that he may "walk in the light;" will remain weak, knowing that he may be girded with "everlasting strength;" and will continue "carnal, sold under sin," knowing that he may enjoy "the glorious liberty of the sons of God." The specific and exclusive object of the following treatise is to make known to all who would know and understand their privileges as "the sons of God" and "believers in Jesus," the forms of divine knowledge above referred to. To the prayerful examination of all who are "walking in the light," or are inquiring after the light, the work is commended, with the fervent desire and prayer of the author, that "their joy may be full."

CONTENTS.

PART I.
OUT OF THE PRIMAL LIGHT INTO DARKNESS.

CHAP.	PAGE
I. THE OFFICE AND WORK OF THE SPIRIT IN CONVICTION OF SIN.	13
II. CHARACTER OF THE CONVICTING ILLUMINATIONS OF THE SPIRIT, AS ILLUSTRATED IN MY OWN EXPERIENCE.	16
III. A GREAT TEMPTATION, A FINAL VICTORY, AND ANOINTING.	23
IV. ASSURANCE OF HOPE.	31
V. THE GIFT OF GRACE.	35
VI. THE TRUE AND PROPER FOOD FOR THE LAMBS OF THE FLOCK.	37
VII. THE FAITH OF THE CONVERT AS ECLIPSED, AND RENDERED WEAK AND INOPERATIVE, BY THE EXAMPLE AND TESTIMONY OF OLD DISCIPLES, AND BY FALSE TEACHING AND FALSE INTERPRETATION OF SCRIPTURE.	52
VIII. TRIAL OF FAITH AND TRIUMPH OF PRINCIPLE.	70
IX. LIGHT AND PRINCIPLES RETAINED THROUGH THE ENTIRE CHRISTIAN LIFE.	77
X. A GROWING DIMNESS OF INNER LIGHT, AND A CONSEQUENT FEEBLE AND SICKLY DEVELOPMENT OF THE INNER LIFE.	79
XI. INTENSE STRUGGLES, CONFLICTS, FIGHTINGS, AND INGLORIOUS DEFEATS	82
XII. LIGHT BREAKING IN.	87
XIII. THE LEGAL AND THE CHRISTIAN SPIRIT.	89
XIV. CONSCIOUS DEFICIENCIES OF CHRISTIAN MINISTERIAL QUALIFICATION.	92
XV. PROTRACTED INQUIRIES AFTER THE MYSTERY OF THE HIDDEN LIFE.	96

PART II.
OUT OF DARKNESS INTO LIGHT.

I. THE LIGHT DAWNING.	105
II. THE LIGHT COME, OR THE BRIGHTNESS OF THE DIVINE RISING.	112
III. SPEAKING TO THE PEOPLE WHEN STANDING IN THE LIGHT.	116
IV. THE RENEWING OF THE HOLY GHOST.	125
V. FREE IN CHRIST.	127
VI. JESUS MANIFESTED TO THE BELIEVER.	131
VII. THE PROMISE OF THE SPIRIT, OR THE DOCTRINE OF THE BAPTISM OF THE HOLY GHOST.	134
VIII. RESULTS OF THE BAPTISM RECEIVED.	147
IX. TRIALS OF FAITH, AND VICTORIES BY THE BLOOD OF THE LAMB AND THE WORD OF HIS TESTIMONY	172
X. SUSTAINING AND ANTICIPATORY GRACE.	182
XI. THE INTERCESSORY FUNCTIONS OF THE SPIRIT.	195
XII. CRUCIFIXION AND SANCTIFICATION OF THE PROPENSITIES.	217
XIII. PARENTAL DISCIPLINE OF THE SONS OF GOD.	230
XIV. EVERLASTING CONSOLATION, OR OUR HIGHEST JOYS WELLING OUT OF OUR DEEPEST SORROWS	237
XV. SPIRITUAL DISCERNING AND ENLIGHTENMENT.	249
XVI. THE LETTER AND THE SPIRIT, AND THE FLESH AND THE SPIRIT.	261
XVII. CHRIST IN US, AND CHRIST FOR US.	267
XVIII. RELIGIOUS JOY.	276
XIX. MISCELLANEOUS TOPICS AND SUGGESTIONS---	282
SECT. I. GIVING TESTIMONY IN RESPECT TO FACTS OF PERSONAL EXPERIENCE.	282
SECT. II. PROPOSED REMEDIES FOR PRIDE OF HEART.	284
SECT. III. CONFESSING SIN.	288
SECT. IV. IMPORTANT MISAPPREHENSION.	290
SECT. V. GREAT AND LITTLE FAITH.	294
SECT. VI. WHEN THE GOSPEL WILL EXERT ITS FULL POWER OVER OUR HEARTS AND CHARACTER.	296

OUT OF DARKNESS INTO LIGHT.

INTRODUCTION.

I AM this day seventy-five years of age. Fifty-eight of these years have been professedly spent in the service of Christ. During this period, I have had varied forms of inward experience, and have observed important facts pertaining to the religious life—experiences and facts, a presentation of some of which may be a matter of interest and profit to all believers, to those especially who are now inquiring after, or are walking in, "the glorious liberty of the sons of God." Especially will this be the case when such experiences and facts shall be placed in the clear light of those teachings of inspiration which bear upon such subjects. The period has arrived in the history of the Church, when, in a sense not common in preceding ages, God, by His Spirit, is "revealing His Son in believers," and causing Him to "be formed within them," and to be "in them the hope of glory." Christ, through the Spirit, is "beginning at Moses and all the prophets, and expounding unto us in all the Scriptures the things concerning Himself" and is "opening our understanding, that we may understand the Scriptures." This He is doing not merely in reference "to what is written in Moses, and the Prophets, and the Psalms, concerning Himself" but more especially amid the higher revelations of the New Testament concerning "the riches of the glory of this mystery among the Gentiles, which is Christ in us, the hope of glory." Everywhere the question is being raised, namely, what are our revealed privileges and immunities as believers in Jesus, and as inheritors, through Him, of "the promise of the Spirit?" When these inquiries shall have been fully answered, "the light of the Church will have come, and the glory of the Lord will have risen upon her," and "the Gentiles will come to her light, and kings to the brightness of her rising." Having sojourned for about eighteen years in the dim twilight of that semi-faith which pertains to Christ almost exclusively in the sphere of our justification; and having, during all these years, "inquired and searched diligently," but vainly, for the revealed and promised "liberty of the sons of God;" and having, during about forty years, dwelt and walked in the cloudless sunlight of "assurance of faith" in the same "Jesus, who is of God made unto us wisdom, righteousness, sanctification, and redemption," and who "baptizes with the Holy Ghost," I have thought that a short account of some of the struggles and defeats experienced in the former state, and of "the spoils won in battle" in the latter, might be profitably "dedicated to maintain the house of God." The fixed habit of my life having been naturally a self-reflective one, has, in a special manner, I judge, qualified me in a good measure for the work before me. As a teacher of mental science, I have constantly habituated myself to a careful analysis of my own mental states, for the purpose of a clear understanding of the faculties, susceptibilities, and laws of my own intellectual, sensitive, moral, and spiritual nature, and that for the purpose of knowing universal mind as it is. I have also been in the equally fixed habit of contemplating my own religious states, emotions, sentiments, purposes, and acts, all my inward and outward experiences, in the clear light of the corresponding truths of the Word of God, and this for the purpose of knowing myself as God knows me. I hear much said in condemnation of the habit of scrutinising our feelings and religious states—utterances which I by no means approve. If we look within, and nowhere else, we shall, of course, gain very little self or divine knowledge. When we look without to Christ, however, the distinctness of our vision of His grace and glory is by no means obscured, but rather brightened, by a distinct consciousness of the results of the vision in our internal experiences. We trust in Christ for the fulfilment of some specific promise in our inner life. The conscious experience of the fulfilment of that promise in that inner life becomes to us a new revelation of His trustworthiness, tends to confirm our faith and love, and qualifies us to testify of His faithfulness before the Church and the world. In the absence of this consciousness the chief benefits of our faith would be lost to us. When, on the other hand, we suppose ourselves to be in the exercise of faith, and the promised result does not arise, we should conclude that a re-adjustment of our relations to Christ should occur. "We believe, and therefore speak." We must be conscious of the believing, on the one hand, and of the speaking, on the other; that is, of the fact of faith and its corresponding results, or we can give no such testimony as this. The same holds true in all departments of the Christian life. Self-reflective circumspection is one of the immutable conditions of a genuine Christian life and experience. We must "ponder the paths of our feet," or "our ways will not be established," and "commit our ways unto the Lord," or "He will not direct our steps." How absolute is the command of the Sacred Word that we shall "examine ourselves whether we be in the faith," "prove our own selves," "prove every man his own work," and "be ready always," "with meekness and fear," "to give an answer to every man that asketh us a reason of the hope that is in us." In knowing Christ as He is, and ourselves as in Him, and in knowing Him and ourselves as He is and we are, we are in the only proper conditions for being and becoming all that is required of us. The plan of Christ is that we shall not only "know that we have eternal life," and that "that life is in the Son," but that we shall be as distinctly conscious of the nature and source of that life. In short, that we shall "know whom we have believed," what we have believed, and what is the consequence of our faith. Without further preliminaries, I now proceed to the accomplishment of the work proposed.

LONDON, *Nov.* 9, 1874.

PART I.

OUT OF THE PRIMAL LIGHT INTO DARKNESS.

CHAPTER I.

THE OFFICE AND WORK OF THE SPIRIT IN CONVICTION OF SIN.

THERE are few subjects about which Christians need to be more fully informed, and about which, as it appears to us, they are less instructed, than about the office and work of the Holy Spirit. There are two distinct revealed relations which He sustains to our race—one to the world, "convincing men of sin, of righteousness, and of judgment," and thereby leading them to Christ; and a promised indwelling personal presence in believers "after they have believed," and, as such, a presence "leading them into all truth," "pertaining to life and godliness." According to the express teachings of inspiration, we know, and can know, divine truth in none of its forms but through a divine insight imparted to us through the Spirit. "The things of God knoweth no man, but the Spirit of God." "No man knoweth the Son, but the Father; neither knoweth any man the Father but the Son, and he to whomsoever the Son will reveal Him;" and the revealed mission of the Spirit is to "take of the things of Christ and *show* them unto us," and to '*show* us plainly of the Father." So distinctly and fully did the apostles recognise their absolute dependence upon the Spirit for right and full apprehensions of divine truth in all its forms, that they teach us that "no man," with any proper apprehensions of the divine import of the words he employs, "can even say that Jesus is the Christ, but by the Holy Ghost."

Individuals are in danger of so preaching Christ, that the hearer, in seeking the knowledge of Him, and a union with Him, is in peril of forgetting his dependence upon the Spirit for the knowledge and union sought after, and of so preaching the Spirit as to induce a forgetfulness of the fact, that the mission of the Spirit is, not to "speak of Himself;" but to "reveal Christ in us," and to "lead us into all truth," and that we are to seek "the baptism of the Holy Ghost," and His continued presence and illumination, as a means to an end, namely, that we may "behold with open face the glory of the Lord," "comprehend with all saints what is the breadth, and length, and depth, and height, and know the love of Christ, which passeth knowledge, that we may be filled with all the fulness of God," "be led into all truth," and "abide in the Son and in the Father." If we seek to know Christ, without recognising our dependence upon the Spirit for that knowledge, or for the abiding presence of the Spirit in our hearts, without seeking such presence as a means of knowing Christ, we shall, in either case alike, fail of our object. If, on the other hand, we seek to "know the only true God, and Jesus Christ whom He hath sent," and seek this as a means of attaining to "the eternal life" which results from that knowledge, and seek "the Promise of the Spirit" as a means of obtaining this knowledge and "the life eternal" thence resulting, we shall not fail of the divine end which we seek. The Church of Christ is the school of God; the things to be learned there are "the things of God;" and the only Being or Teacher in that school who knows these things, and can impart to us a real knowledge of them, "is the Spirit of God." When we seek a knowledge of these things in filial dependence on our great Teacher, "the Spirit of God," we "shall know the things which are freely given us of God," and "which He hath purposed for them that love Him."

The characteristics of the knowledge which we receive of the truth, through the teachings of the Spirit, require a passing notice in this connection. Our apprehensions of divine truth assume two forms—that of *belief*, characterised by greater or lesser degrees of conscious certainty; and that of *absolute knowledge*, which, like our demonstrative convictions, utterly exclude all doubt. The latter is the form of knowledge always obtained through the illuminations of the Spirit.

Under His illuminations we not only believe in, but "*know* God and Jesus Christ whom He hath sent;" we "*know* that we have eternal life;" we '*know* the things which are freely given us of God;" and '*behold* with open face the glory of the Lord." In His convicting illuminations, the truth of God becomes "a *discerner* of the thoughts and intents of the heart;" that is, the sinner has a direct, intuitive, and absolute knowledge of his own heart, his own moral self and moral life, as God sees it. In such convictive process two distinct revelations of truth are simultaneously made to the mind—God in His moral purity and excellence, and in His sovereign claims upon our supreme obedience and regard, on the one hand, and the heart and moral life as related to God's purity, excellency, and absolute authority, on the other. As God and the heart are thus set over against each other before the mind, it is made to know, and that absolutely, the utter godlessness, sinfulness, and infinite criminality of its unregenerate life. The sinner absolutely and intuitively recognises himself as having been, as an offspring of God, in God's world, and as having been under infinite obligations to have sought the knowledge of Him, and to have rendered supreme obedience to His will, and yet to have been literally and utterly "Without God in the world," and to have entertained no respect for His will or character. It is under such convictions that men are brought to the exercise of "repentance towards God, and faith towards our Lord Jesus Christ."

CHAPTER II.

CHARACTER OF THE CONVICTING ILLUMINATIONS OF THE SPIRIT, AS ILLUSTRATED IN MY OWN EXPERIENCE.

The Wanderer Lost through Misdirection.

I WILL now elucidate the above statements by a reference to facts of my own experience. When, at the age of seventeen years, and while engaged in teaching school, I was led, during the progress of a revival of religion which occurred in the place where I then was, to think with deep seriousness upon "the things which concerned my peace," I was made distinctly conscious that the final question of my soul's eternity was then and there to be determined. Hence the intensity of interest with which I contemplated the result of that divine visitation. Having from childhood been educated amid "the straitest sect" of the Calvinistic faith, regeneration, the beginning and source of the religious life, was regarded by me, and rightly so, if I had been correctly taught, as a change of the moral and spiritual *nature* of the soul—a change in which the creature is wholly passive, and which is the exclusive result of a sovereign act of God; and the question whether that change was to be wrought in me, depended not at all upon what I should or could do, but upon a decree immutably fixed in the Divine mind from eternity. My whole being was consequently centered upon the inquiry, not what I should, but what God would do in the matter of the change referred to? I began to pray, and did so, not knowing whether I was acting for my good or ill, but under the distinct impression, having ever been so taught, that with God "even my prayers were an abomination." No one urged upon me "repentance toward God, and faith toward our Lord Jesus Christ;" but all held before me the sovereign election of God, and His exclusive agency in regeneration. In one of the meetings, we were absolutely assured, in so many words, that if we had not been from eternity elected to eternal life, our salvation was impossible. This, as the speaker afterwards informed me, he said especially on my account. I conversed much with Christians and ministers, and that not to learn what "I should do to be saved," having been absolutely taught that I could do nothing whatever effective in the matter, but to know from their experience whether God was, or was not, likely to produce in me the regenerating change under consideration; and whether, if I was to be saved, the period of that change was near or remote. Thus inquiring, and thus waiting, the agony of suspense which I endured deepened at length into the rayless midnight of blank despair. During the many days and nights in which I wandered on in this "blackness of darkness," I came to understand fully the meaning of those words of inspiration, "In the evening thou shalt say, would God it were morning; and in the morning, would God it were evening." Each hour, between the setting and the rising of the sun, seemed an eternity; and I would say to myself, "I would give the universe, did I possess it, if I could see the sun once more." As soon as I saw his face, I would exclaim, "I would give the universe if I could see him set in darkness again." The fountain of life was dried up within me, and I often said to myself, "Were all the world mine, I would freely part with it for the privilege of shedding a single tear." At length all my sensibilities seemed to fail, and I descended into a state of almost emotionless despondency. While in this state, I went home and spent an evening with my mother. I told her that I had but one desire, and that was to be a Christian. I was absolutely assured, however, that I was not one of the elect; that God, consequently, would never regenerate me; and that she must expect to see her only son thereafter, not as he had been, but as a reckless reprobate in the world. To me no other destiny seemed possible. She insisted that the change had already occurred in my inner life. But so I viewed my own condition and prospects.

The Great Revelation, and consequent Passage from Death unto Life.

I had continued in this state but a short time, when a new revelation—I know not what else to call it—was made to my mind—an open vision of the character, glory, and love of God on the one hand, and of my own entire moral or spiritual life on the other. In this manifestation I apprehended, with absolute distinctness, God as having ever loved me with a more than parental love, and as having ever been ready to receive me, pardon me, love me, and care for me, as a child, had I confessed my sin to Him, implored His pardoning mercy, and sought His favour. In the light of the face of God as turned towards me, I saw with equal distinctness that my whole heart and entire moral life had been in total alienation and estrangement from Him. I had never sought to know Him, or asked for His favour and care; had never recognised His parental love and kindness; had never entertained the least respect for His will, sought to please Him in anything, or done the right or avoided the wrong, because He required it. In other words, my entire moral life had been an utterly godless one. Every moral act of my entire existence, whether such act had been, without reference to the motive or intent which prompted it, in the form and direction of the right or the wrong, "evil, and only evil continually." Not an act of my life had been performed from that sacred respect for the will of God and the law of duty—the respect which renders, or can render, any act morally virtuous. In other words still, I saw with perfect distinctness that the moral depravity of my entire moral life had been total and absolute. At the same time I perceived, with equal distinctness and absoluteness, the infinite *criminality* and *ill-desert* of such a life, and its utter forfeiture of the Divine favour to eternity; that, in consequence of a life of such utter voluntary alienation and estrangement from such a Being—a Being of such ineffable love, glory, purity, and perfection, and Him, too, my Creator, my Redeemer, my Preserver, and infinite and boundless Benefactor—that for such alienation and estrangement from such a Being, I had utterly forfeited all claims to His mercy and favour, both now and for an eternity to come. On this subject I had no more doubt than I had of my own existence. Under these convictions my mind turned with shame from the face of God, and, with utter reprobation upon my own moral self and life. "I abhorred myself and repented as in dust and ashes." At that time, not knowing what my God would do with me, I said distinctly and definitely, that if God should "cast me off for ever," I would stand before the universe and affirm the sentence to be just. The thought of *continuing* in such alienation and estrangement from such a Being became also more to be reprobated and fearful in my regard than perdition itself. In this state of mind, when alone with God, "I bowed the knee" before Him, and confessed that I had no right to ask or expect any favour at His hands, and that my whole eternity hung upon His mere grace and mercy. One favour I would venture to ask, that I might be kept from ever returning to that state of alienation from Him in which my life had been spent, and that I might have grace to appreciate His love, excellence, and glory; to love and venerate Him, and have a sacred respect for His will. If He would grant me this, I would accept of anything in time and eternity that He might appoint me. This was the exact substance and form of that prayer. I had no sooner pronounced these words, than I was consciously encircled in "the everlasting arms." I was so overshadowed with a sense of the manifested love of a forgiving God and Saviour, that my whole mental being seemed to be dissolved, and pervaded with an ineffable quietude and assurance. I arose from my knees without a doubt that I was an adopted member of the family of God. With "the peace of God, which passeth all understanding," pervading every department of my mental nature, I could look upward, and, without a cloud between my soul and the face of God, could and did say, "My Father and my God." Such was my entrance into the inner life. Let us now consider

Certain important Lessons taught by the Facts above Presented.

The Nature of Sin.—If we would understand sin as God regards it, we should contemplate it just as the Spirit presents it to the mind when He induces conviction of sin. Sin, as the Spirit of God convicts us of it, is always apprehended as exclusively a *personal* matter, a state of the inner man, a form of voluntary moral activity, on account of which the soul has justly forfeited the eternal favour, and as justly incurred the endless displeasure of God. As revealed to the mind by the Spirit, and the conscience enlightened by the Spirit, sin and infinite ill-desert, a hopeless forfeiture of the favour of God, are inseparably united. God is apprehended as having, on account of His relations to us as our Maker, Redeemer, Preserver, and infinite Benefactor, and, also on account of His infinite natural and moral perfections, infinite claims upon our love, veneration, and obedience. The soul is also revealed to itself as having been, in all its moral activities, in voluntary alienation and estrangement from all the claims of God and of His moral law upon it. The soul is revealed to itself as having come into this state, and continued in it, not from necessity, but choice. In my own case, for example, I was convicted of no sin of my ancestry, near or remote, and of no form or degree of demerit for anything which did attach to me personally, and to no one else but myself. Nor was I convicted of ill-desert for anything in or about myself but alienation and estrangement from God, His character, His will, and the law of duty—alienation and estrangement in which I was consciously voluntary. The same holds in all other cases. Under the convicting power of the Spirit, every man is convicted of personal criminality, and nothing else; of "knowing God and not glorifying Him as God;" of knowing Him as our Maker, Preserver, Redeemer, and infinite Benefactor, and yet withholding gratitude from Him, of knowing His will, and refusing obedience to it. Every individual, also, when convicted by the Spirit of sin, or of voluntary estrangement from God, from His will, and the law of duty, apprehends, with absolute distinctness, that that estrangement has been *total*, and has been equally so in respect to all forms of moral activity, whether externally right or wrong. When the Spirit renders the truth "a discerner of the thoughts and intents of the heart," every man, whatever the visibilities of his life may have been, and however amiable certain of his natural temperaments may have been, perceives with perfect absoluteness that no moral act of his unregenerate life was prompted by that motive and intent which render such act morally virtuous, or such that the conscience or God can regard, or ought to regard, as an act of obedience to the Divine will and the law of duty. Regeneration is not an advance from a low state of moral goodness to one that is higher, but an entrance into a state *entirely new*. The words of inspiration, "If any man be in Christ, he is a new creature; old things have passed away, and behold, *all* things have become new," are just as true of any one man as of any other; and this passage from the old state to the new is just as immutably necessary to eternal life in the case of any one unregenerate man as it is in that of any other. Any other view of sin, or of the natural state of man, is in open contradiction to all that Christ, Moses, the prophets, apostles, and the Eternal Spirit, teach us of "what is in man."

Reasons of the Objections of Individuals to the Evangelical Faith.

We now perceive the reason of the *objections which individuals entertain to the principle and doctrines of the evangelical faith*. All such objections take their origin and form from a want of a true apprehension of sin, and of the actual condition of man as sinner. When any individual, whatever his previous views may have been, apprehends sin as it is, sin as God and the conscience divinely enlightened view it, when any man perceives his own moral life as it stands related to the will of God and the law of duty, all his objections to the doctrines of the Trinity, atonement, salvation on the condition of "repentance towards God and faith towards our Lord Jesus Christ," and "eternal judgment," disappear at once. When man knows himself as he is, he becomes absolutely conscious that that faith, with all its revelations, must be true, or he is hopelessly lost. A very highly-educated and intelligent unbeliever, for example, once listened to a discourse which we delivered on the subject of regeneration. In that discourse, the actual character of the natural man was set forth, and the necessity of the change, represented by the term regeneration was verified. The truth, as presented, he afterwards stated, "commended itself to his conscience." On his way from the house of God, these thoughts passed through his mind: "What a fool I have been! If I had this religion, what injury could it do me? It might, on the other hand, be to me an eternal benefit." With these thoughts pressing upon his mind, he on the next Sabbath listened to a discourse from the text, "By the deeds of the law shall no flesh living be justified: for by the law is the knowledge of sin." In that discourse the nature of the moral law, and man's relations as a sinner to that law, were as clearly elucidated as we were able to do it. As the man listened to these expositions, he said to himself, This, as I absolutely know, is the moral law, and these are my conscious relations to that law. If, now, there is no redemption for me in Christ, I am without hope for eternity." Thus, through "the knowledge of sin," he was led directly to Christ, and few men ever evinced a purer faith in Christ than did this man in his subsequent life. Hence it is that the Spirit first convinces of sin, as the means of inducing faith in Christ as a saviour from sin. Such, also, is the fixed tendency and aim of all true preaching of "the everlasting gospel." A ministry whose fundamental aim, and the fixed tendency of whose ministrations are not to convince men of their sin, and hopeless ruin in sin, and thus to lead them to Christ, is "a plant which our heavenly Father has not planted."

The Witness of the Spirit.

We may now understand also, in one of its essential forms, "the witness of the Spirit" to our sonship with God. Much is said upon this and kindred subjects in the New Testament. When, as shown above, I, for example, was brought into a certain state of utter self-abandonment and dependence upon the mercy and grace of God in Christ, I was made absolutely conscious that God had pardoned and accepted me. I was as absolutely—I could not tell how—assured of this, as I was that I existed at all. This, as I understand it, is one of the forms in which "the Spirit bears witness with our spirits that we are the sons of God." The Spirit, and He only, knows when we are accepted, and He only can make us absolutely conscious of the fact. When, in connection with implicit faith and consecration on our part, He manifests God to us as our Father and portion, then "the Spirit bears witness with our spirit," our conscious trust and consecration "that we are the sons of God." When He imparts to us "full assurance of faith," "full assurance of hope," and "full assurance of understanding," we have the witness of the Spirit that we are being "taught of God," and are, consequently, "His sons and daughters."

CHAPTER III.

A GREAT TEMPTATION, A FINAL VICTORY, AND ANOINTING.

For some months after I had found peace and assurance of acceptance, my spiritual state was rather of a *negative* than *positive* character. I had become dead to the desire of wealth, and all my plans of ambition—plans which I had, with the intensest interest, cherished from childhood up—were wholly relinquished. Even the idea of acquiring a liberal education—the cherished thought of my young life ever since the subject had been suggested to my mind—was wholly dropped out of my regard. One thought only possessed my whole being—that of "walking with God," and this in the retired circle of private life. Had I been educated in the Catholic faith, my controlling religious tendencies, had nothing occurred to give them a higher directions, would have unquestionably drawn me in the direction of monastic retirement. I had not continued long in this state before the aspirations of my old nature began to revive, and to draw me with greater and greater strength in the backward direction towards the worldly life. This influence reached its highest power in the early spring; and on the day of the town and state elections, when all my young associates were assembled, under my eye, and in the immediate presence of my father's dwelling—assembled for those amusements in which I had formerly so intensely delighted, it seemed that the concentrated powers of "the world, the flesh, and the devil," and that in their accumulated strength, were brought to bear upon my young and susceptible mind, to induce me to join that company, and, in doing so, to make a final choice of the worldly, instead of the religious life. As soon as I had completed the task assigned me, I turned for the forest, and, in the heart of the same, spent the day with God. There, in deep "fellowship with the Father and with His Son Jesus Christ," I became "crucified to the world, and the world to me." From that good hour I have never felt the least temptation to return to the worldly life. In that "house of God and gate of heaven," also, my Christian life passed over from the negative to a *positive* state. I became distinctly conscious that I was called of God to be in the world as Christ was in the world, to do all I could to bring the world back to God. I then and there felt myself girded for the purposes of that calling with a strength not my own. I left that forest with the distinct consciousness that I was a dedicated servant of Christ, and was endued with a divine power for that service—a power of which I had never heard before, and knew not by what name to call. That dedication has remained. Becoming early conscious that I was called to the ministry, I set about the needful intellectual preparation. During the progress of my liberal education, I was often told by individuals who best understood my natural adaptations, that I ought to enter the army, or become a statesman. Having received the full persuasion that I could better serve Christ as a preacher of the everlasting gospel than in any other sphere, I never felt the least drawings in any other direction. Whatever others might prefer, with me the idea of "saving a soul from death," and putting that soul in possession of the treasures of eternity, has rendered as "dross" and "loss" the wealth and the honours of this world.

Nor was my action for doing service for Christ delayed. I immediately set about persuading my associates. One of them was soon converted, and afterwards became, and continued till his death, a central light in the leading church in the city of Buffalo. Many of the others were so influenced, that, not long afterwards, they became members of the Church of God. The next winter, in my eighteenth year, I was called to teach school in a very ungodly neighborhood, where there was not within more than three miles of my schoolhouse a single individual who could take part with me, singing excepted, in any religious meeting. I soon organised two meetings for each week, none speaking or praying in those meetings but myself, until I was joined by young converts. As the result of those meetings, a church, consisting of from thirty to fifty members, a large majority of whom were from these converts, was immediately after organised in that place—a church which remains until this day. Such has been "my manner of life from my youth." All other forms of wisdom have even appeared "foolishness" to me, as compared with that higher wisdom which "winneth souls." Some profitable lessons may be learned from the facts now before us. Among these I notice the following:—

Common Defect in Christian Character.

We notice, in the first place, what may be regarded as the most *common defect in Christian character* in those cases where we must suppose that there has been a real entrance into the religious life. In most cases, perhaps, the spiritual life process never advances beyond the passive state above described. There has been, in the experience of such individuals, real conviction of sin, genuine "repentance towards God, and faith towards our Lord Jesus Christ," and conscious assurance of pardon and peace with God. Here, however, the process of renewal stops. There is, on the other hand, no dedication for positive and active service as servants of Christ, and no "anointing," or "endowment of power from on high" for such service. Religion, in all such cases, is passive rather than active, negative rather than positive, and purely receptive rather than aggressive. Individuals present themselves to Christ to be saved, and not, in addition to this, as "living sacrifices, holy" (dedicated for active service), and, for this reason, especially "acceptable unto God." They, judging from their lives, regard themselves as "called with an holy calling," for the mere attainment of personal salvation, and not to "hold out the word of life," to "shine as lights in the world," and to do efficient service in the great work of "perfecting the saints," and "saving souls from death." "The Spirit of the Lord God" is not upon them as He was upon Christ, and God has not anointed them as He did Christ, to "preach the gospel to the poor," to "heal the broken-hearted," to "preach deliverance to the captives, the recovery of sight to the blind," to "set at liberty them that are bruised," to "preach the acceptable year of the Lord, and the day of vengeance of our God." Yet every believer is as really called to a positive and supremely dedicated mission in the work of "seeking and saving that which was lost," as was Christ. How can we otherwise be among those who are "the light of the world," and "the salt of the earth?"

In this passive, negative state, if we remain therein, we are, according to the express teachings of the Bible, in one of the most perilous conditions to the Christian life possible, a condition from which there is a perpetual peril of out "falling away" into a state from which "it is impossible that we should be renewed again unto repentance." As the only condition of escaping such peril, the apostle exhorts believers to "leave the first principles of the doctrine of Christ,"—the immature and passive state in which the mind is occupied almost exclusively with the matter of our personal salvation, the state in which we are perpetually, in consequence of relapses into sin, "laying again the foundation of repentance from dead works, and of faith towards God,"—and to "go on unto perfection," that mature, supremely dedicated, sanctified, and divinely-anointed state, in which Christ is "glorified in us," because we "abound unto every good work." Had I, for example, continued in the passive and unanointed state to which I have referred, there would, with perfect certainty, have been a resurrection of the power of worldly propensities, and of prior worldly loves and aspirations, which would have insured open apostasy, or a gradual dying out of the religious life, until, with perhaps a name to live, I should have been "dead while I lived." Two young men of most eminent talents once, as members of the same class, entered one of our American colleges, each having the ministry in view. One of them, during the progress of his education, in a state of supreme dedication to Christ, sought a divine anointing for his work. As a consequence, he became one of the most eminent and useful ministers of the gospel known in the United States, "died in the Lord," and in heaven his name is as "ointment poured forth." The other, when he made a public profession of his faith, presented to the Church a written statement of his early experience. All wondered at the account given, and not a doubt rested upon any mind of the genuineness of his conversion. He continued, however, in the passivity of his first faith. As a consequence, there was a resurrection of his early ambitions, and, under the temptation, he turned aside, and entered the legal profession. He became a world-renowned statesman, but died a confirmed drunkard. Reader, are you in Christ as "a branch that beareth not fruit?" If you continue so, as Christ is true, you will be "cut off," and reserved for "the burning."

What we should always do when under Temptation.

We notice, in the next place, what we should always do when, under temptation, we fall into sin, or when we find ourselves under temptation to sin. In the first case, most Christians simply confess the wrong, and seek pardon for the same. This they should do, but by no means stop here. They should reflect upon the cause of their fall, and seek to have that cause removed. Their recovery in such cases will always be permanent. The celebrated preacher and theologian of America, Dr. Hopkins, for example, was afflicted with a very ungovernable temper. He had a brother-in-law, a member of the legal profession, who was an infidel. This man was accustomed to say to his family, "Dr. Hopkins is, at heart, no better man than I am, and I will prove it to you one day." One evening, Dr. Hopkins called upon his brother-in-law to adjust some business matters in which they were mutually concerned. The infidel, knowing well the weak point in the Doctor's character, set up most unrighteous claims, and that for the specific purpose of exciting his anger. The attempt was a success. Dr. Hopkins left the house in a rage, closing the door behind him with much violence. "There!" said the infidel to his family; "you see now the truth of what I told you, that Dr. Hopkins is, at heart, no better man than I am; and now I have got my foot upon his neck, and I will keep it there." That, reader, is the infidel heart the world over. Dr. Hopkins, however, went immediately to his closet, and spent the entire night there in prayer to God. As the morning dawned, an ineffable peace, quietness, and assurance, pervaded his whole being. Hastening to his brother-in-law's residence, he confessed, with tears, to him and his family, the sin which he had committed in their presence, not saying one word about the graceless provocation which had occasioned the sin. As the man of God retired, the infidel said within himself, "There is a spirit which I do not possess, and that spirit is undeniably divine." Thus convicted, he became a Christian, and a preacher of the gospel which he had once despised. Thirty years subsequent to this occurrence, Dr. Hopkins stated, that since that memorable night, no temptation or provocation that he had received had ever once stirred a motion of that evil temper within him. Let all believers imitate this sacred example, and carry, not only their sins, but their propensities which tempt them to sin, to "a throne of grace," and "the very God of peace will sanctify them wholly,"—so subdue and sanctify those propensities, that they will not only cease to tempt us to sin, but will prompt to the opposite virtues. An evil propensity sanctified, as it will be, when presented for that purpose, at "a throne of grace,"—becomes, ever after, a permanent incentive to all that is well-pleasing in the sight of God. How important that all believers should understand this great fact!

Other Christians equally err when subject to temptation to sin. Under the pressure of the temptation, they suffer a thoughtless curiosity to draw them towards the scene which awakens desire, where they look upon the face of sin, instead of promptly turning away from the temptation, and getting as near to God as possible. In the circumstances in which I was at the time of the great temptation above referred to, many would have determined to visit the scene where the temptation lay, with the purpose of going there and looking on as a mere spectator. Under the influence to which they would thus subject themselves, they would be induced to "deny the faith," or their faith would be so weakened as to render a fall almost certain under future temptations. By taking the steps I did, I gained a permanent victory over the propensities through which I was thus strongly tempted. This should always be the case when tempted: we should always turn from the temptation towards the face of God. We shall then not only be kept for the moment, but shall always become endued with a new power from on high for a certain triumph under future "trials of faith."

Light upon the Doctrine of the Baptism of the Holy Ghost.

The facts above presented also throw some light upon that central doctrine of the Bible—*the baptism of the Holy Ghost*. When I went out of that forest, for example, I went out not only in the consciousness that I was "not of the world," that I was emancipated from its entanglements, and that I was, for life and an eternity to come, a consecrated servant of Christ, but that, for my mission and work, I was endued with a power not my own. Of the nature of that power, as I have said, I was utterly ignorant; of its presence I was absolutely conscious. From that hour I began literally to "read my Bible with new eyes." The leisure moments of the following summer were spent in the study of that "dearest of books, that excels every other," in communion with God, and in labours to bring my young associates to Christ. In the meetings where I taught school the next winter, I always prayed three times. We commenced the meetings with singing. Then followed a prayer, and the reading of a chapter from the Bible, followed by a very few remarks from me. We would then sing again, and I would pray a second time. The reading, the remarks, and singing followed as before, and the exercises would be closed with another prayer, followed by singing. As soon as I began to pray, I became conscious of an enlargement, and freedom, and power of utterance at which I wondered with unutterable wonder. The same was true of the audience. Strong men and women were awestruck, and yielded to the convicting influence which pervaded the assemblies. The giant fighter of all that region—a region where men were accustomed to knock each other down with terrible violence—attended those meetings. Even he was overpowered, and became a babe in Christ. Afterwards, I received similar enlargement in speaking for Christ. In the last place where I taught school, a revival of religion commenced in that school, a revival which spread all over the whole society around. During this period I held three meetings each week, the schoolhouse being always filled to its utmost capacity. In these meetings, I uniformly spoke for a period of at least from one-half to three-quarters of an hour. Myself and all the people felt that the power of utterance of which I was possessed was not my own, but a God-imparted gift. I overheard, for example, a company of young men speaking upon the subject. The oldest and most intelligent among them remarked that "of one thing he was certain, that the power under which that teacher speaks is not his own, but is divine." Of the same fact I was myself equally assured.

We have here, as I understand the subject, the beginnings of those divine baptisms, and endowments of power from on high, promised to all believers in the Bible. With singleness of purpose and object to be "not of the world, as Christ was not of the world," to be "sent into the world as He was sent into the world," and to be sanctified for our life, mission, and work, as He "sanctified Himself" for His, we seek unto

God, in the name of Christ, for mercy and grace to be and to do all that He wills, and to finish the work which Christ has appointed us, as He finished the work which "the Father gave Him to do." While in this state of total separateness from the "world, with its affections and lusts," and of supreme consecration to Christ, a divine influence and power comes over us, by which we become consciously "crucified unto the world, and the world to us," and we begin to live as "Christ lives in us," an influence and power by which "the eyes of our understanding are enlightened," so that "we, beholding with open face the glory of the Lord, are changed into the same image from glory unto glory," and consciously "having all-sufficiency for all things, we abound unto every good work." Here we receive "the promise of the Spirit," "the baptism of the Holy Ghost," the promised "endowment of power from on high." Without this "anointing" the entire body of believers are a "feeble folk;" with it, none are "sickly or feeble" in all that flock. "He," on the other hand, "that is feeble among us is as David," "more than a conqueror through Him that hath loved us," while "the house of David" (the leaders of the flock) "are as God, as the angel of the Lord before Him." Here, also, we have a vision of the approaching future of the "Zion of our God." The time is near when all Zion's "children will be taught of the Lord, and great will be the peace of her children," all God's "servants and handmaidens will prophecy," because they shall all be "baptized with the Holy Ghost," and "a little one shall become a thousand, and a feeble one a strong city."

CHAPTER IV.

ASSURANCE OF HOPE.

THE view which the Holy Spirit gave me, at the first, of the godless worldly life which I had led, has remained to this day, but was, from time to time, during subsequent years, renewed with most impressive distinctness. About one year after my conversion, for example, while sitting in a family circle where I was boarding at the time, a vision of that godless life was most impressively presented to my mind. To the circle around me I remarked that I was horrified and affrighted in view of the life which I had led. Yet I had not been an immoral youth. On account of my well-known attainments and moral reputation, I had, the year before, been selected to teach the school in one of the most Christian, moral, and intelligent districts in all the region round. It was that total alienation and estrangement from God, and that total want of respect for His will and the law of duty, which made that life appear so fearful to me. Such revelations of my former moral self and life induced me to make it a subject of most earnest prayer, that I might never return to that godless state, on the one hand, and, on the other, might have grace to "keep myself in the love of God," during my future sojourn on earth. At length, I attained to a full assurance that I was, not only then an accepted servant of Christ, but should have grace to continue such even unto the end. In this assurance, I have done service for Christ up to the present. Not a shadow of doubt rests upon my mind that I am His for eternity, and in such utterance, as it seems to me, all believers should "walk with God." We should recognise ourselves, and receive, through the Spirit, an inward assurance that our union and fellowship with Christ is, not only for the future of life, but for an eternity to come; that we are united to him by "a covenant of salt," an "everlasting covenant." This, as I judge, is what the Scriptures call "assurance of hope." Two common errors here present themselves—errors which require special consideration.

By Asa Mahan.

Wrong Advice to those Seeking the Higher Life.

In listening to advice often given to those who are seeking the rest of faith, I hear things said which I cannot approve. Such persons are told to seek for grace to be holy at the present moment, to learn to "love moment by moment," with no concern about their *future* obedience. Now the Scriptures, as I read them, teach us expressly and most abundantly to entertain deep concern, not only about present but future sanctification, and teach us to exercise present faith for the latter as well as for the former. Paul, for example, entrusted his immortal interests to Christ for future as well as for present keeping. "I know whom I have believed, that He is able to keep that which I have committed unto Him against that day." The promises have a specific reference, not merely to present, but to future keeping, and pledge to our present faith *preserving* as well as *instant* grace. We are expressly authorised to trust "the very God of peace," not only for the present, to "sanctify us wholly," but to "preserve us blameless unto the coming of our Lord Jesus Christ." We are exhorted to "take unto ourselves the whole armour of God," not only for safety against present perils, but that we may be "able to stand in the evil day" which may come. It should be our constant aim, not only to be "made perfect in love" for the passing moment, but to be "rooted and grounded in love." All our separations from sin, and dedications and consecrations to Christ, should be for the eternal future as well as for the present, and our faith in divine keeping should have an equal reference to both. He only attains to the full "rest of faith" who has the assurance, as all may have, that he is in Christ, not only for the passing moment, but will have "grace to" abide in Him. As a means of such an abiding, I, for one, seek to have "the body of sin destroyed," on the one hand, and on the other to be so sanctified in "my body, and soul, and spirit," that I shall have "a divine nature" which shall always effectively draw me into "fellowship with the Father, and with His Son Jesus Christ." "Let us, as many as would be perfect, be thus minded."

Influence of such Assurance.

I often hear it said, also, that if we had an assurance of future keeping and final salvation, we should become careless about present obedience. When I hear such suggestions, two thoughts commonly present themselves to my mind—that the individuals who present such suggestions are in a very selfish state, on the one hand, and have utterly false apprehensions of the nature of "assurance of hope" on the other. The object of Christian faith and hope, with them, seems to be mere security of final salvation. The object real Christians desire and hope is present and future "walking with God,"—and "fellowship with the Father, and with His Son Jesus Christ." The central element of Christian hope in respect to heaven is that we shall then be "like Christ,"—because "we shall see Him as He is." "Every man that hath *this* hope in Him (Christ) purifieth himself, even as He is pure."—Nothing else but a supreme desire and aim for present purity can result from such a hope. The individual whose assurance of final salvation induces present carelessness in respect to fellowship with Christ, and present indifference in respect to moral purity, ought to know that at the last his "hope will be as the giving up of the ghost." Supreme selfishness, and not the love of God and holiness, is at the basis of all his religious aspirations and hopes. Such persons also are in equal error in regard to the *nature* of this "assurance of hope." There are no such elements as these in it—that we can "live after the flesh and not die;"—that we "shall be made partakers of Christ,"—but upon the condition that we "hold the beginning of our confidence steadfast even unto the end;" that we shall be "kept from falling" without faith, watchfulness, and prayer on our part; and that, in dependence upon divine aid and grace, we are to "keep the faith," "finish our course,"—and "work out our own salvation." How can an individual, impressed with the necessity of fulfilling all these conditions or failing of eternal life, have "assurance of hope"—in regard to that life? The individual who possesses this assurance, I reply, looks to Christ, and seeks by faith and prayer not only to be "rooted and grounded in love," and to be "confirmed, settled, and strengthened" in His obedience, but to be equally confirmed in the spirit of watchfulness against all occasions of falling, and all the evil incitements in his own nature and the world around him. Because he is consciously confirmed and endued with power in all these respects, and has full faith in future grace "for every time of need," he cannot but "serve God without fear," and in "full assurance of hope." The absolute assurance with which I, for example—and my case is but the common one in all such instances—have served Christ these many years has never induced me to entertain for a moment the presumption that I could take a step in the direction of disobedience without peril to my immortal interests, or that I could fail to "keep my body under and bring it into subjection,"—without "being myself a cast-away." In the early years of my Christian life, I "fled youthful lusts" as I would flee from the approaching wave of devouring lava. On account of the known influences which pervade such scenes, I have never, since "I named the name of Christ," attended a theatre, a circus, or racecourse and have never allowed an idle curiosity to induce me to draw near and look upon the face of sin, any more than I would to gaze upon the face of the Second Death. Within the circle of conscious safety I have found all the amusements and social gratifications which my very strong and buoyant social nature has demanded. Yet I "serve God without fear," and in "full assurance of hope."

When, a few years since, in full possession of my faculties, I lay for about two weeks so near eternity that it was apprehended that each breath might be my last, I had no disposition then to "cast away my confidence," and had no more doubt of my salvation than I should have were I in heaven. I have no more disposition to forsake Christ now, or to doubt of His eternal love and favour, than I had then. Yet I know well that I must "fight the good fight," "finish my course," and "keep the faith," or not receive "the crown of righteousness." The same is true of all who have *Christian* "assurance of hope."

CHAPTER V.

THE GIFT OF GRACE.

"UNTO me," says the apostle Paul, "who am less than the least of all saints, is this grace given, that I should preach among the Gentiles the unsearchable riches of Christ." The view which the Spirit of God gave me at the first of my actual condition and deserts as a sinner, on the one hand, and of what the grace of God had done for and conferred upon me as "a believer in Jesus," on the other, has ever held my mind in continuously growing sympathy with the above sentiment of the apostle, and has constantly, in my apprehensions, rendered more and more wide and deep, and seemingly impassable, the gulf between the state in which I deserve to be and what, by the infinitude of divine grace, I am permitted to be and to become. The language in which I was, during the early years of my Christian life, accustomed to express my ideas upon the subject was the following:—"What a privilege it is to be a Christian! to be the follower, and bear the name, of such a Being as Jesus Christ!" What gave me most power with Christians and sinners was the manner in which I was accustomed to utter such words. The distance between personal desert and the privileges of grace conferred has ever appeared infinite, and is constantly becoming more and more impressive. When we think of Christ as having "loved us and given Himself for us," when Gethsemane and Calvary are present in thought, we cease to wonder that "by the cross" Paul was "crucified unto the world, and the world to him," and that suffering for Christ's sake was regarded by him as a gift of "infinite grace to vileness given." With what ineffable sweetness do the words come to the heart, "Unto you it is given, in the behalf of Christ, not only to *believe* on Him, but also to *suffer* for His sake!" With what unutterable wonder do we contemplate the fact, that God not only invites us to such service, but that what we "do in the name of Christ" is, in His regard, "of great price," and that He holds in reserve infinite rewards for the same! That wonder reaches its consummation, when we contemplate the fact that we are "called with an holy calling" to do service, not as mere servants or friends, but as "the sons and daughters of the Lord, the Almighty." "Behold what manner of love the Father hath bestowed upon us, that WE should be called the sons of God." I could not regard myself as a Christian at all did I regard in any other light my place as a member of the sanctified family, and as a labourer in the sphere to which Christ has assigned me, and if I did not "bear the cross" with this sentiment, "God forbid that I should glory, save in the cross of our Lord Jesus Christ, by whom the world is crucified to me, and I unto the world." Many who bear the name of Christ seem to regard Christian service, not as an ineffable privilege, a gift of grace, but as a heavy yoke and wearisome burden, which are to be endured as little and as unfrequently as possible. Such individuals may well question the genuineness of their faith. Are they not "enemies of the cross of Christ?" The true believer finds rest under the burden and yoke of Christ, and "quietness and assurance for ever" under the pressure of the cross.

CHAPTER VI.

THE TRUE AND PROPER FOOD FOR THE LAMBS OF THE FLOCK.

No prophet, apostle, or teacher of truth ever received a more important commission than that committed by our Saviour to Peter, in the words, "Feed my lambs." All believers, whether young or old, at the time of their conversion, enter the fold of Christ as lambs of the flock, and all need, as the immutable condition of their privileged future growth and development as "believer in Jesus," the same, in all essential particulars, kind of care, nourishment, instruction, and admonition. All at this primal, critical, and determining period of their new life, must, as "new-born babes, desire the sincere milk of the Word,"—and must be furnished with, and taught to feed upon, the same, that "they may grow thereby," —or they will, with perfect certainty, without a reconversion to their primal childhood state, become feeble and sickly weaklings during their future Christian life, if they do not become "dead while they live." No teacher of truth, whether in the ministry or out of it,—and all in the school of Christ, and that before they have been long in that school, "ought to be teachers,"—no teacher of truth, we say, ever put to himself a question of higher importance than this, namely, What is the food proper for these lambs of the flock? or, What is this "sincere milk of the Word," which these "new-born babes" should "desire" and be taught to feed upon? In other words still, What are those primal truths and principles of "our most holy faith," into which the young convert must be fully instructed, and with which he must be deeply impressed, as the revealed condition of his "growing into Christ in all things," and thereby attaining to a perfected manhood in Him, "unto the measure of the stature of the fulness of Christ?" Let us see if we cannot find an answer to these momentous questions. As a means to this end, let us first consider the actual condition of the young convert, when, as a lamb of the flock a "new-born babe,"—he is committed to the care of the ministry and membership of the churches, his heaven-appointed teachers; we shall then best know his needs, and the kind of instruction and influence demanded in his new condition.

Actual State of the Young Convert

As an illustration and example of the actual spiritual state of all genuine converts, at the beginning of their new life, permit me to refer to my own case, at the time when I became conscious that God, for Christ's sake, had forgiven my sins. Two characteristics, as we have seen, peculiarised that state, and separated it from all forms and developments of the worldly life, to wit—a deep abhorrence and reprobation of my former moral self and life, together with a supreme desire and choice to be free from sin in all its forms, and a corresponding appreciation of moral purity, with a supreme desire and choice to be, in all respects, conformed to the will of God and the law of duty. Aside from these two positive elements—the desire to be free from sin, on the one hand, and the intense "hungering and thirsting after righteousness," on the other—my state was almost exclusively, as I have stated, a negative one. I had almost no conception whatever of the nature and character of "the new life," or of the means and conditions of "the holy living" to which I had been called. The foundation for the new life, as is the case with all true converts, was well laid; but of the means and conditions of perpetuating and perfecting that life, and of the new direction which my activities were to take, I was indeed "a babe in Christ,"—and had "need of milk, and not of meat," had need to be taught "the first principles of the oracles of God."

When I went out of that forest a consciously dedicated and anointed servant of Christ, I was in equal ignorance of the nature of the service to which I was called, and of the conditions on which I could be furnished and girded with strength for that service. I knew Christ well in the sphere of justification, or the pardon of sin, but knew nothing of Him in that of our sanctification, and had never heard of Him, or thought of Him, as "the Son of God who baptizes with the Holy Ghost." Of the idea of "the life of faith," and of the life revealed in the words, "I in them, and Thou in me, that they may be made perfect in one," I was as ignorant as an unborn babe. Had any one come to me in my prayerful study of the Bible, and put the question, "Understandest thou what thou readest?" my proper answer would have been, "How can I, except some man shall guide me?" Such, at their best estate, is the condition of all young converts, when first entrusted by our Saviour to the ministry and the churches, and that with the solemn admonition to those who "should be teachers," "Feed my lambs."

The Peculiar Forms of Instruction and Influence to which the Young Convert should be subject.

A ready answer may now be given to the question, By what forms of instruction and influence may these primal and supreme necessities of the convert be met? One great demand of his being, the pardon of his sins, has been fully met. When he becomes conscious of sin, he knows well just what to do, and where to go. "The throne of grace" is before him, and there stands his "Advocate with the Father." He draws near, and receives conscious freedom from "all condemnation." What he now needs to be taught most fully is, his relations to Christ in the whole matter of sanctification, as well as of justification; that we are just as "complete in Him" in the one relation as in the other; that His power to "save unto the uttermost them that come unto God by Him" is equally absolute in all relations, and circumstances, and particulars in which salvation is needed by us, and that we are just as absolutely authorised to trust Him to "sanctify us wholly," as to justify us fully, and to "keep us in perfect peace," and possess us with "fulness of joy," as to free us from all condemnation. Especially does the convert need to be most fully instructed in regard to the privileges and immunities which he has in Christ as "the Mediator of the New Covenant." Permit me here to cite a single inspired statement of the provisions of this covenant. "Then will I sprinkle clean water upon you, and ye shall be clean: from ALL your filthiness and from ALL your idols will I cleanse you. A new heart also will I give you, and a new spirit will I put within you; and I will take away the stony heart out of your flesh, and I will give you an heart of flesh. And I will put my spirit within you, and cause you to walk in my statutes; and ye shall keep my judgments, and do them." "Thus saith the Lord God; I will yet for this be inquired of by the house of Israel (believers), to do it for them." Now the convert needs not only to be instructed into the full meaning of this covenant, as expressed in the Old and in the New Testament, but to be assured that it is both his privilege and duty to look to God through Christ to have all this rendered real in his experience, and that when he shall "count him faithful that hath promised," God will "do exceeding abundantly above all that we ask or think," and so purify and sanctify us, that "when our iniquity shall be sought for, there shall be none," and when our sins are inquired after, "they shall not be found."

Of equal importance is it that the convert shall be as fully instructed in regard to the nature and extent of God's "exceeding great and precious promises," how they put us in possession, when embraced by faith, of "all things pertaining to life and godliness," that "by THESE," and not by our own resolutions and vain endeavours; "we may become partakers of the divine nature, having escaped the corruption that is in the world through lust;" and that when, by faith, we plead these promises at "a throne of grace," God will keep us from "falling,"—"sanctify us wholly," "preserve our whole spirit and soul and body blameless unto the coming of our Lord Jesus Christ," and that God will "make all grace abound toward us, that we, always having all-sufficiency in all things, may abound to every good work." This also the convert should be taught, that "all the promises are yea and amen in Christ Jesus," and that, as "a son of God," and "joint-heir with Christ," he has an absolute title to them all, and that in all their fulness.

In a very special manner should the convert be most fully taught, in respect to his relations to Christ, as "the Son of God who baptizes with the Holy Ghost," what are to be his privileges and immunities when "the promise of the Spirit" is fulfilled in his experience; how open will then be his visions of "the glory of the Lord," and of "the love of Christ;" how changed he will become "into the same image from glory to glory," and be "filled with all the fulness of God;" and finally, how impossible it will be for him, unless he shall be "endued with power from on high," to become what he is divinely privileged to become, or to "fight the good fight," "finish his course," "keep the faith," and finish the work which Christ has given him to do. Let us contemplate, in this connection, a single passage of Scripture. "He that believeth on me, as the Scripture hath said, out of his belly shall flow rivers of living water. (But this spake He of the Spirit, which they that believe on Him should receive; for the Holy Ghost was not yet given, because that Jesus was not yet glorified.)" What the convert needs to be taught is, that it is his absolute duty and privilege to become possessed of all that is here promised; that the immutable condition of his obtaining this infinite good is, that "the Holy Ghost shall come upon him, as He did upon the apostles at the beginning," and that his first and most imperious duty and necessity is, that he shall wait upon Christ for "the promise of the Spirit," as they did. Of what infinite importance it is that he should not be permitted to rest until he has "received the Holy Ghost."

Not less important than all the above is it that the convert should be early instructed and admonished of the necessity laid upon him that he shall "hold the beginning of his confidence steadfast, even unto the end" of his heaven-appointed mission and work as a servant of Christ, and of the infinite and eternal consequences which are pending upon his fidelity as a member of the family of God, as "a believer in Jesus," and as called of God to "shine as a light in the world." As he enters the Church, and takes the vows of God upon him, he should be most fully admonished that, as a branch of the sacred vine, he is expected to "abide in Christ," and glorify the Father by "bearing much fruit;" and that, if he shall fail to do this, he will be rejected as "reprobate silver," and, as a withered branch cut off from the vine, be reserved for the burning.

I refer to but one other need of the individual under consideration, and a most imperious necessity this is. I refer to the *testimony* of old and experienced believers, who will testify to him, from the conscious facts of their inner lives, to the truth of all that has been above stated. He should be assured, as the result of their observation and experience, that every believer is "complete in Christ," that we "can do all things through Christ which strengtheneth us," that He does "baptize with the Holy Ghost," that He is "able to save unto the uttermost all that come unto God by Him," that in "tribulation, or distress, or persecution, or famine, or nakedness, or peril, or sword," "we are more than conquerors through Him that hath loved, us," and that "neither death, nor life, nor angels, nor principalities, nor powers, nor things present, nor things to come, nor height, nor depth, nor any other creature, shall be able to separate us from the love of God which is in Christ Jesus our Lord." Under such testimony, and in the presence of such revealed provisions of grace, privileges, "enduements of power from on high," and such "exceeding great and precious promises," how readily would our converts "enter into the rest of faith," gird "on the whole armour of God," and take rank among the disciplined soldiers of the cross!

It is well known that at the battle of Waterloo a considerable portion of the army of the Duke of Wellington, as far as his home-troops were concerned, consisted of new recruits—volunteers, who had never seen war before. In all the home-regiments, such recruits were intermingled with old veterans of former campaigns. On the evening prior to the great battle, every such veteran, it is said, set about preparing his new associate for the coming conflict, assuring him that they had only to obey orders, and, under their great commander, victory was sure; that he had never lost a battle—that his wisdom was fully adequate to every exigency that could occur; that he had fully calculated upon the resources at his command, and knew how to use them, so as to render success and the glory of their country a certainty. I became acquainted, several years since, with one of those volunteers, then a venerable man, and a leading member of a church in the State of Ohio. At the time of the battle under consideration, he was but eighteen years of age; and at Quatre-Bras had slept, on the night after the bloody scene there, on the field, amid the dying and dead of both armies. At Waterloo his regiment occupied the center of the English line, and suffered more than almost any other on that day, he being one of four of a company of upwards of sixty that answered at the roll-call at the close of the day. "At one time, to open a passage for their cavalry into the hollow square where I stood," he remarked, "the front in which I was being eight deep, the French led up two cannon, and placing them hub to hub, fired two rounds before we could silence those guns. At each fire, every man on each side of the line where I stood fell, the gaps being instantly filled up, our line happening to be in the center of the range of those guns." "Did you not run?" I exclaimed. "We never thought of it," was the reply. "The only thought which possessed our minds was to 'do our duty,' and 'stand in the evil day.'" Such are new recruits under the influence of the example and testimony and admonition of old veterans. Such should be the old soldiers to the young and new volunteers in "the army of the living God "and "the great Captain of our salvation." When this shall be the case, as ere long it will be, then indeed will "the weapons of our warfare be mighty through God to the pulling down of strongholds." As long as these new volunteers, and old soldiers, too, are taught, however, that they certainly will sin, they will, by their continuous lapses and backslidings, do little more than spend their religious lives in laying over and over again, "the foundation of repentance from dead works, and faith toward God."

The Kind of Instruction given, or "the First Principles of the Oracles of God," as taught to Young Converts by our Saviour and His Apostles.

It may be important for us to stop right here for a few moments, and contemplate the kind of spiritual nourishment with which Christ's lambs were fed, "the sincere milk of the Word," administered to "the new-born babes" in the Church by our Saviour Himself and by His inspired apostles. Clear light on all such inquiries is furnished us in the New Testament. The Sermon on the Mount is our Saviour's first discourse to the collected multitude of His early converts. Here, of course, we should expect to find the true and proper food for His lambs. Such, in fact, are the peculiar characteristics of this divine discourse.

In verses 3-12 of the fifth of Matthew, we have, for example, a specific statement of the essential elements and characteristics of the new life into which these new converts had just been introduced, and of the entire cluster of the divine virtues of which they had, by divine grace, become possessed; and these virtues specified in the very order in which they are always actually developed in Christian experience. And what "exceeding great and precious promises" are hung out to the faith of all who possess these virtues! The first step into the new life is into that poverty of spirit in which the soul, conscious of its infinite ill-desert, and of its hopeless self-induced ruin in sin, renounces all self-dependence and all finite trusts, and "commends its spirit," and all its mortal and immortal hopes, to the mercy and grace of God. Blessed are such, says our Saviour; they shall be put in possession of "the everlasting kingdom," to attain which, they put their trust in Me. The next step is into that state in which the mind "sorrows for sin," and "sorrows after the Lord." Blessed are such, exclaims our Redeemer; God "hath anointed Me to bind up the broken-hearted," and these mourners shall have "everlasting consolations and good hope through grace." The next form of virtue which the new life takes on is meekness, the necessary product of "poverty of spirit and godly sorrow,"—meekness, "the ornament of the meek and quiet spirit, which is, in the sight of God, of great price." Blessed, says our Saviour, are the possessors of this true and beauteous grace; their wealth shall be infinite, "no good thing shall be withheld from them."—When the mind has passed through the process of "repentance toward God, and faith toward our Lord Jesus Christ," and has taken on "the ornament of a meek and quiet spirit" before God, it then becomes possessed of one supreme desire, the state represented by the words, "hungering and thirsting after righteousness," the desire and choice to be perfectly free from all sin, and to be correspondingly pure in the sight of God.

What does the Saviour absolutely promise to such, to all who trust in Him, as "the Mediator of the New Covenant,"—to have the provisions and promises of that covenant fulfilled in their experience? This, we answer, and nothing less than this, that they shall obtain what they desire—"THEY SHALL BE FILLED." Our Saviour now tells us what the convert is to expect as, in the possession of these divine virtues, he advances onward in the direction of the new life upon which he has entered. He will himself abound in deeds of mercy, and will "receive wages, and gather fruit unto life eternal." In the possession of the pure heart which Christ shall give him, he shall "see God," and "his fellowship shall be with the Father and with his Son Jesus Christ." As a world-peacemaker, always seeking to make peace between men and God, and to bind the race together in the bonds of universal brotherhood, he will be known and designated as one of the sons of God. As a world-peacemaker, and in the practice of righteousness, "bonds and afflictions," or persecutions await him. Enduring these, however, great joys here, and immortal fruitions hereafter, are in reserve for him. When will those who have received from Christ the commission, "Feed my lambs," furnish them with such pure and unadulterated food as this?

Let us advance a little further into this primal discourse of Him who "spake as never man spake." In verses 13-16 of this chapter, our Saviour sets before these young disciples the relations which, as possessed and in the exercise of these virtues, on the one hand, or as having lost the same, on the other, they sustain to the world. In the former state, they are "the salt of the earth," and "the light of the world;" in the latter, they are the most hurtful in their influence, and themselves in the most hopeless and perilous condition possible. Let us attentively read the passage:—"Ye are the salt of the earth; but if the salt have lost his savour, wherewith shall it be salted? it is thenceforth good for nothing, but to be cast out, and to be trodden under foot of men. Ye are the light of the world. A city that is set on an hill cannot be hid. Neither do men light a candle, and put it under a bushel, but on a candlestick; and it giveth light unto all that are in the house. Let your light so shine before men, that they may see your good works, and glorify your Father which is in heaven."

Christ would have the convert impressed with the deep and omnipresent conviction that he is called, by "a divine and holy calling," to occupy an influential place among that "sacramental host," upon whose fidelity the destiny of the world is suspended. At what pains, also, were the inspired apostles to impress the same truth upon all believers, young and old. "God," they assure us, "who commanded light to shine out of darkness, hath shined in our hearts," not merely that we might be saved ourselves, but "to give"—to the world around us—"the light of the knowledge of the glory of God in the face of Jesus Christ;" "Among whom ye shine as lights in the world;" "Holding forth the word of life." Equally explicit and impressive were our Saviour's instructions to those young converts in regard to their relations to sin. They were to understand, that whenever their heart should condemn them of aught that was wrong, God would accept of no service at their hands until that wrong was adjusted, and that they must hasten that adjustment at the peril of their immortal interests. "Agree with thine adversary quickly"—

lest the case be handed over to "God, the Judge of all." Under the same peril, also, was the convert to separate himself totally from all things which he could not retain or use without sin. That your whole body should not be cast into hell. "Brethren," says the apostle, "if a man be overtaken in a fault, ye which are spiritual restore such an one in the spirit of meekness; considering thyself, lest thou also be tempted." "Brethren," says another apostle, "if any of you do err from the truth, and one convert him, let him know, that he which converteth the sinner from the error of his way shall save a soul from death, and shall hide a multitude of sins."

Every convert, if we would copy after our Great Teacher, and those who were taught and inspired by Him, should be deeply impressed with the fact that his first, and every other, step in the direction of sin, is a step in the direction of death, a step from which he must be converted, or "die in his sins." "If ye live after the flesh, ye shall die." God forbid that I should ever teach the convert, or any other believer, that he can cease to "shine as a light in the world," can cease to glorify God by not "bringing forth much fruit," and continue in a justified state.

In this divine discussion also, the convert is taught that his subjection to the will of Christ is to be absolute and undivided; that no other form of service will be accepted; that he is to have but one care, and that to please Him who has "called him to glory and virtue;"—that the obedience expected of him is to be in full accordance with that rendered in heaven; that, as a son of God, his virtues are to be a copy of those of his Father above, and that he is to be "perfect, as his Father in heaven is perfect." All these things the Saviour impressed upon those young disciples, upon the lambs of the flock before Him, without a single intimation that He did not expect them to obey strictly all that He had taught them. On the other hand, He closed that discourse with the solemn asseveration that the eternity of His hearers, and of all who should hear what they had heard, was pending upon their doing, or not doing, His words. He did not teach them that they were not liable to sin, that they never would sin, or that if they should sin they would be hopelessly lost. He did not teach them, however, that they would sin, or were expected to sin. He did teach them, on the other hand that they could not sin without thereby imperiling their immortal interests, and that nothing but immediate repentance, in case they did sin, could rescue them from the perils of the second death. Every utterance of our Saviour, on the other hand, tended immutably and most emphatically to impress those young disciples with the deep conviction that the full and absolute obedience required of them they were expected to render, and nothing whatever is said to indicate a limitation to the obedience which was expected. How careful was our Saviour to impress all converts, and all believers too, with the truth of their absolute completeness and all-sufficiency in Him, and to fix their faith upon Him, as "He that baptizeth with the Holy Ghost." "All things are possible to Him that believeth." "He that believeth in me, as the Scripture hath said, out of his belly shall flow rivers of living water." "I am the Resurrection and the Life." "He that followeth me shall not walk in darkness, but shall have the light of life." "How much more shall your Father in heaven give the Holy Spirit to them that ask Him." "I will pray the Father for you, and He shall give you another Comforter, that He may abide with you for ever." In all the above instructions, our Saviour has clearly taught us, "who ought to be teachers," how, and upon what, to "feed His lambs."

In regard to the manner in which inspired apostles, in obedience to the precept of our Saviour, "Feed my lambs," taught young believers, we have a specific example in the two epistles to the Thessalonians, the first epistles ever written. Paul, as we are informed, during his first journey through Macedonia, spent "three Sabbaths" at Thessalonica, and there, on account of the uprising of the Jews, was, with Silas, "sent by night unto Berea." During the short period spent in the former city, many were converted and organised into a church. While at Athens, or immediately after his arrival at Corinth, the apostle wrote the first, and quite soon after, the second of the epistles under consideration. Here, consequently, we have a specific example of the kind of instruction, of "the sincere milk of the Word" which Christ would have furnished for "new-born babes,"—all of those to whom these epistles were addressed being such. These epistles not only present us with examples of the proper food to be administered to "the lambs of the flock," but as clearly reveal the kind of instruction which the apostle had given these young converts while among them. Let us, for a moment, contemplate some of the prominent features of these epistles.

In the first place, the apostle sets out before these converts himself and associates, as men of God, believers in Jesus, who, by faith in Him, had been "sanctified wholly," and had in God's sight, and before their converts, led holy, just, and blameless lives. "Ye are witnesses, and God also, how holily and justly and unblameably we behaved ourselves among you that believe." How did such examples and such testimony tend to "confirm, settle, and strengthen" the faith of these converts in Christ, as "able to save unto the uttermost them that come unto God by Him"! Having thus set before these converts himself and associates, as thus "dead unto sin, but alive unto God through Jesus Christ," the apostle then sets before these same converts their privileges "as believers in Jesus,"—with the form and degree of sanctification to which they were called through faith in Christ. "And the very God of peace sanctify you wholly; and I pray God your whole spirit and soul and body be preserved blameless unto the coming of our Lord Jesus Christ. Faithful is He that calleth you, who also will do it." Every Greek scholar is aware that the original word rendered *wholly* is one of the strongest words known in the Greek, or any other language—a word made up of two others, one of which means *all*, and the other *perfection*. The passage might be literally rendered thus—"The very God of peace sanctify you in all respects to perfection." In this passage, therefore, these converts were absolutely assured that they were called of God to a state, and to a future life, in which they would be wholly sanctified and blameless in all their moral activities, and that God would thus sanctify and preserve them, they trusting Him to do it for them. Nothing whatever is said in either of these epistles to limit the blameless purity to which the apostles and his associates had attained, and to which these converts were authorised to expect to attain. Similar testimony did the apostle everywhere give to his own sanctification, and to the blamelessness of his life before God and men. "I am crucified with Christ;" "by whom I am crucified to the world, and the world unto me;" "I have learned, in whatsoever state I am, therewith to be content;" "I can do all things through Christ which strengtheneth me;" "whom I serve with a pure conscience;" "Herein do I exercise myself, to have always a conscience void of offence both toward God and toward men;" "Be ye followers of me, as I am of Christ;" "Those things which ye have both learned, and received, and heard, and seen in me, do; and the God of peace shall be with you." While "the promises" lift their divine forms before us, how important to young believers that they should have before them also such living exemplifications of the great truth that "all the promises are Yea and Amen in Christ Jesus, to the glory of God the Father."

We positively learn from these epistles also, that, in their earliest experience, these converts had been carefully taught, and had received and realised in themselves the promise of the Spirit. Having reminded them that "the gospel came not unto them in word only, but also in power, and in the Holy Ghost, and in much assurance," and that they had "received the Word in much affliction, and joy in the Holy Ghost," he gives them two admonitions, which evince what they had been taught and had personally experienced on the subject under consideration. The admonitions are these: "Quench not the Spirit—Despise not prophesying." Those only, according to the express teachings of the New Testament, who have been "baptized with the Holy Ghost" do prophesy. This central doctrine of Christ, then, Paul and his associates had carefully taught these converts, and they had received it, and were then in the full possession and exercise of "the spiritual gifts" which attended this baptism. The example of Paul in this case was carefully and specifically followed by all the apostles relatively to all who "believed in Christ through their words." Their first concern everywhere was, that all their converts should be early "baptized with the Holy Ghost."

So prominent and all-impressive, also, were the teachings of Paul by word and by his "first epistle, in respect to the eternal judgment," that these converts were led to expect its immediate occurrence. To remove this impression was the special object of the second epistle. All the other apostles were in full accord with him in their teachings on this subject. The results in experience of their new life—results which these converts were taught to expect—we learn from such admonitions as the following:—"Rejoice evermore. Pray without ceasing. In everything give thanks; for this is the will of God in Christ concerning you." This is the specific kind of spiritual food with which Christ would have all His under-shepherds "feed His lambs." No wonder that, of converts thus taught, Paul, a few months after they had been in Christ, could give such testimony as the following:—"And ye became followers of us, and of the Lord, having received the Word in much affliction, with joy of the Holy Ghost; so that ye were ensamples to all that believe in Macedonia and Achaia. For from you sounded out the word of the Lord not only in Macedonia and Achaia, but also in every place your faith to Godward is spread abroad; so that we need not to speak anything." Converts thus instructed never fail to "shine as lights in the world."

In Heb. vi. 1-5, the apostle gives a specific statement of those "first principles of the doctrine of Christ" into which all believers were then fully instructed at the commencement of their new life, primal truths which all true converts did receive. These truths are represented by the words "repentance from dead works," and "faith toward God," "the doctrine of baptisms and laying-on of hands," of "resurrection of the dead," and "of eternal judgment." All who received these truths by faith were "enlightened," "tasted of the heavenly gift," "were made partakers of the Holy Ghost," and "tasted the good Word of God, and the powers of the world to come," the "enduements of power" which peculiarised the new dispensation. The baptisms here referred to have, of course, a special reference to "the baptism of the Holy Ghost," of which that by water is the symbol. It is not by the latter, but by the former, that the believer is "baptized into Christ," is "buried with Him by baptism into death," becomes "dead unto the world, and the world to him," "dead indeed unto sin, and alive unto God through Jesus Christ our Lord." "The laying-on of hands," in the apostolic and primitive Church, had, not as now, a reference to dedication to the ministerial and other special offices, but had an almost, if not quite exclusive reference to the "baptism of the Holy Ghost." Hence it was that upon all converts and believers who had not "received the Holy Ghost since they believed," hands were laid, and that for the specific purpose that the subject, in connection with the ordinance, might "receive the Holy Ghost." At the laying-on of the hands of Ananias, Paul was not ordained to the ministry, but "received sight," and "was filled with the Holy Ghost." The gift that was in Timothy, and which he was admonished to "stir up," was not mere authority to preach the gospel—a strange gift that to be "stirred up,"—but "enduement of power from on high," which that young disciple had received in connection with the "laying-on of Paul's hands," and those "of the Presbytery." Hands were then laid upon individuals who were to enter upon new duties, as was the case with the seven deacons, and with Paul and Barnabas when about to be sent on their new mission; and were laid, not to confer mere authority, but that the subjects might receive "enduements of power" for their special duties. With the apostles, no believer was prepared for making the requisite advancement in "the new life," for "growth in grace," and for "shining as a light in the world," until, after the exercise of "repentance from dead works, and faith toward God," he had been "enlightened," had "tasted the heavenly gift," had been made a "partaker of the Holy Ghost," had consequently "tasted the good Word of God, and the powers of the world to come," and had been fully instructed in the doctrine of "the resurrection of the dead and of eternal judgment." These were "the first principles of the oracles of God," the primal truths, "the sincere milk of the Word," into which, first of all, the new converts were fully instructed by the men of God, whom Christ inspired and commissioned to "feed His lambs." An army thus instructed and disciplined at the beginning, of course "subdued kingdoms, wrought righteousness, obtained promises, stopped the mouths of lions, quenched the violence of fire, escaped the edge of the sword, out of weakness were made strong, waxed valiant in fight, turned to flight the armies of the aliens," and brought the world upon its knees before God. In such a host, young volunteers will "endure hardness, as good soldiers of Jesus Christ," even as delicate females and young children never became "faint or weary," but endured the tortures of the rack, of fire, and the cross, with all the patience, power, and assurance of the oldest disciples. When will the Church, with her pastors and teachers in the lead, "inquire after the old paths," in which apostles, and martyrs, and primitive believers "walked in the light of God?"

CHAPTER VII.

THE FAITH OF THE CONVERT AS ECLIPSED, AND RENDERED WEAK AND INOPERATIVE, BY THE EXAMPLE AND TESTIMONY OF OLD DISCIPLES, AND BY FALSE TEACHING AND FALSE INTERPRETATION OF SCRIPTURE.

Influence of False Teaching and Example

EVERY one who will carefully reflect upon the spirit of self-abandonment, of humiliation, meekness, and "hungering and thirsting after righteousness," which the Spirit of God always induces in the mind of every genuine convert, will perceive that such "a babe in Christ" will readily receive, and embrace by faith, "the first principles of the oracles of God," "the sincere milk of the Word," when the same is properly ministered, and that nothing can tend so effectively to weaken and render inoperative his faith as to imbue him with the assurance that the freedom from sin and the righteousness which he so supremely aspires after, he is never to attain in this life.

Set before him the dogma, and that as a revealed truth of God, that, at the best estate to which he will ever attain by faith in Christ, he will find himself "carnal, sold under sin," and find it the fixed law of his moral activity that, when he shall "will to do good, evil will be present with him," and that "the good which he shall will to do, he will not do," and "the evil which he shall will not to do, he will do;" and where is the rational hope that he will ever become "rooted and grounded in love," "strong in the Lord, and in the power of His might," and "grow up in Him"—unto the measure of the stature of the fulness of Christ,"—or even fail to lose the ardour and freshness of his first love? Suppose that the old veterans at Waterloo, instead of teaching the young volunteers lessons of absolute obedience, and inspiring them with the assurance of victory under their great commander, had assured these new recruits, and that as from the Duke himself that no soldier, since the first organisation of the English army, hath been able fully to obey the orders he receives, "but daily doth break them in thought, word, and deed," and that, in special crises, their fidelity always fails; that the obedience which each soldier purposes to render, he does not render, and the disobedience which he purposes to avoid, he perpetrates—what kind of a battle would that under consideration have been? What would armies become, were they organised, disciplined, and made to act under the omnipresent influence of such a sentiment? Can the influence of the omnipresence of the same identical sentiment be less disastrous in "the army of the living God," under "the great Captain of our salvation?" What if children in all families and schools were required to commit to memory such a catechism as this: No child, since the Fall, hath been able perfectly to obey the commands of its parents or teachers, but "daily doth break them in thought, word, and deed?" What if these children were rendered everywhere familiar with the idea that their parents, and all the men and women whom such children hold in the deepest veneration, were in the daily habit, when they were children, of perpetrating such disobedience? What would our children and scholars become under such teachings? What but lawless and shameless violators of their sacred obligations? Can the influence of the same sentiment be less disastrous in the family and school of God? Are all the laws and principles of mind reversed when we attempt to act religiously? Must there not be something fatally wrong in the teachings which our converts and members of churches very commonly receive in regard to the expected omnipresence of sin in the hearts and lives of believers? Must there not be some fundamental misapprehension in regard to the meaning of those texts of scripture which are supposed to teach the universal and continued sinfulness of believers in this life? Did any preacher ever witness a revival of religion, or an advance in holiness in the Church, through the preaching of the dogma that all believers, at their best estate, "find a law that, when they would do good, evil is present with them," and find themselves "carnal, sold under sin?" Can any one designate any good which has ever resulted from the use which has been made of the texts under consideration? Has our Saviour undertaken to educate the divine family, and discipline "the army of the living God," upon principles which would, with infallible certainty, induce lawlessness and disorder in every other department of human activity?

At one time, when I was a child, for example, my parents sent me several times to a neighbor to bring home some sugar which he owed them. The box in which the sugar was placed was, in my regard, a sacred thing. I did not even look into it. The last time I went on such errand, however, the children of that neighbor gathered round me, as I was about to leave, and addressed me in these identical words—I remember them well:—"Asa, you will eat some of that sugar before you get home." I denied the imputation. Yet I did that very thing, and the putting the thought into my mind was the only cause of my so doing. Suppose, now, that my parents, before sending me on such an errand, had given me a solemn command not to touch the sugar, and made me promise not to do it, and had then informed me that no child "since the Fall" had been able to carry such a box without appropriating a portion of its contents; that they, and Washington, and Paul, and the mother of Jesus, had always committed such acts under similar circumstances, and that I must "grow in grace" by taking less and less on each successive errand. We know well that such instruction would render all children graceless thieves. Can similar sentiments relatively to sin have an influence less disastrous upon the obedience of the children of God?

When will "masters in Israel" and members of our churches consider that the immutable laws of mind render it impossible for us, when we hold it as a revealed truth of God that we shall sin "in thought, word, and deed," and shall not fully obey the divine will, even to *intend* not to sin at all, or to render perfect obedience? How often do we hear it said that the individual who aims at the moon will shoot higher than he who gives his weapon a lower level. But does any man, can any man, point his weapon at the moon seriously intending to hit that object? So, no man can sincerely intend to accomplish any result while he seriously believes that his best endeavours will never enable him to reach that result. If God requires us to hold it as a revealed truth that we shall at no time fully meet His will, He requires us to hold a truth, the belief of which renders it impossible for us even to intend the obedience which He requires.

The sentiment under consideration, also, and the construction given to those passages which are supposed to teach that sentiment, gives, in the judgment of those who hold it, a kind of divine sanction to the sins consciously committed. That Christ is distinctly revealed in the Scriptures as able to save us in this life, from all sin and render our obedience "perfect and entire, wanting nothing," and to induce in us all the faith requisite to our sanctification in this divine form, all admit. If He requires us to believe that He will not thus sanctify us, or induce in us the faith requisite to this end, it must be because he prefers that we should be partially under sin, rather than wholly saved from it. There is no escaping this conclusion. Why should we desire, or seek, or strive to be more perfect in our obedience than Christ really chooses that we should be? Such is the practical sentiment which really lies in the heart of the mass of professing Christians who are consciously "carnal, sold under sin." They never, with "godly sorrow" repent of those sins, or confess them as if they were consciously criminal on their account. One of the facts which horrified me when a young convert, fearing sin more than I did perdition, was the shocking indifference with which old professors spoke of and confessed their sins. When I would expostulate with them upon the subject, they would reply, not by confessing their infinite criminality, but by reminding me that even Paul had a "thorn in the flesh," was not perfect, but "carnal, sold under sin;" and that God would soon "teach me the plague of my own heart," by letting me slide back from my "first love" into the state in which they then were. This is the exact influence and necessary result of this hateful sentiment in the churches. Regarding their carnalities, worldly mindedness, heart-backslidings, and shortcomings as the inevitable conditions of their religious life and experience, they come to be possessed of a gloomy content with their state, being quite satisfied if they are still conscious of "an aching void" left by "the joys they knew when first they saw the Lord."

When the young convert, in the simplicity of his new faith, in the ardour of his first love, and with his insatiable "hungerings and thirstings after righteousness," enters upon "the highway of holiness," what does he find? Do old professors rise up around him to tell him of the glorious victories which he is called to win "by the blood of the Lamb and the word of his testimony," of his "completeness in Christ," of the all-sufficiency of His grace, of His power to "save unto the uttermost them that come unto God by Him," and in every condition of existence, and against all assaults from "the world, the flesh, and the devil," to render them "more than conquerors through Him that hath loved them?" Do those who have accepted from Christ the sacred command and commission, "Feed my lambs," tell him of the "enduements of power," the divine enlightenments, the transforming and open visions of the divine glory, of the divine fellowships, the indwellings, onenesses "in Christ and the Father," and of the "all sufficiencies for all things," and of "the exceeding great and precious promises" in reserve for him? On the other hand, he does find the mass of believers all around him, believers old and young, a sickly and "feeble folk," all crying to Him—

> "Look how we grovel here below,
>
> Fond of these trifling toys;
>
> Our souls can neither fly nor go
>
> To reach eternal joys."

The worst of all is, that even his appointed teachers impress him with the conviction that this is as high a spiritual state as he can really expect in the fold of Christ; that none are saved from sinning here; that all, on the other hand, are, at their best estate, "carnal, sold under sin," and will continue to repeat the despairing cry, "O wretched man that I am! who shall deliver me from the body of this death?" until the bonds of the flesh shall be broken by death. What can be expected of our "new-born babe" under such nourishing as this? What, but that his new-born joys shall die out within him, and he be left a stranger to all the fulnesses of joy, triumphs of faith, and divine fellowships, represented in the Scriptures as the common privilege of all believers in Jesus. This I can say as the result of all my observations, of more than fifty years' continuance, that there is no relation of cause and effect more fixed than that between the sentiment under consideration, and the absence of that form of experience represented by the following promise of our Saviour: "He that believeth in me, as the Scripture hath said, out of his belly shall flow rivers of living water." He that enters the service of Christ fully expecting to "sin daily in thought, word, and deed," will, as surely as lead thrown upon the surface of water will sink to the bottom, become a backslider. No convert, I am quite sure, can hardly strive more earnestly than I did to retain his first footing; yet the evil came, and it seemed to me a necessity of my faith. To me it now appears a near approach to treason for an individual to enter the divine service with any expectation or calculation other than implicit and absolute obedience to "every word that proceedeth out of the mouth of God," to every indication of the will of "the great Captain of our salvation."

Texts of Scripture supposed to Teach the Omnipresence of Sin in the Hearts and Lives of Believers.

Let us now, for a few moments, turn our thoughts to those passages of Scripture which are supposed to teach the omnipresence of sin, and disloyalty to our God and King, in the hearts and lives of all believers in Jesus. Of the Old Testament, I call to mind but two or three passages which are cited to prove this doctrine. In his prayer at the dedication of the temple, Solomon (Kings x. 46) makes this statement, "If they sin against Thee (for there is no man that sinneth not)." The utmost that can be made of this passage is, a confession of what all admit to be true, to wit, the universal sinfulness of the race. The words employed limit the meaning of the speaker to this one idea. To suppose that he was thinking at all of what the saints of God and believers in Jesus had attained to in ages past, and would attain to in ages to come, is one of the most preposterous constructions of the words employed of which we can form a conception. The real meaning of the passage, however, as fully shown by Dr. Clarke, may be thus expressed: "If they sin against thee (for there is no man who *may* not sin);" that is, if they shall do what all men living are liable to do. This is the exact meaning of the original Hebrew, and renders the passage a very impressive one.

In Job ix. 20, we find the following confession: "if I justify myself, mine own mouth will condemn me: if I say I am perfect, it also shall prove me perverse." Suppose that all this was true of Job at the time he made this confession. He speaks here of himself alone, and of no other human being. The fact that he was then morally imperfect no more proves that no believer will, to the end of time, be "redeemed from all iniquity," and rendered wholly pure, than the confession of David to the sins of adultery and murder proves that all Christians are guilty of these identical sins. Job, however, is speaking not at all of his moral state at that moment, but of his whole past life. "He could not enter into judgment with God," he tells us, "because he had sinned." To attempt self-justification would insure his condemnation, by adding to his criminality and perverseness. For an individual to confess, in view of his whole past life, that he is a sinner and not perfect, and to confess that he is now in sin, are two confessions totally distinct from one another. It is to imperfection, and that exclusively and specifically, in the former, and not in the latter sense, that Job confesses in this passage; and in this sense, all believers will have occasion, to eternity, to affirm themselves sinners and imperfect.

In Psalm cxix. 96, the sacred writer thus speaks: "I have seen the end of all perfection; but Thy commandment is exceeding broad." The term *but* is put, in the translation, in italics, to indicate that it is not in the original. Here it is said that the Psalmist affirms that he has seen that all believers will, from the beginning to the end of time, be, and continue to be, morally imperfect. A wilder, and more unauthorised exposition, I venture to affirm, can hardly be given of any passage. The term "end" here undeniably means, not the limit or termination, but the *consummation*. The sacred writer is contemplating the exceeding broadness, or unlimited application, of God's commandments, and affirms that he here perceives the consummation of all perfection. The absolute perfection of the divine law, and nothing else, is affirmed in this passage. No reference whatever is had to the relations of any being to that law.

In turning to the New Testament, we first notice the inference deduced from 2 Peter iii. 18, "But grow in grace, and in the knowledge of our Lord and Saviour Jesus Christ." Growth in grace implies, it is said, an advance from one degree of sinfulness to another less sinful. The command "Grow in grace," therefore, implies the present sinfulness of all believers. According to this construction, we have undeniably an absolute command from God, not to break off all sin at once, but to do this *gradually*. We should, therefore, sin against God, by disobedience to a command requiring us to "grow in grace," or give up sin gradually, if we should now wholly cease sinning. This construction also convicts our

Saviour Himself of positive sinfulness. In Luke ii. 52, it is positively affirmed that Christ did "increase" or grow in grace,—the original word, there rendered "favour," being the same as that rendered "grace" in the passage under consideration. The command "Grow in grace, and in the knowledge of our Lord and Saviour Jesus Christ," will be binding, and equally so as now, upon believers to eternity. As their capacities shall increase and expand, they will eternally advance in holiness and knowledge. We are required to grow "in wisdom and in favour (grace) with God and man," just as, and in no other sense than, the youthful Jesus did thus grow.

In Phil. iii. 12, Paul, it is said, affirms his own moral imperfection: "Not as though I had already attained, either were already perfect." Why do not individuals, before they put such a construction upon these words, consider carefully what the apostle says in verses 15-17 of this same chapter? Let us read these verses. "Let us therefore, as many as be perfect, be thus minded: and if in anything ye be otherwise minded, God shall reveal even this unto you. Nevertheless, whereto we have already attained, let us walk by the same rule, let us mind the same thing. Brethren, be followers together of me, and mark them which walk so as ye have us for an ensample." It is undeniable that the apostle uses the term "perfect" in two senses in this chapter—senses in one of which he affirms himself not to be, and in the other to be perfect, and, in the latter sense, unqualifiedly requires us to copy his example.

Now Greeks, to whom the apostle was writing, were in no danger of misunderstanding him in the two distinct and separate senses in which he employs the term in this passage. With them, those who were victors on the racecourse, and were crowned as such, were called perfect, the perfected ones, or those who had attained to perfection in glory. Those who were running for the prize, and put forth their utmost energies to gain it, were perfect, not in glory, but as far as present duty was concerned. Paul represented himself as running a race, "not as uncertainly," but with "assurance of hope,"—a race, not for a "corruptible," but for an "incorruptible crown." Until he had "finished his course," he could not have, or had not "attained," the crown, and was not perfect—that is, perfected in glory. This he was "following after." As a runner for the crown, however, he was doing all he possibly could, and was in this sense perfect, that is, in the matter of present duty. "This one thing I do, forgetting those things which are behind, and reaching forth unto those things which are before, I press toward the mark for the prize of the high calling of God in Christ Jesus." Here we have a specific description of a perfect runner, and as such, that is, as far as present duty is concerned, Paul does claim perfection, and requires us, and that unqualifiedly, to copy his example. Paul then does here present himself, not as perfected in glory, but as an example of a morally perfect man. It is very remarkable that the dogma of the continued sinfulness of all believers in this life is, by learned theologians, based upon arguments the validity of which, in the same form in which they are put, implies equally the sinfulness of our Saviour, "who knew no sin." If the command," Grow in grace," implies present sinfulness, actual growth in grace, which is, as we have seen, absolutely affirmed of Christ, implies His prior sinfulness. If the mere declaration of Paul, "Not as though I were already perfect," implies his then sinfulness, what must we think of the testimony of our Saviour in regard to Himself; to wit, "I cast out devils, and I do cures today and tomorrow, and the third day I shall be perfected?"—the identical word and form of the word in the original which Paul applies to himself when he says, "Not as though I were already perfect." Both Christ and Paul looked forward to a perfected state to which neither had then attained, and this fact no more implies present sinfulness in one case than in the other.

But what must we think of I John i. 8, "If we say that we have no sin, we deceive ourselves, and the truth is not in us"? What must we think of the Biblical knowledge of those who assume, without careful inquiry, that we are here taught that, if we say that we are not, at this moment, sinning against God, we are self-deceived, and are not Christians? If we put this construction upon the passage—and we must, in order to deduce from it the doctrine of the omnipresent sinfulness of all believers in this life—we must affirm that such men as Wesley, Finney, Athanasius, Chrysostom, and all the leading fathers and members of the primitive Church, were never born of God. The apostle, in this connection, is speaking of two classes of persons,—one "who confessed their sins," and the other who denied that they had sins to confess—that is, affirmed that they "had not sinned," the true and proper meaning of the words, "we have no sin." When the Saviour said, "He that is without sin among you, let him first cast a stone at her," who does not perceive at once that the meaning is, let him do this who is not conscious of ever having sinned? This epistle, as we are informed, chap. ii. 26, was expressly written to guard believers against certain seductive errors then being propagated in the Church. "These things have I written unto you concerning them that seduce you." Of these seducers there were then two prominent classes—Judaising teachers, who denied their need of salvation by faith, on the assumption that they were not sinners at all, or had never sinned, and false apostles, who "turned the grace of God into lasciviousness," affirming that, as "salvation is by faith, and not by works," believers can live as they list. This first error the apostle meets by affirming that "if we say that we have no sin" to be forgiven and cleansed from—that is, affirm that "we have not sinned," the form in which the idea represented by the words "if we say we have no sin" is expressed in the last verse of this chapter—"we deceive ourselves, and the truth is not in us," on the one hand, and "make God a liar, and His word is not in us," on the other. Nothing can be more evident than is the fact that by the words, "if we say we have no sin," and "if we say we have not sinned," the apostle means the same thing, and in neither form of representing the same idea has he any reference whatever to the dogma of the omnipresence of sin in "believers in Jesus." What a mass of palpable contradictions this dogma imputes to the apostle in this epistle! Look at one or two examples. "Whosoever abideth in Him sinneth not." Whosoever saith that he abides in Him, and "has no sin"—that is, that he does not sin "deceiveth himself; and the truth is not in him." "Herein is our love made perfect." If we say that our love is made perfect, thus fulfilling the law, we are self-deceived, and not Christians at all. A construction which thus "turns the Word of God into foolishness," is evidently "a plant which out heavenly Father has not planted." The second form of error above referred to, the apostle meets by such utterances as the following:—"He that saith, I know Him, and keepeth not His commandments, is a liar, and the truth is not in him."

One additional passage demands our special attention—I refer, of course, to Rom. vii. 5-25. Permit me to state right here two well-known facts bearing very fundamentally upon the exposition we should give to this passage: that up to the time of Augustine in the fifth century, the entire primitive Church, who received the Epistle to the Romans directly from the apostle, understood him to refer in that passage to a legal, in contrast with a Christian experience; and that from that time to the present this passage has been so understood and expounded by the most influential commentators on the Bible throughout Christendom. The bearing of the passage in favour of the doctrine under consideration, if it can be made to favour that doctrine at all, is of the most doubtful character possible, and can never be properly used by the advocates of this doctrine as one of their valid proof-texts. Such a doctrine ought to be based upon none but passages whose meaning is most plain and decisive. If we will turn to chap. ix. 30-32 of this epistle, and carefully read these verses, we shall find the key that will clearly open the real meaning of the passage under consideration, together with the entire reasoning of the apostle in the chapter which follows. Let us read the verses to which I have referred:—"What shall we say then? That the Gentiles, which followed not after righteousness, have attained to righteousness, even the righteousness which is of faith. But Israel, which followed after the law of righteousness; hath not attained to the law of righteousness. Wherefore? Because they sought it not by faith, but as it were by the works of the law. For they stumbled at that stumbling-stone." Turning to Rom. vii. 5-25, we find there the record of an attempt to "attain to the law of righteousness," and a total failure to attain the end sought, an endeavour "by the works of the law," and that without Christ and without faith in Him. A more clear and specific exposition of the method in accordance with which the Jew sought righteousness cannot be given, nor a clearer statement of his failure to attain the end he sought. The individual whose struggles are described in this passage, instead of attaining to righteousness in any form, fails in every endeavour, does not the good he purposes to do, and does the evil which he resolves not to do; "finds a law that, when he would do good, evil is present with him," while "the law in his members wars against the law of his mind (his conscience), and brings him into captivity unto the law of sin which is in his members;" renders him "carnal, sold under sin," and compels him to bear about "a body of death," from which he vainly endeavours to free himself. The only reference to Christ that there is in this passage is the thankful one, that through Him there is deliverance from the bondage previously described. If to endeavour to attain unto righteousness, and utterly fail in every purpose and endeavour, and thus to endeavour without Christ and without faith in Him, is Christian experience, then the passage under consideration describes such experience. If, on the other hand, we do, through faith in Christ, "attain to righteousness," are "made free from the law of sin and death," become "more than conqueror through Him that hath loved us," and "rejoice in hope of the glory of God," then the passage under consideration, what it specifically does do, describes the experience of the Jew, a legal in opposition to a Christian experience.

When we turn to chap. viii., we here find Christ, and faith in Him, and consequently find freedom from all condemnation—freedom from the law of sin and death, "the righteousness of the law fulfilled," "the spirit of adoption" abiding in the heart, hopes full of immortality, and "the world, the flesh, and the devil" overcome "by the blood of the Lamb and the word of His testimony." He reads the Epistle to the Romans to his own terrible loss who stumbles upon Rom. vii. 5-25, the single phrase, "I thank God through Jesus Christ our Lord" excepted, as descriptive of "the life by the faith of the Son of God."

The language employed by the apostle in this passage renders it demonstrably evident, also, that he is here speaking of himself not as a believer walking by faith, but of his former experience as a Jew "seeking righteousness by deeds of law." "When we were in the flesh," in our carnal, unrenewed state, he says, "the motions of sin, which were by the law, did work in our members to bring forth fruit unto death." He then goes on to show that while the law is blameless, "holy, just, and good," all his endeavours to "attain to righteousness" through it were perfectly abortive. Up to verse 14, he uses the past tense in speaking of his own experience, and refers specifically to his fleshly and legal experience. From verse 14, he continues his former representation of his unregenerate and legal experience, but changes the tense in which he speaks of himself. "We know," he says, "that the law is spiritual; but I am carnal, sold under sin." Having used the present tense in speaking of the law, he was required, by a law of the Greek language which scholars well understand, to use the same tense also in describing his own experience, though his past and legal one. Lest he should be misunderstood, however, he defines and specifies, in verse 18, the state to which he does refer. "I know," he says, "that in me, that is, in my flesh" (in my unrenewed state), "there dwelleth no good thing." If any shall imagine that the apostle is here speaking of his life of faith, and revealing its abortiveness, Paul surely is not responsible for the error, he having taken such special pains to guard against it.

Some individuals do not know how to reconcile certain expressions of Paul in this passage with the idea that he is here speaking of himself as an impenitent sinner, and not as a Christian. He speaks of himself, for example, as "delighting in the law of God after the inward man," as doing, when he sins, "what he hates, and not what he would," and that it is not "he that does it, but sin that dwelleth in him." And he concludes the chapter by saying, that "with the mind he served the law of God, but with the flesh the law of sin." This, it is thought by some, can be true only of Christians.

Turning now to Ezek. xxxiii. 31, 32, we have a revelation of the Jewish mind in exact accordance with the above representations of the apostle:—"And they come unto Thee as the people cometh, and they sit before Thee as my people, and they hear Thy words, but they will not do them: for with their mouth they show much love, but their heart goeth after their covetousness. And, lo, Thou art unto them as a very lovely song of one that hath a pleasant voice, and can play well on an instrument: for they hear Thy words, but they do them not." To the same effect are the words of God through the prophet Isaiah (Isa. lviii. 1, 2)—"Cry aloud, spare not, lift up thy voice like a trumpet, and show my people their transgression, and the house of Jacob their sins. Yet they seek me daily, and delight to know my ways, as a nation that did righteousness, and forsook not the ordinance of their God: they ask of me the ordinances of justice, they take delight in approaching to God."

What makes sin so "exceeding sinful" is the fact that, when men do the evil, they, from the necessary laws of their "inner man," their moral nature, disapprove, reprobate, and even hate what they do. Whatever men may do, their consciences are on the side of God and duty, and often impel them to purpose to do the good and avoid the evil. Hence the old maxim that "the path to hell is paved with good resolutions." If men would obey their consciences, and yield to the impulsions of their moral nature, they would obey the law of God; yet, through enslavement to their carnal nature, they do "obey the law of sin." This is just what the apostle means when he says, "With the mind I myself serve the law of God, but with my flesh the law of sin."

It is also a remarkable fact that much of what the apostle says in this passage is an almost verbatim copy of the utterances of heathen authors upon the same subject. "He that sins," says one of them, "does not what he would; but what he would not, that he does." Another affirmed of himself that he knew the wrong, and yet did it, and approved of the right, and yet did the wrong. Xenophon tells of one individual who, when reproved by Cyrus for a gross wrong, replied thus (we give an exact copy of the sentiment expressed, but not of the words employed)—"Surely," said the accused, "I must have two natures. For it cannot be the same nature which approves and delights in what is right and just, and yet does the wrong. When the good nature prevails, we do the right; and when the bad, we do the wrong."

If Rom. vii. 5:25 is a representation of Christian experience as realised in the case of Paul, that is, of such experience in its highest forms, then is the gospel as utterly powerless in the matter of sanctification as is the law, and Christian experience at its best estate is void of Christ and of faith in Him; is utterly powerless against the carnal propensities, and is no better than that of the Jew on the one hand, and of the heathen and all evil-doers on the other; while all the statements in the eighth chapter are false and absurd. What must we think, for example, of the affirmation that one who is presented as "carnal, sold under sin," and as, in every conflict with evil principles, suffering an inglorious defeat; is in "tribulation," "distress," "persecution," "famine," "nakedness," "peril," and "sword;" that such an one is even in all these things more than a conqueror, through Him that hath loved us?" So in all representations. If, on the other hand, we understand, with the entire primitive Church and the ablest commentators in the world, that Paul, in this portion of Romans vii. describes, and intends to describe, a legal, in contrast with Christian experience, and in the eighth chapter to set in contrast before us "the glorious liberty of the sons of God," through "the blood of the Lamb and the word of His testimony,"—then Paul is throughout self-consistent and divinely instructive in his teachings.

There is one passage (Gal. v. 17), which has been thoroughly misunderstood and misapplied in respect to the subject under consideration. The passage reads thus:—"For the flesh lusteth against the Spirit, and the Spirit against the flesh: and these are contrary the one to the other: so that ye cannot do the things that ye would." This passage has been understood to teach, that the flesh, our sinful lusts, on the one hand, and the Spirit of God on the other, are in constant conflict with each other in the heart and mind of every believer. Under such circumstances, "he cannot do what he would;" that is, fully obey, or "walk in the Spirit," but must alternate in his activity between the two. In other words, the Spirit of God, in conflict with the flesh, has not power to hold our propensities in subjection, and set us free to do the will of God. In other words still, while the Spirit, as we are taught elsewhere, is "stronger than he that is in the world," Satan, He has not full power against the flesh. Is this what the apostle meant to teach here? "God forbid." The direct opposite is the undeniable meaning of the inspired writer. In the verse preceding he says, "Walk in the Spirit, and ye shall not fulfil the lusts of the flesh." The reason why this must be the case is given in verse 17, that under consideration; and the reason specifically assigned is this: the flesh and Spirit are opposites, "two masters," each the absolute antagonist to the other, and when you are under the control of one, that of the other is excluded. Hence, if you "walk in the Spirit," "ye cannot do the things that ye would," if under the control of the flesh. When will believers cease misreading their Bibles, and so misreading them as to insure their continuance under the dominion of the flesh?

It has been supposed by some, that in the petition, "And forgive us our debts, as we forgive our debtors," our Saviour intended to teach the universal and continued sinfulness of believers in this life. From the fact that our Saviour has taught all believers to put up the petition, "Thy will be done in earth, as it is in heaven," why do not these same individuals infer that the time will come when the divine will will be thus done on earth? The words employed authorise the latter inference quite as absolutely as they do the former. Besides, we have in the Bible inspired prayers for the forgiveness of sins committed many years prior to the putting up of the petitions referred to. The Psalmist, for example, when advanced in years, prayed that God would not "remember the sins of his youth, nor his transgressions." Advancing as we are "to the judgment-seat of Christ," and subject to perpetual wrong from others, we shall, whether now under sin or not, ever have occasion to pray that we may be forgiven at that day, as we do "forgive men their trespasses."

The whole design of our Saviour in teaching us to hold in perpetual remembrance the sins of our past lives, and to pray that, as we forgive, we may be forgiven, is made void by the inference under consideration. The fact, on the other hand, that He has specifically revealed Himself as having made full provision for our entire sanctification, and is able to "save us unto the uttermost;" that, on condition that we "inquire of Him to do this for us," God has absolutely and specifically promised thus to sanctify us; that "this is the will of God, even our sanctification;" that, as "the Mediator of the new covenant," Christ is revealed as ready to do this for us; that He has commanded us to "be perfect as our Father in heaven is perfect," and has, finally, required all believers, in all their prayers, to pray that God's "will may be done in earth as it is in heaven;" all these great and all-impressive revelations of God do impart to us the assurance that this, the united and inspired prayer of all the saints, will be consummated in the experience of the Church in this world.

The Influence of the Construction which has been put upon the Passages above considered.

For centuries, the mass of believers have fully tested the influence upon their faith and inner life, and upon their views of the most important revelations of scripture, of the construction which has been put upon the few passages above considered. In experience, this construction has, undeniably, rendered backsliding, "the leaving of the first love," the almost immutable law of the inner and outer life of believers—a law which has, in fact, rendered their path, not "as the shining light, which shineth more and more unto the perfect day," but as the evening twilight, which deepens on into greater and greater darkness, "until an almost fixed state is reached—a state in which "neither sun nor stars appear"—a state in which there is more of care than of peace—more of doubt than of assurance of hope—more of an "aching void within" than singing for joy of heart—more of groaning than of inward shouting—more of weakness than of strength—and more of defeats than of victories "through the blood of the Lamb and the word of His testimony." Such facts, everywhere visible, and all occurring under specific teachings in respect to the religious life, ought surely to induce "the masters in Israel" to inquire seriously whether there have not been serious misapprehensions in regard to the real teachings of the Word of God in respect to "the high way of holiness."

The construction under consideration has also been "a veil upon the hearts" of believers and their teachers whenever they have read the provisions and promises of grace, as revealed in the Scriptures, for "the glorious liberty of the sons of God" in this life. If, for example, we accept of Rom. vii. 7-25 as a revealed presentation of the religious life at its best estate, as we must do if we accept it as teaching the characteristics of that life, we must limit, by what is revealed in this passage, all that is said in the eighth chapter and elsewhere about the provisions and promises of grace for our present sanctification and joy in God. When Paul, for example, tells us that "the law of the Spirit of life in Christ Jesus hath made me free from the law of sin and death," and "in all these things we are more than conquerors through Him that loved us," we must not understand him to designate any freedom or form of victory incompatible with what is implied in the words "I am carnal, sold under sin," and "I find a law that, when I would do good, evil is present with me."

When Paul says, "I can do all things through Christ which strengtheneth me," we must not understand him to mean that he finds any strengthening grace in Christ through which he will not be compelled to say, "The good that I would I do not, but the evil which I would not, that I do." When we read, for example, that "Christ is able to save them to the uttermost that come unto God by Him," and that God is "able to do exceeding abundantly above all that we ask or think," we must not expect that anything will be done for us to relieve us from "captivity unto the law of sin which is in our members." When we read, "He that believeth in me, as the Scripture hath said, out of his belly shall flow rivers of living water," we must understand that nothing is promised here to relieve us from the cry, "O wretched man that I am! who shall deliver me from the body of this death?" When we pray, "Thy kingdom come; Thy will be done in earth, as it is in heaven," we must bear in mind that nothing more is to be expected from the prayer of all the saints than this, that in our most perfect obedience we shall be constrained to say, "That which I do I allow not; for what I would, that do I not, but what I hate, that do I." Permit me here to request of the reader a careful reading of the following words of our Saviour, and then an equally careful comparison of the same with the passage from Romans vii. now under consideration. "Neither pray I for these alone, but for them also which shall believe on me through their word; that they all may be one, as Thou, Father, art in me and I in Thee, that they also may be one in us; that the world may believe that Thou hast sent me. And the glory which Thou hast given me I have given them, that they also may be one, even as we are one: I in them, and Thou in me, that they may be made perfect in one; and that the world may know that Thou hast sent me, and hast loved them, as Thou hast loved me." All this undeniably relates to believers in this life. Is nothing here prayed for? and are we here authorised to expect nothing more nor better than is disclosed in this portion of Romans vii.? I rejoice to know that the hearts of believers are being "turned unto the Lord," that "they may know the things which are freely given us of God," and that, as a consequence, the veil which the construction has put upon the passages above considered is being "taken from their hearts."

CHAPTER VIII.

TRIAL OF FAITH AND TRIUMPH OF PRINCIPLE.

AT the time of my conversion, sectarianism in its most embittered forms ruled in all the churches. Most of the denominations also were divided into schools and parties, each of which held the doctrines of the others in the intensest reprobation; schools and parties giving rise in several instances to new and hostile sects. Under such circumstances, the conviction took an early and a distinct form in my mind, that in all these sects and schools and parties there was much of truth, with more or less of intermingled error; and that, if I should make it my simple inquiry, "What is truth?" and be guided in my inquiries, not by prevailing opinion around me, but by an exclusive and prayerful reference "to the law and to the testimony," I should probably be at home nowhere but with my own conscience and my God, and should in important respects—all differences, however trivial in themselves, being then deemed important—be esteemed, even by my own sect and, school and party, as unsound in the faith. Hence it was that, before I had been a believer for a single year, the question was distinctly submitted to my deliberate moral election—to wit, By what law should my future inquiries after truth and duty be directed? Shall I take unquestioning rank as a member of some sect, school or party? Or shall I be the honest and earnest scholar of truth itself; with my intellect, my conscience, my God, and His Spirit, law, and testimony as my authoritative leaders and guides? Such questioning I was not long in deciding; and fixing permanently my life principles, I determined that, as I had opportunity, I would, with all care and candour, examine all the principles and doctrines of all churches, sects, schools, and parties, and as fully as possible weigh all the real evidences for and against their truth, and then, holding my mind in an even balance, let the weight of evidence, and nothing else, determine my convictions and course of conduct, accepting whatever consequences agreements and disagreements with popular sentiments might bring upon me. To this principle I have, since that good hour, sacredly and deliberately aimed to conform in the formation of all my opinions, beliefs, doctrines, and principles, in every sphere of thought and activity in common.

This utter renunciation of the fear of man, and this deliberate election of the fear of God as my immutable motive in determining all questions of truth and duty, was not made without much inward pain and self-crucifixion. I did not know Christ then as I do now, and was not "in Him, and He in me," then as now. As a consequence, it was not then, as it is now, "a small thing to be judged of man's judgment." Yet, painful as it was, the election was made, and has ever remained as the fixed law of faith and conduct. As the result of inquiries conducted in the strictest adherence to such principles, I have never for a moment stood outside the circle of the evangelical faith, but have ever maintained a fixed position in the center of that circle. The doctrines of the divine origin and authority of "that dearest of books, that excels every other"—of the Triune God—of the mystery of the incarnation, "God manifest in the flesh"—of the universal sinfulness of man—of atonement through the death of Christ—of the necessity of regeneration through the Spirit as the immutable condition of our "seeing the kingdom of God"—of "repentance from dead works, and of faith towards God"—of "the resurrection of the dead"—and of "eternal judgment"—all these and kindred doctrines I hold as of infinite importance in themselves, and as verified revelations from God, and hold them with the distinct consciousness that I must thus regard them, or cease to "walk in the light," and be determined in all my convictions by valid evidence. On other questions of vital interest relatively to the revealed privileges and immunities and "high callings" in this life of "believers in Jesus," my sacred convictions—convictions induced by the most careful and devout study of the Word of God—my most sacred convictions, I say, have constrained me to take open issue with the popular faith of the class of believers with whom I was ecclesiastically connected, and of the great majority of evangelical denominations, and hence have often found myself as a stranger among my own people. As I advance near the setting sun of life, however, I have the unspeakable satisfaction to know that these very doctrines, the holding of which was imputed to me as heresy of the most dangerous character, are becoming vital centers about which, in all these denominations, Christian thought is now revolving.

Having for nearly sixty years been a disciple of truth under the principles above stated, it will not be deemed out of place if I should offer a few considerations to commend these principles to the implicit regard of all who would "walk in the light of God." The spirit of manly, Christian independence demanded by these principles does not permit us, it should be borne in mind, to regard or treat with contempt, but with deep respect, the doctrines of the churches, or the opinions and sentiments of those who differ from us. This spirit does require us, on the other hand, to examine, with all candour and care, all such doctrines, opinions, and sentiments, to compare them with searching scrutiny with the Scriptures of truth, the law, and the testimony, and to accept or reject them as we find them to accord, or not to accord, with these all-authoritative and unerring standards. This spirit is also at an equal remove from that latitudinarianism, miscalled liberality, which regards with indifference all questions pertaining to truth and error, and blindly fellowships each alike. This spirit, on the other hand, not only "loves righteousness and hates iniquity," but, with equal fervency, loves truth and hates error, carefully discriminates between the right and the wrong, the true and the false, and has fellowship, only with truth and goodness, and always, in questions of truth and duty, searches and decides in the fear of God alone. Why should this be the fixed law of thought and action with us?

This, I remark, in the first place, is the identical spirit, and these are the identical principles, specifically and absolutely imposed in the Scriptures upon every "believer in Jesus," as of absolute authority in all his inquiries after truth and duty. In the Bible we have set before us "one Lawgiver," "the Father, of whom are all things, and we in Him, and one Lord, Jesus Christ, by whom are all things, and we by Him;" one Lord, who is Himself "the way, and the truth, and the life," and who is the exclusive source "of all rule and all authority." All believers, as Christ absolutely informs us, are "sons of God,"—sons sustaining to each other the relations of "brethren." "All ye are brethren." "They," He further says, "that are appointed to rule over the Gentiles exercise authority over them;" "but it shall not be so among you." Religious teachers, and all who do, in certain relations, bear rule in the churches, are absolutely prohibited from "exercising lordship over God's heritage." Paul, while, as an inspired teacher of truth, he did claim for what God communicated through him absolute authority, was careful to inform believers that, as an individual, he had no "dominion over their faith." While listening to teachers, each hearer is required to judge for himself of the truth or error of what he hears. "Let the other judge." Each believer is further required to "prove all things"—that is, to discriminate for himself between what is true and what is false, between what is right and what is wrong, and to "hold fast that which is good." When Christ required His followers to "beware of false prophets" or teachers, and gave the test, "their fruits," by which the true ones are to be distinguished from the false, He makes each hearer an independent judge of what he hears. There is no principle which is more distinctly revealed and absolutely imposed in the Scriptures than this. Let me add here, that no individual will more readily and cordially submit to the brotherhood, and to his religious teachers, in all things not pertaining to the conscience, than will the believer who is most absolute in his subjection to the spirit and principles under consideration. Within the holy of holies of the conscience, he knows but one Lawgiver and one Lord, and but one rule of faith and conduct, the Spirit and Word of the living God. Outside of this sphere, he will most cordially "make himself all things to all men."

In exercising this absolute and exclusive respect for the Word and will of God in all questions of truth and duty, we become absolutely entitled to the promise, "they shall all be taught of the Lord," and shall consequently be infallibly taught "in all things pertaining to life and godliness"—that is, in regard to all things requisite to our highest moral purity, peace, and blessedness, and fruitfulness in every good word and work" here, and to assure for our selves "an abundant entrance into the everlasting kingdom of our Lord and Saviour Jesus Christ." "He that followeth me," says our Saviour, "shall not walk in darkness, but shall have the light of life." We do not, as He expressly teaches us, become followers of Christ and believe in Him, as He specifically requires, until we have "forsaken all" for Him; and He, by a deliberate act of moral election on our part, becomes, to the exclusion of human authority, "our wisdom, righteousness, sanctification, and redemption." When He thus becomes the supreme Lord of our intellect, conscience, and will, then He becomes responsible to give us the Holy Spirit, through whom, in all that pertains to "life and godliness," we shall "walk in the light, as God is in the light." Outside of this sphere, and in respect to all questions not requisite to our highest moral purity, peace, and usefulness, and final salvation, we shall, with all others, be liable to err in judgment. In "the highway of holiness," on the other hand, "God will be our everlasting light," and "our feet shall not stumble." When human teaching and authority, whatever its form or source may be, becomes our light, a veil passes between our hearts and "the light of God," and no promise comes to us that we shall be "taught of God."

Our *convictions* of truth, when the knowledge of it is sought by searching the Scriptures in the fear of God alone, will have infinitely greater influence in moulding the heart and character than when the same truth is received on human authority, whatever the form of such authority may be. To hold the truth itself as a part of the creed of our sect, or party, or school, and to hold the same truth as that which God hath taught us, and as coming to the heart and conscience from Him, impart to that truth entirely diverse influences over the mind. He that has sought the truth for himself, and has gone to God's treasury to find what he seeks, has an assurance that he is "walking in the light of God,"—an assurance otherwise impossible. In presenting that truth to others, he will always speak with the firm assurance of an original witness, consciously testifying "what he has seen and heard." That, on the other hand, even if it chance to be true, which, without original inquiry, we have accepted as a mere tenet of our sect, school, or party, we can never have any such assurance about, can by no possibility act as a vitalising power in our own hearts, or inspire us with courage and assurance when we present it to others. What gave Paul, for example, such utterance and power as a minister of the everlasting gospel was the absolute consciousness that the gospel which he preached was not after man, that he "neither received it of man, neither was he taught it, but by the revelation of Jesus Christ." So, when our dwelling-place is not the undigested teachings of our sect, school, or party, but the Word of God, when we walk up and down amid the great revelations of that Book, and all our convictions take conscious form from a direct and divinely-illumined vision of those revelations, then "will our righteousness go forth as brightness, and our salvation as a lamp that shineth" We shall not "despise prophesyings," or religious teachings; but we shall "prove all things," and thus discern and "hold fast that which is good." The mere disciple of the sect, school, or party, not only does not receive truth in any form as from God, but never embraces it in its unadulterated form. The truth which he happens to find is always weakened or neutralised in its influence by the interminglings of error.

When all believers in common, I remark finally, shall inquire for truth, and determine all questions of doctrine and duty in the fear of God alone, and shall avail themselves of all human helps, but regard the same as human and nothing more, then, and only then, will that unity of spirit, and of views of truth, duty, and order obtain which God desires to see, and the honour of our divine religion among men demands. All having a common source of truth and standard of judgment, and all directed in their thinking and judging by a common divine illumination, and all, with singleness of purpose and object, seeking to know God's truth and will as God apprehends, and would have us apprehend them, and all entertaining a sacred respect for the right of private judgment in every member of the sanctified family, discord in the household of faith would be impossible; while in all essentials there would be absolute unity, and in all non-essentials there would be universal charity. This is the unity which Christ prayed for in the behalf of all who believe in Him, and God desires no higher unity than this.

I will here give two examples of the influence of the spirit and principles under consideration: When I became a student in college, I found that my roommate and myself, though members of the same denomination, and fully agreeing in the essentials of the evangelical faith, held antagonistic views on questions of doctrine then deemed of almost fundamental importance. In our room, angry debates often occurred between him and friends of mine who agreed with me in doctrine. In such disputes I took no part whatever. When we were alone, however, I would freely question him about his views, and draw from him a clear statement of his reasons for holding the same. If I differed from him, I would fully state to him the points of disagreement, with my reasons for my own views, and my objections to his, asking him, at the same time, to furnish me fully with his objections to the views which I had advanced. With such statements our discussions always terminated. We had been together but a few weeks when my associate thus addressed me—"Roommate, I will confess this to you, that you always treat my views and arguments with perfect candour." In my own secret thoughts, I thus replied, "Before we graduate, a perfect unity of judgment will obtain between us on all the questions about which we now so widely differ." The result was as I anticipated. I cannot designate a single doctrine about which our views were opposed when we took leave of each other. When a student in theology, leading members of the institution, who belonged to the opposite schools into which the now United Presbyterian Church was for a time divided into two distinct denominations, organised a society for the purpose of a comparison of views upon the identical principles above indicated. Our object was to know one another, for the united purpose of finding the truth. The result was the same, unity of "mind and judgment" among all the members of that society, and that, without exception, the same unity as obtained between my roommate and myself. "I would to God" that all teachers and pupils of God's truth would "go and do likewise."

CHAPTER IX.

LIGHT AND PRINCIPLES RETAINED THROUGH THE ENTIRE CHRISTIAN LIFE.

As I am about to speak of a seeming decline of the vitality of the inner life, it may be expedient, for the purpose of being fully understood, to notice briefly certain essential views of truth and principles of action which have remained permanent. The distinct apprehension which I at first received of the total alienation and estrangement of the unregenerate heart from God, His will, and the law of duty—of the infinite ill-desert of sin—of the absolute necessity of the new birth to an admission to the kingdom of God—of the doctrine of atonement through Christ—of "repentance from dead works, and faith toward God"—of "eternal judgment"—and of the necessity of a holy life as the condition of final admission to the kingdom of light, never became dim, or lost their impressiveness over my mind. Hence, before and after my entrance upon the ministry, I retained power to impress the truth of God effectively upon the human heart, as thousands of converts, who afterwards evinced the genuineness of their conversion by their Christian lives, bear witness. Nor am I conscious of ever having swerved from the strictest adherence to the principles above elucidated in all my inquiries after truth and duty. Nor have I ever allowed any considerations of personal popularity or pecuniary loss or gain to have the remotest influence in determining my open avowals of what I honestly regarded as true or false, right or wrong. In all my ministrations, I have been conscious of but one motive, namely, by what form of ministrations and course of life can I bring the greatest number of men to Christ, and do most for the edification of the Church? Nor for a single day or hour of my Christian life have I allowed myself in the commission of any known sin or in the neglect of any known duty; and when conscious of wrong to God, man, or a child, I have made it the fixed law of my life to make immediate confession and reparation. So far "I have fought a good fight, and have kept the faith." Nor do I record these facts as claiming special credit on their account. They belong to what I regard as constituting mere *essentials* of common Christian character. Without these I could not, in my own regard, be an honest or a Christian man. I state these facts that I may not be misapprehended in what follows. This fact I may also state here: in my own Christian life, I have never been what I regard as a backslider, that is, one who has been in voluntary estrangement from God and the law of duty. From the beginning I have sought the light, and uniformly walked in it, as far as vouchsafed to me.

CHAPTER X.

A GROWING DIMNESS OF THE INNER LIGHT, AND A CONSEQUENT FEEBLE AND SICKLY DEVELOPMENT OF THE INNER LIFE.

YET, as years passed on, the inner light in which I had walked began gradually to grow dim, and continued to become more and more so, until at length my dwelling-place was in the darkened twilight of the Sun of Righteousness. Under such circumstances, the inner life took on a comparatively sickly hue, and an unhealthy growth and development. One of the marked characteristics of the state to which I descended was the gradual decay and dying out of the inward peace and joy in God which the first love had induced and so long perpetuated. In this state, the gospel of Christ stood out before the mind as a divinely-originated and perfected system of eternal truth, a system absolutely adapted to approve itself to the intellect, and demand the supreme subjection of the will, and yet comparatively void of power to move and mould the affections, stir and break up and purify the great deep of emotion, and thus to vitalise and perfect the inner man and the outer life. To accomplish any such results as these, the gospel must attain to an equal and full control over all the susceptibilities, faculties, and activities of our nature, and never does, and it never can, have this all-renovating and all-vitalising power but after we have received "the promise of the Spirit," and Christ is formed within us, and dwells in us, "the hope of glory." If, on the other hand, after the light and joys of the first love have developed our susceptibilities, and created in us a relish and desire for such forms of blessedness, that light and those joys shall pass away, or become less divine than they once were, they will leave "an aching void" behind, a painful sense of emptiness and want, which will render us more unhappy than we were before "we tasted the heavenly gift." In the depth of mind, there will be a perpetual cry, "Oh, that I knew where I might find Him" and yet God will seem to be not near, but afar off, so that we cannot behold Him, or "approach near, even unto His seat." The Word of God will be to us "a sealed book." We may read it diligently, with all the helps which we can obtain, and we shall yet find little there to vitalise the inward deadness, or show us the face of God. "We fear the Lord, and yet walk in darkness and have no light." All this was especially true in my own case. My early joys had been very deep, and, to all around me, surprisingly long continued. As a consequence, few could have felt their loss as I did.

In this state, common disappointments and bereavements have an afflictive and painful power to which unconverted persons are comparative strangers. It is this fact which has given rise to the satanic lie that the path to heaven is a thorny one, while that to hell is strewn with flowers. This idea would be true, however, were the Christian life to be passed in the state under consideration. Such was my experience during the period of this eclipse of the face of God. Losses, perplexities, disappointments, and bereavements, had a power to induce mental pain and suffering of which I had no conception before. To all eternity, it seems to me, I can never forget the pure agony which I experienced when God took from us, in succession, two infant children, each that "thing of beauty," of about four months of age, one our first-born son, and the other our little daughter. The first died on Sunday morning, and I felt constrained to preach to my people that forenoon. Those two countenances, as I looked upon them for the last time, have ever since remained before my mind with the same distinctness as if the vision had occurred but one hour ago. Of what occurred on the way to and from those burying-places, I have never been able to recall a single instance. I have only a faint recollection of seeing two little coffins let down gently into "the lap of God." Such was the effect of afflictive providences upon my sensitive nature, then so highly developed, but so barren of spiritual peace and joy of heart. So intense was the pain induced by events of the character under consideration, that I often thought with myself that there "was no sorrow like unto my sorrow," and with that sorrow no divine consolations seemed to be intermingled. Such I believe to be the case with all Christians where, with the fervour of their first love, their early religious joys have passed away. They may *love* the world, but can never again *enjoy* it as they once did, and in the world, and away from God, they will suffer from worldly tribulations as none others can suffer.

Another peculiarity of the state under consideration is a renewed vitalisation of the evil propensities and their action, with an intensity unknown in the prior worldly life. As afflictive providences now pain us more than formerly, so cares, perplexities, disappointments, and provocations disturb our peace, ruffle our passions, and irritate our tempers, more than before religious content, peace, and joy had place on our minds. Hence it is that one of the most patience-taxing and disagreeable individuals in the family, in the social circle, and in all the relations of life, is the Christian who has experienced deep religious joy and peace, and has lost "the blessedness he once spoke of." In no circumstances do "roots of bitterness," when they do "spring up," bear such lasting and bitter fruit as when they spring up in churches in which there has, in former years, been the most abundant Christian love, unity, and joy in God. Hence it is that there are no prejudices so strong, no strifes so relentless, and no controversies so embittered, as the so-called religious, and no hate so deep as the *odium theoloicum*, the theological hate. It is a truth of inspiration, a truth verified also by universal observation and experience, that when we have once had a consciousness of "the gladness and deep joy" of the religious life, and have lost that blessedness, we descend to lengths, and breadths, and depths of unhappiness never before experienced. "The last state of that man is worse than the first" becomes true of us, in exact proportion to our loss of the spirit or joys of the new life.

CHAPTER XI.

INTENSE STRUGGLES, CONFLICTS, FIGHTINGS, AND INGLORIOUS DEFEATS.

IF the reader can form the conception of an individual whose fixed and abiding aim and purpose is "so to exercise himself as to have always a conscience void of offence toward God and toward man," and has not lost this purpose—an individual, however, who has had very deep and abiding joy in God, and does not now know "the joy of the Lord," as "his strength;" if the reader can conceive of such an individual, in the state above described, entering into a resolute conflict with the newly-vitalised and ever-active evil propensities and tempers within him, and that with an inflexible determination to subdue and hold them all in subjection, he will form some conception of the conflicts and defeats which I experienced during six or eight years of my Christian life. With me, then as now, covetousness, evil intent, however secret, and evil desire inwardly entertained and cherished, carefulness about the future, discontent with our lot, evil-speaking, yielding to the promptings of envy or anger, "and such like," are sin. Yet how to avoid the sin I found not. Evil incentives were all around me, and evil propensities answering to the same, and always kindled into a flame the moment they were touched with the spark of temptation, were within; and temptation always came suddenly, and took the will captive before reflection was possible. How often did I say to myself; "If I could only have time for reflection, when beset with unexpected temptation, I could be the victor in the conflict." Before reflection could come to my relief, however, the evil was done, and I was in captivity. I then read my experience in the seventh chapter of Romans, and a bitter experience it was.

Under such circumstances, two courses, supposing a more excellent way than either is not open to us—two courses remain for the believer. He may give the conflict over as a hopeless endeavour, and, in a kind of gloomy content, let his evil passions and temper have dominion over him. Or he may, notwithstanding the odds against him, maintain the conflict, and, by repentance and faith in Christ, recover from his lapses when they do occur. The latter course I adopted, and maintained unerringly. The former many seem to adopt, and do it at the infinite peril of their immortal interests. No individual can allow sin to lie upon his conscience unrepented of and unforgiven without throwing himself into the arms of the second death. Since then, I have learned "the more excellent way" referred to. Christ, when this way has been learned, takes away our sins by destroying and taking away the power of those evil principles and propensities within us—principles and propensities which induce us to sin—and putting within us His own "love of righteousness and hatred of iniquity," and thus rendering holiness as natural to us in our new, as sin was in our old life. I tried, to my deep and abiding sorrow, the common and old way for years, before I inquired and searched diligently "for the new and living way," "by which I now draw nigh unto God," and "full grace to help in time of need."

The Causes which led to such Results

When any important event occurs, we naturally inquire for the reason or cause of such occurrence. If we should form our judgment of the duration of the primal joy of the new life from a consideration of the new relations into which the mind is then introduced, its relations to God, and to its own mortal and immortal interests, and also from the positive representations of Scripture upon the subject, we should conclude that this joy will not only steadily increase, but will be eternally enduring. In the pardon of sin, and in our adoption as the sons of God, the good received, and the grace and love manifested in the same, is each infinite. In being "turned from darkness unto light, and from the power of Satan unto God," no change in character and relations like this can occur in the experience of rational minds. Surely the blessedness resulting from such experiences might be expected to be eternally enduring. That it should be thus enduring, accords with the express revelations of the Bible. "Jesus answered and said unto her, Whosoever drinketh of this water shall thirst again: but whosoever drinketh of the water that I shall give him shall never thirst; but the water that I shall give him shall be in him a well of water springing up into everlasting life." "He that believeth in me, as the Scripture hath said, out of his belly shall flow rivers of living water." "These things have I spoken unto you, that my joy might remain in you, and that your joy might be full." "Ask, and ye shall receive, that your joy may be full." "In whom, though now ye see Him not, yet believing, ye rejoice with joy unspeakable, and full of glory." "Thy people shall all be taught of the Lord, and great shall be the peace of thy people." "For the Lord shall be their everlasting light, and the days of their mourning shall be ended." "Everlasting joy shall be upon their heads; they shall obtain joy and gladness, and sorrow and sighing shall flee away." "We joy in tribulation also." "In all these things we are more than conquerors, through Him that hath loved us." Such is the revealed blessedness—blessedness in this life—of those who walk in "the highway of holiness." We often hear it said that religion does not consist in feeling, whether joyful or sad. This is true. Yet "the fruit of righteousness is peace, and the effect of righteousness, quietness and assurance for ever." "The fruit of the Spirit is love, joy, peace," &c. An experience in which we are not "kept in perfect peace," in which "the peace of God, which passeth all understanding, does not keep our hearts and minds by Christ Jesus," in which we do not "rejoice evermore," and "our joy is not full," is not normal but abnormal Christian experience. Nor will any believer ever become "rooted and grounded in love" unless "the joy of the Lord is his strength." We cannot "know and believe the love that God hath unto us," and our love not "be made perfect;" and we cannot be "made perfect in love," and "all fear not be cast out," and our "joy not become full," because "our fellowship is with the Father and with His Son Jesus Christ." The time, I venture without fear to predict, is not distant when, with the Christians of that generation, the great mystery in the history of the Church will be the fact that, for long periods, believers in Jesus sighed, and cried, and searched after "the blessedness they knew when first they saw the Lord," "the soul-refreshing views of Jesus and His Word" which they then enjoyed, and talked and sang to one another about the "aching void" which that blessedness and those views had left in their hearts. No believer who will be advised by me will rest, or "give God any rest," until Christ is in him as the Father is in Christ, and he has "Christ's joy fulfilled" in his heart.

But how does this joy in God pass away? Most commonly, I answer, through sin for which the "heart condemns" the subject, and the sin is left upon the conscience unrepented of and unforgiven. In my own case, this was not the cause after which we are seeking. There has never been a period in my Christian life when I did not cherish a sacred respect for every form of the known will of God, or when "my heart condemned me" and I did not seek prompt forgiveness; yet there were years in which I "feared the Lord and trembled at His word," and still "walked in darkness and had no light." How did I lose that primal blessedness? In the first place, I answer, I *expected* to lose it. That I should lose it was a fixed article of the creed in which I had been taught from the beginning. In the heart of every believer whom I knew, and of whom I had heard or read, that blessedness had faded out. In my experience this joy passed away so gradually and imperceptibly that very little alarm was excited. As the light faded, I read my experience and inward life very distinctly in the seventh chapter of Romans, which, as I honestly supposed, reveals that experience and in the best form to be expected this side heaven or the hour of death. The wretchedness that I experienced, and the abortive efforts I made to recover my former standing and overcome my evil tendencies and besetments, revealed to me, as I supposed, the fact that I was then in the identical moral and spiritual state in which Paul was when he wrote this and his other epistles. Thus, by my own faith and views of the express teaching of inspiration, was I frozen in, and that in "a land of darkness as darkness itself; where the light is as darkness."

Nor had I, at that time, any views of Christ, of the provisions of His grace, or of the power of the Spirit—views which had the remotest efficacy to relieve my difficulties, or reveal the path which would have conducted me out of that "darkness into God's marvellous light." I knew Christ almost exclusively in the single sphere of our justification. Hardly "by the hearing of the ear" had I any knowledge of Him as our sanctification. Of "the promise of the Spirit" I was in total darkness. I consequently had no idea of what is meant by all that is revealed of

Christ as a manifested, personal presence, "formed within us, the hope of glory," and, with the Father, "making His abode with us." All the promises and revealed provisions of grace were limited and eclipsed by what was supposed to be revealed of Christian experience and privileges in the chapter referred to, and other falsely interpreted passages. Yes, reader, I was in that dim twilight of a semi-faith, because, while I was studying diligently—and this is not wrong—what was called the great doctrines, my imperious need, as I afterward found, was "some one to teach me what are the first principles of the oracles of God." Had some one thus taught me, how long would I have remained in that dark and dreary waste? No longer than I did remain after the highway of holiness was opened upon my vision. If you, reader, are now dwelling in these low grounds, heed the voice which comes to us from God out of heaven, calling upon the sacramental host to go forward, and ascend those "delectable mountains" whose cloudless summits are ever warmed and illumined by the life-giving beams of the Sun of Righteousness.

CHAPTER XII.

LIGHT BREAKING IN.

In the moral and spiritual state above indicated, I entered, about the eighth year of my Christian life, upon my studies as a student in theology at Andover, Massachusetts. Our Biblical Professor was the celebrated Biblical scholar, Rev. Moses Stuart. In the progress of our Biblical studies, we came at length to the seventh chapter of Romans. Our learned Professor, to the surprise of not a few of his pupils, laid out all his learning and talents in rendering it demonstrably evident that the specific object of the apostle in this chapter is to elucidate a legal in distinction from a proper Christian experience. The express object of the entire epistle, as he showed us, is to elucidate and verify the doctrine of salvation in its entireness, salvation by faith, as opposed to the Jewish error of salvation by deeds of law and patriarchal descent. In the first five chapters, the Christian doctrine of justification by faith is most fully stated, elucidated, and verified, in opposition to the Jewish error of justification by deeds of law. In the next three chapters, a precisely similar course of demonstrative reasoning is pursued relatively to the fundamental doctrine of sanctification by faith, as opposed to the Jewish error upon the same subject. In the portion of the seventh chapter devoted to the subject, the apostle details, in fact and form, his own abortive legal experience as a Jew, and in the eighth chapter details, in contrast with his former legal self and life, his Christian experience as a believer in Jesus. The contrast is most instructive and impressive. In the former state he was always under condemnation, bringing forth fruits unto death; in the latter, he was free from all condemnation, because he was justified freely by divine grace, and "dead indeed unto sin, but alive unto God through Jesus Christ our Lord." In the former state, in every purpose of obedience, and in every conflict with his evil propensities, "the law in his members," he suffered a sad and inglorious defeat, and was a stranger to victory in all its forms; in the latter state, in every condition of existence, and in every conflict with the powers of sin, he was "more than a conqueror through Him that hath loved us." In the former state, he found "a law that, when he would do good, evil was present with him;" in the latter, "the law of the spirit of life in Christ Jesus made him free from the law of sin and death." In the former state, "he was carnal, sold under sin;" in the latter, he was the Lord's freeman, "delivered from the bondage of corruption into the glorious liberty of the children of God." To explain the experience detailed in Romans vii. as Christian experience, is to annihilate, as our Professor showed us, all distinction between sanctification by faith and "by deeds of law," between the experience of the Jew and that of the Christian, and to affirm faith in Christ to be just as inoperative in the matter of sanctification as is the law. The views which our Professor presented, accord, as he rendered undeniably evident, with those received by the entire primitive Church directly from the apostle himself, and with the expositions of a vast majority of the most distinguished commentators of all ages. We were finally shown, by numerous quotations from heathen authors, that the experience portrayed in this seventh chapter is identical with that of men living in sin, as portrayed by such writers, and that their language, in most important respects, perfectly corresponds with his upon the same subject. All our ideas of the Christian life, as we were shown, are marred when we identify the legal experience described in Romans vii. with the Christian experience described in the next chapter, and in other parts of the Bible.

The argument of our Professor was most manifestly unanswerable, and with the conviction induced, rays of light began to pierce "the horror of great darkness" in which my mind was involved. The supposed revealed necessity, that the believer shall remain "carnal, sold under sin," and carry about with him in his "captivity under the law of sin" and death "the body of this death," was taken away, and I was set free to inquire, and soon began most eagerly to inquire, in other portions of the Word of God "for the things which are freely given us of God." The manner in which these inquiries were pursued, together with the results, will be disclosed hereafter.

CHAPTER XIII.

THE LEGAL AND THE CHRISTIAN SPIRIT.

As much is being said in the churches about a legal righteousness and righteousness by faith, or the legal and Christian spirit and method of righteousness, it may be important for us to stop right here for a moment, and see if we cannot obtain clear and distinct apprehensions of these two distinct and opposite spirits and methods of righteousness. At the time when Paul wrote the Epistle to the Romans, the Jew stood out before the world as the advocate and representative of the doctrine of justification by deeds of law and of legal righteousness, while the Christian stood forth as the advocate and representative of the opposite doctrine, that of justification and sanctification both by faith. The object of the apostle in this epistle (I repeat what I have stated in substance before) is to elucidate these two distinct and opposite methods of righteousness as advocated and represented by these two classes of individuals.

In doing this, the apostle gives the Jew full credit for all that could be claimed in his behalf. "Israel," or the Jews, had "a zeal for God," "followed after the law of righteousness," "rested in the law," "made his boast of God," "knew His will," approved the things that are more excellent," and "had the form of knowledge and of the truth." Yet, in seeking righteousness "by deeds of law," the Jew failed in the end he sought both in the matter of justification, on the one hand, and sanctification on the other—utterly failed in both particulars. This he did for two reasons. The fact that he, in common with all the race, had sinned, and come short of the "glory of God,"—a fact which rendered it absolutely impossible that any human being shall be justified "by the deeds of the law." The Jew also, notwithstanding his "approval of the law," and "delight in it after the inner man," and frequently renewed efforts and purposes of obedience, utterly failed to render the obedience purposed and required, because the evil propensities in man are stronger than the conscience and the will. The Christian, on the other hand, in seeking righteousness by faith, does "attain to righteousness" in both particulars, because that in Christ provisions absolutely adequate and efficacious do exist for the full justification and sanctification of all who believe in Him.

To understand clearly the nature of the legal spirit, as it is in itself and as represented by the Jew in his "following after righteousness," we have only to recur to the efforts which Paul represents his countrymen as putting forth in the direction of obedience to "the law of righteousness." Representing himself as a Jew, and as he once was, the apostle thus speaks:—"To will is present with me; but how to perform that which is good, I find not. For the good that I would, I do not; but the evil which I would not, that I do! "That which I do, I allow not; for what I would, that do I not; but what I hate, that do I." In examining all the above statements, we find, on the one hand, the presence of a clear apprehension, inward approval of, and even inward delight in, what the law requires. We find also purposes and efforts to render this obedience; but, in every single purpose and endeavour, a total failure "to do that which is good,"—the good to do which there is a readiness to will. We find, on the other hand, the total absence of all recognition of the fact of self-impotence and dependence upon divine aid, or any aid whatever beyond self, to do the good—the total absence, consequently, of faith in Christ for "grace to help" human impotency. In other words, every purpose is formed and every effort put forth in the exclusive spirit of self-sufficiency and self-dependence. This is the legal spirit in its nature, essence, and form. The language of this spirit is, "The man that doeth these things shall live by them" "I will do them, and live thereby." The language of faith, on the other hand is, "We are not sufficient of ourselves to think anything as of ourselves, but our sufficiency is of God," and in Christ we do "have all-sufficiency for all things," and may consequently "abound to every good work." The legal spirit boasts of its strength, is full of good purposes, but is utterly powerless to "do that which is good." The spirit of faith, on the other hand, recognises and confesses to total self-impotence, and yet is ever girded with all-sufficient strength, because "its hope and trust is not in self, but in the living God."

I may illustrate these two opposites by a reference to my own case. In the matter of justification, my self-renunciation and dependence upon the grace of God in Christ were absolute. Here, consequently, I had "assurance of hope." In that of sanctification, on the other hand, whenever I failed in my purposes of obedience, after confession and the consciousness of forgiveness, I would say to myself "I know of but one thing to do, and that is, to renew my purpose of obedience and start anew." I record the very words I was accustomed to repeat to myself under the circumstances referred to. As a consequence, my renewed purposes were as abortive as my former ones had been, and I read my experience in the seventh chapter of Romans. Whenever, and to what extent, and in what form soever, reader, you may purpose obedience, resolve to start anew in the divine life, and do this expecting thus to obey because you have purposed to do so, you will read you future experience just where I read mine, and will never find "deliverance from the body of this death." The reason is, that all such purposes and efforts are not of faith, but purely legal. If on the other hand, "with purpose of heart you shall cleave unto the Lord," and while you do so you shall, with a distinct recognition of your total moral impotency for anything good or right, recognise in Christ an infinite fulness for all your necessities, and shall put full trust in Him, as your all-sufficient "wisdom, righteousness, sanctification, and redemption," then will "your righteousness go forth as brightness, and your salvation as a lamp that shineth," and your stability in love and obedience be "as Mount Zion, which cannot be moved, but abideth for ever." The reason is, that "the life which you now live in the flesh is by the faith of the Son of God, who loved you, and gave Himself for you." Such is the distinction between the legal and Christian spirit and method of righteousness.

CHAPTER XIV.

CONSCIOUS DEFICIENCIES OF CHRISTIAN AND MINISTERIAL QUALIFICATION.

When the Spirit of God is about to open upon the mind some new and fundamentally important aspect of divine truth, or to impart some new, and fresh, and vitalising aspect of what we really knew before, and this as a means of lifting us to new and far higher forms of "the hidden life" than we were formerly possessed of, He commonly, first of all, renders us distinctly conscious of some, specific inward spiritual want—a want which what we now know of the gospel is not adapted to meet—a want, however, to meet which fully and perfectly the new manifestation is absolutely adapted. We are thus led to inquire and search diligently after this manifestation which God has prepared for us, and which the Spirit, through these "unutterable groanings," is preparing us to receive; and when we have been induced to "search for God" in these new and living manifestations, and to "search for Him with all our hearts, and with all our souls," we "find Him," and find Him as "our everlasting light, and the days of our mourning are ended." The brightest of all "the signs of promise," in regard to the near future of Zion, is the fact that the conviction is everywhere obtaining among evangelical Christians that they are living far below their revealed privileges—that everywhere they are being pressed with a common, and conscious, and specific *want* and *desire* for something higher and better than they have hitherto enjoyed—and that with the conviction that there are in Christ provisions fully adequate to meet these necessities. These wants will never be met by looking back to "the blessedness we knew when first we saw the Lord," or to "the soul-refreshing view of Jesus and His Word" which was once enjoyed. As far as the mount of justification is concerned, the joys of pardoned sin, and the "soul-refreshing view of Jesus and His Word" there enjoyed, God is saying to His people, "Ye have compassed this mountain long enough." Inquire now for "the rest that remains for the people of God," for "the rising of the Sun of Righteousness with healings in His wings," for "the promise of the Spirit," for the open-faced "beholdings of the glory of the Lord," for the divine fellowships, and for the coming of Christ and the Father to "make their abode with you," so that you may know in experience what your Redeemer meant when He said, "I in them, and Thou in me, that they may be made perfect in one; and that the world may know that Thou hast sent me, and hast loved them as Thou lovest me." Nothing but these eternal verities will meet and satisfy the great want that is now pressing upon believers.

In my own case, "the aching void" which the passing away of my primal religious joys had left in my heart, together with the conscious fact that nothing in my then views of the gospel seemed to have power to bring back that blessedness, and with constant failures of my best resolutions, rendered me continuously conscious of the fact that I had somewhere missed my way, and needed some one to teach me the secret of the inner life, as that life is portrayed in the Scriptures. However clear and distinct my views of the system of Christian doctrine one fact I knew, and was distinctly conscious of, that my inner life did but very partially accord with that which Christ has promised to believers. My thirst was not quenched, nor were the waters which Christ had given me "within me as a well of water springing up into everlasting life;" nor was "my joy full;" nor did I have an experience of what our Saviour meant when He said, "He that believeth in me, as the Scripture hath said, out of his belly shall flow rivers of living water." Hence the continued inward cry, "Oh, that I knew where I might find Him!" and where is the key that will unlock the mystery of my inner life, and show me "the living water?"

I had not been over six or seven years in the ministry before far more than as many hundred converts were added to my own and other churches around me, and that through my direct instrumentality. As soon as these converts multiplied before me, the command came distinctly home to my mind, "Feed my lambs." I looked over the churches to which I ministered, and perceived that the membership of the same were, almost without exception, in a sickly and feeble spiritual state, none of them having "princely power with God and with men," none of them "kept in perfect peace," or "rejoicing with joy unspeakable and full of glory." In the visible presence of such facts, another precept came home with similar distinctness to my mind, "Feed my sheep." The two precepts under consideration, as I clearly understood them, required that those young converts and feeble believers should be so instructed that "they might grow up into Christ in all things," "attain to the measure of the stature of the fulness of Christ," be "thoroughly furnished into every good work," "rejoice ever more," and be "filled with all the fulness of God." This was the unmistakable pattern of the New Testament saint, as distinctly drawn by the pen of inspiration. I was myself consciously not *such* a saint, and was darkly ignorant of "the way, the truth, and the life" by which I could attain to a personal realisation of the revealed divine ideal before me. How could I lead "the flock of God" in a way unknown to myself? He that would, as required, *feed* the flock, must in his own experience, as I clearly saw, *lead* the flock. What he has himself "*seen* and *heard*," that he must "testify" to believers. What is expressly required of the religious teacher—and all believers should, in their diverse spheres and measure, be teachers—what is required of the religious teacher, I say, is that he shall, in his inner and outward life, be a living exemplification of the life-imparting power of the truth which he teaches—"an epistle of Christ," "known and read of all men" as such. This deep consciousness, thus induced, of most essential personal and ministerial deficiency, developed in the depths of my inner being a sense of a specific and overshadowing want, together with an irrepressible desire to discover the divine secret or manifestation by which that want would be fully met, I will relate a single fact as illustrative of the mental state to which I refer. At the close of a protracted meeting of about one week's continuance—I was President of Oberlin College then—upwards of two hundred and fifty individuals separated themselves from the congregation, and seated themselves in front of the preacher's stand as converts and inquirers, all but a few of them being of the former class. As I looked over that mass, I said to myself, "If any one was present who could direct me into 'the new and living way' after which I am inquiring, I should take my place among these converts and inquirers." Such was the sentiment that was omnipresent in my mind during the years of my Christian and ministerial life of which I am now speaking.

CHAPTER XV.

PROTRACTED INQUIRIES AFTER THE MYSTERY OF THE HIDDEN LIVE.

UNDER the influence of this sentiment, I entered upon the most careful inquiries after "the hidden mystery" of the divine life. In my researches into the Scriptures, "a veil" was upon my heart—the veil of false doctrines and false interpretations of the Word of God in regard to the condition and privileges of believers in this life—a veil which must be "rent from top to bottom" before "the way into the holiest of all can be made manifest" to the inquirer after "the things which are freely given us of God." This veil for years, notwithstanding my careful and prayerful study of the Scriptures, darkened my apprehensions of what now appears as the plainest teachings and "first principles of the oracles of God." How plainly marked are these "first principles," "the sincere milk of the Word," in partaking of which the convert cannot but grow up into the stature of a perfected manhood in Christ Jesus! "So foolish was I and ignorant," that years of painful research passed before I "looked into the perfect law of liberty."

My Biblical researches, however, were not in vain. I early became absolutely convinced that there are most distinctly revealed, whatever my views about the sinfulness of all believers in this life, "better things" than the ministry and churches around had attained to—"better things," towards which their poor experiences had hardly approached. Instead of there being among us "no sickly nor feeble ones," almost all in common appeared to be smitten with a kind of spiritual paralysis. The "feeble among us were not as David," always conquerors; nor was "the house of David," the leaders of the sacramental host, "as God, as the angel of the Lord before Him," nor was holiness unto the Lord "upon "the bells of our horses." We were not "filled with all the fulness of God," nor was "He doing for us exceeding abundantly above all that we ask or think." If the promises do not authorise us to expect *all* that they seem to pledge to our faith, they certainly do require us to ask and receive more than we do obtain. Such were the conclusions forced upon my mind by the careful study of the revealed provisions and promises of grace.

With special interest did I study the recorded experiences and attainments of the apostles and their associates. There all was in palpable contrast with what was passing in the interior of my own mind, and what I saw around me. They "mounted up on wings as eagles," while "our souls could neither fly nor go to reach eternal joys." They ran without weariness, while we fainted in walking. They were "careful for nothing," while we were "careful and troubled about many things." They had "learned in whatever state they were therewith to be content," while we were "weary, tossed with tempest, and not comforted." They "rejoiced evermore," and that "with joy unspeakable and full of glory," while we talked, and sang, and prayed, and inquired after "the blessedness we knew when first we saw the Lord." They were possessed of "full assurance of hope," "full assurance of faith," and "full assurance of understanding," and of God "as their everlasting light;" while we were perturbed with doubts and fears, and "walked in darkness, and had no light." In view of such palpable facts and revelations, I was accustomed to say to myself:—I know that myself and believers around me have diverged somewhere from "the highway of holiness," and are walking in a dim twilight, when we should be "walking in the light of God," with no clouds between us and the Sun of Righteousness. I know that there is a secret about "the life of God in the soul of man," a secret not yet revealed to me, but which would be manifested, if "I should wait for the vision, while it tarried."

I made, also, the most careful inquiries of the most spiritual believers, ministers and others, that I met with, about this one subject. As soon as I met my old friend, Professor Finney, whom I had not seen for years, I made the most earnest and diligent inquiries of him. I found all, however, in the same darkness on this vital question that I was.

I finally took up the memoirs of the holiest persons I heard of—memoirs of such individuals as David Brainard, Edward Payson, and others, and read them for one exclusive purpose—the discovery of the one secret under consideration. I arose from the perusal of such books with bitter disappointment. These men of God had the same difficulties in their experiences that I had, the same struggles and defeats, the same ignorance of God as their "everlasting light," the same absence of "the rest of faith," and the same ignorance of the remedy to the evils which pressed upon them, and of the divine secret after which I was inquiring. This consolation remained to alleviate the disappointment referred to:—If these men, with myself, and all with whom I conversed, have failed to discover this "hidden mystery," Paul, and Peter, and John did know it, and what God revealed to them He will make known to me, if I faint not in my inquiries and in prayer. "Faint, yet pursuing," was my continued maxim. "Yes," I would exclaim, "in due time I shall reap, if I faint not."

But for the reason that what follows next in order is requisite to a full understanding of these facts of my own interior life—facts tending to throw light upon the conditions of attaining to a full fruition of "the liberty of the sons of God,"—I should omit the remainder of the present chapter, there being the appearance of a desire for self-glorification, seeking which all should regard as a grievous sin against God. What I am to state, however, are merely certain facts of plain Christian fidelity—facts occurring in circumstances which then "tried men's souls." The fidelity manifested by myself was common with thousands of ministers who stood by God's truth, and vindicated the rights of His poor, in that "evil day."

Immediately after I became pastor of one of the Presbyterian churches in Cincinnati, Ohio, the Anti-Slavery agitation began to move the whole American mind. Such was the all-pervading influence of the Southern States at the time, however, that a vast majority of even our Northern population, including that of the ministry and membership of our churches, took open ground against the agitation; the opposition, also, taking on the most embittered form conceivable, an open determination being everywhere avowed to put down the disturbance even by mob violence. These were the days in which Pro-Slavery Mobs occurred in such cities as Boston and New York, and the martyr Lovejoy was murdered in cold blood in the State of Illinois.

Immediately after my removal to Cincinnati, I was elected a trustee and member of the Prudential Board of the trustees of Lane Seminary, a theological institution on the hills that overlooked the city. In the upbuilding of that institution, and in securing for it the services of the celebrated Rev. Lyman Beecher, D.D., as its president and professor of theology, I took a very active part, having drafted the letter afterwards published in the Doctor's Memoirs, the letter addressed by the trustees of the Seminary to his church in Boston, to persuade them to consent, for the sake of higher interests, to part with their beloved pastor. The coming of such a man, with an able corps of associates, drew, almost at once, to the institution a large number of students from all parts of the country. Of these young men, Dr. Beecher, on a visit to the Eastern States, stated publicly that he had never in his life known so large a body of young men among whom there was such an amount of talent and piety. On coming to the institution, a very large portion of the students connected themselves with my church, and attended upon my ministry, very few of them joining any other church in the city. Such facts brought me visibly into very direct and influential relations with the Seminary.

The second year of Dr. Beecher's administration, by consent of the Faculty, the students held a discussion of a week's continuance on the then all-agitating subject of slavery. The result of that discussion was, that, with very few exceptions, those students became avowed abolitionists, and organised themselves into a society for the promotion of their sentiments. Among the young men who joined this society were a number from the Southern States, two of them sons of a distinguished Presbyterian minister in the State of Alabama. All such individuals, as they were well aware, were, by the position they had assumed, self-banished from their native States and their homes, it being certain that their lives would have been taken had they ventured even to visit their parents.

The facts above stated, as they were noised abroad through the papers, startled the nation, and threw the city into the most violent agitation. By men of the highest standing, the levelling of the institution to the ground was openly spoken of, while my visible connection with the students centered public reprobation upon myself. To indicate somewhat the extent and violence of that reprobation, I would give the following statement. As our two little daughters, one five and the other three years of age, were upon the sidewalks, they were stoned, and obliged to flee for their lives—were stoned, I say, by the children in the streets, because their father was an abolitionist. For months, when we lay down at night, we did so apprehending that our dwelling might be mobbed before morning. Under such circumstances, the Faculty of the Seminary called the students together, and entreated them to quiet the public agitation by disbanding their anti-slavery organisation, and refraining from all public discussions of the subject. The young men were told that their principles were right, and their spirit worthy of all commendation. It was unwise for them, however, to take public grounds so far in advance of public sentiment. "I have ever," said one of the most influential members of the Faculty, "made this a fixed principle of my life, never to become the open advocate of any cause until public sentiment has become sufficiently advanced to sustain me in the position I have taken; and I urge you, young gentlemen, to act upon the same principle in the case before you." The students did not accept such counsels as wise and prudent, however, and did not dissolve their society.

Before the mob of the city was organised, the, spring and summer vacation, of three months' continuance occurred, and the Faculty, all but one, went to the East, and the students dispersed; myself, on a four weeks' vacation, visiting my friends in western New York. During this interval, I had a full opportunity to judge of my situation, and calculate my future. But a few weeks before, the terrible Pro-Slavery Mobs had occurred in the city of New York, and everywhere public sentiment burned with the intensest indignation against the abolitionists. I said to myself distinctly: "If I identify myself with truth and right and God's poor and oppressed ones, as I must do, or violate my conscience and the will of my Divine Sovereign, I shall lose my place as pastor in Cincinnati. In that case, no important church in the country will be open to me. I shall, consequently, be necessitated to spend my life as pastor of some obscure church in the country." Such were the facts as they then presented themselves to my mind. I did not hesitate, but determined to accept the consequences of "serving God with a pure conscience." I claim to have done nothing more than, as I have said, a common Christian duty, and what thousands of my associates in the ministry would have done in my circumstances, and, in substance, did in theirs.

With such apprehensions distinctly before my mind, I returned to my people in the city, where many had said that I would never dare to show my face again—I, in my absence, refusing to preach as a candidate in one of the most important churches in the portion of the country I visited, and that for the reason that I was sure that no man with my sentiments could then be settled over any such church. I had been at home but a few hours, when I received a notice to attend a meeting of the Prudential Committee of the Seminary. At this meeting a code of laws for the Seminary was submitted, a code dissolving the Anti-Slavery Society among the students, prohibiting public, and even private, discussions of slavery on their part. The clause prohibiting private conversation upon the subject was omitted from the code as finally passed by the trustees. A clause more arbitrary than this was inserted—a clause giving the Prudential Committee absolute power to turn any student out of the Seminary when they should think it necessary so to do—a clause which was inserted for the openly avowed purpose of preventing the return of certain of the most prominent and able advocates of the anti-slavery cause. It was this clause which opened the eyes of the public to the monstrous character of the whole code, and secured an extensive sympathy with the students. When the vote on the code was about to be put, I, for the purpose of gaining time, remarked that we had no power to pass any laws whatever, this power being exclusively lodged with the trustees. This was assented to, and the committee adjourned, with the avowed determination that a meeting of the trustees should be called as soon as allowable. I at once sent a letter to Dr. Beecher, informing him of what was being done, and urging him to return at once with his associates, and prevent the impending evils, as I was sure that the Seminary would be dismantled should any such code as was being proposed be adopted. None of the Faculty returned, however—Dr. Beecher even stopping in the interior of the State of

Ohio until after the trustees had acted. When the Board met, I was, against my choice, compelled to take a stand more publicly and openly than I had ever done before. I must acquiesce in, or protest against, a code of laws which my conscience and judgment reprobated as opposed to the inalienable rights of human nature, to public morals, and the interests of humanity—a code which prohibited candidates for the Christian ministry from all concerted discussion and action in respect to fundamental questions concerning the rights of prostrate and downtrodden human nature. At the meeting of the Board, the statement was openly made that, at the anniversaries at the East, a consultation had been held by the leading presidents and officers of colleges and theological seminaries East and West, and it had been unanimously agreed among them, that in them all laws like those then before that Board should be passed, and that they were waiting our action. As I heard that announcement, this thought passed through my own mind: "The first institution that shall pass such laws must be crushed; that will deter the others."

When my course relatively to these laws become known, my separation from the fellowship of the ministry and membership of all the churches, my own excepted, and from the common civilities of the people of the city, became, as I expected it would, complete. Outside this one circle, there was in the city none so poor as to show me common respect. At this time, our Methodist brethren held a camp-meeting some twenty-five to thirty miles from the city, and that upon ground where they had, prior to this, held similar meetings for many years in succession. At this meeting the ministry found themselves utterly powerless to move at all the vast congregation before them. After consultation they sent for me, they being aware of the power which God had before given me on such occasions. As I took my stand, on my arrival, in the presence of the vast crowd before me, a consciousness of divine power came over me of which I had never had an experience before. During the progress of the discourse the hearts of the crowd were moved by the power of the truth and of the Spirit, "as the trees of the wood are moved by the wind." At the close of the discourse, sinners of all classes, and in astonishing numbers crowded to the places of inquiry. The whole following night was spent by ministers, without sleep at all, in directing inquirers to Christ, and a revival of religion occurred which is spoken of by people in the city and all that region to this day. When I witnessed these results, this sentiment forced itself upon my mind: "He always wins who sides with God," and always wins such victories as his heart most desires. During one of the intervals of worship, I retired into the forest for personal meditation and prayer. While there, with a sense of painful loneliness and isolation which it is impossible to describe, I lifted my eyes and heart above, and said in words to my Father in heaven, that "I was willing, if need be, to be alone and to be despised in the world; but there was one thing that I did desire, and would venture to ask: that I might be conscious that my heart was pure in His sight, that I might *see* God, and live and walk in the manifested light of His countenance. If God would grant me this one infinite good," I added, "I would accept of any burdens or afflictions that He might lay upon me." That was the distinctly uttered vow which I took with me from that forest. I have passed through heated furnaces and deep waters since that time, but have never taken back or regretted that vow. The brightness of the final "rising of the Sun of Righteousness" did not come at that moment. The era was very near, however, when "God did become my everlasting light, and the days of my mourning were ended."

When the students returned to the Seminary, they met in the chapel, and sent a committee to the Faculty, requesting that the new code of laws might be read and expounded to them. When this was done, and the privilege of discussing among themselves the character of the laws was positively denied them, absolute submission or a departure from the institution being demanded, one of the young men rose and said, "We may have, at least, this privilege, to say openly, as a body, whether we will or will not submit to these laws. I therefore request every student who will, with me, refuse such submission, and request of the Faculty a dismission from the institution, to rise to his feet." All but about one dozen arose, and having received their dismission, left. A wealthy citizen, a brother-in-law of the late Chief-Justice Chase, promptly furnished the seceders comfortable accommodation a few miles out of the city, and the great philanthropist, Arthur Tappan of New York city, sent five thousand dollars in money to aid them in prosecuting their studies in their new location. In a few weeks these young men were quietly pursuing their studies, while the Faculty of Lane Seminary were alone, presiding over a dismantled institution. No other college or seminary followed the example of that one in passing laws to suppress among students the discussion of the great moral and religious questions of the age. The January following, 1835, I received an appointment to the presidency of Oberlin College, and during the progress of that year, I found myself at the head of an institution with about five hundred students in attendance, with the students who had left Lane Seminary and others pursuing their theological studies under Professor Finney as their professor of theology, and Professor Morgan, who had been dismissed from Lane Seminary on account of his anti-slavery principles, as their professor of Biblical literature. Oberlin College is the first institution of the class that opened its doors wide for the education of humanity, without distinction of race, colour, or sex. "He hath said, I will never leave thee, nor forsake thee."

I have this to record about my church in Cincinnati: Most of its members, upwards of two hundred in number, were converts under my ministry, their number being but sixteen when I became their pastor. During the period to which I have referred, those older members and young disciples stood around their pastor like a Spartan phalanx, and were about to add two hundred dollars to my salary when I was called from them. Some time after I left, they called as their pastor one of the most open and fearless abolitionists in the United States, and stood by him, as they had done by me, until he, Dr. Blanchard, was called to the presidency of an important college in the State of Illinois. I never doubted the revelation of God, that "godliness is profitable unto all things, having promise of the life that now is, as well as of that which is to come."

PART II

OUT OF DARKNESS INTO LIGHT.

CHAPTER I.

THE LIGHT DAWNING.

THE baptism of power for the conversion of sinners which I received at the camp-meeting referred to was retained when, in the early spring of 1835, I assumed my duties as President of Oberlin College. At the institution, in connection with the labors of Professor Finney, and in five protracted meetings held by myself, more than one thousand souls were hopefully converted prior to the middle of March of the next year. With very few exceptions, these converts evinced by their subsequent lives the genuineness of their conversion. Yet the conscious deficiencies above described remained, and pressed upon me with a weight never before experienced. Aside from my new relations to the churches, I had under my immediate care hundreds, and in successive years was likely to have thousands, of youth who would, after passing under the instruction of myself and associates, go out into the world to teach what we had taught them, and to represent Christ as we had represented Him in our instruction and example to them. "Has not God," I asked myself with the most deep and solemn interest, "in reserve for 'those that love Him,' 'some better things' than I, through my experience and present knowledge, am able to make known to these young disciples and to the churches round me? It must be so," I replied; "and if it be possible I will, by the grace of God, be both in experience and knowledge abundantly furnished for the good work before me.'" In accordance with this purpose, I made careful inquiry of Brother Finney and our associates. I found their minds, like mine, to be in darkness, just where, and about what, I was seeking light. In my researches after the mystery of the hidden life, I was, consequently, thrown back upon the Word of God and prayer for divine enlightenment.

During the second summer of our residence at Oberlin, a meeting in a large tent, furnished us by friends in New York for such services, was held in the vicinity of Mansfield, Ohio—a meeting attended by great congregations of unregenerate persons and of Christians. While many of the impenitent were hopefully converted, the preaching and exhortations had a wonderful effect upon professors of religion, not a few of whom gave up wholly their old hopes, and started anew for the kingdom of God. Among the individuals of this latter class was one minister of the gospel, who arose in the congregation and presented himself as a subject of special prayer, saying to us that, after the most careful self-examination, he had come to the deliberate conclusion that up to that time he had never been a converted man. In giving his reasons for that conclusion, which he did very clearly, "the thoughts of many hearts were revealed," and a large number of professing Christians saw themselves, in the light of the statements made, "weighed in the balances, and found wanting." Oh, that the same searching process might go through all our churches throughout the world! How many who are now resting upon their lees would be saved from that final catastrophe in which their "hopes shall be as the giving up of the ghost"!

The facts above stated rendered that meeting remarkable in the churches in all that region of country. Upon myself, the effect was to quicken and intensify the inquiry which I had been pursuing for years. What shall be done, I inquired, for these young converts and these believers, all of whom have started anew, and not a few have, for the first time, really "tasted that the Lord is gracious"? Shall all these be started upon that old track where backsliding is a certainty? Or shall they be set forward upon that "new and living way," where "their feet shall not stumble"? While pressed with such questions as these, I took up a little volume, that providentially lay by me, a volume entitled, "Clarke on the Promises," and read, on the title-page, this passage "Whereby are given unto us exceeding great and precious promises: that by these ye might be partakers of the divine nature, having escaped the corruption that is in the world through lust." No words can describe the effect which the reading of that passage had upon my mind. I seemed at once to be fanned by "the wings of that morning" whose everlasting light was about to dawn upon my waiting spirit. I looked at the passage, and deeply pondered every clause and leading word of it.

2 Peter i: 4 *Explained and Elucidated.*

Let us tarry for a few moments under the shadow of the great revelation before us, while I shall endevour to set before the reader the views of truth and the way of life opened upon my mind as I continued to reflect upon this wonderful utterance: "Whereby," that is, as the verses preceding show, "through the knowledge of God, and of Jesus our Lord." In this knowledge, "divine power hath given unto us all things that pertain unto life and godliness, through the knowledge of Him that hath called us to glory and virtue." We think of the holy and godly life required of us in the Scriptures. Everything requisite to the full realisation of that life in our experience is conferred upon us as a gift of grace, through the revelation of God in Christ. In knowing Christ, and the Father in and through Christ, we have all the knowledge, and all the forms and sources of influence and power, requisite to our being, becoming, and doing all that is required of us, and to assure for ourselves all the good that "God hath prepared for them that love Him."

In addition to all this, there are given to us specific *promises*, "promises exceeding great and precious." "What are divine promises?" I asked. In every such promise, as I at once perceived, God designates some specific blessing requisite to our purity, peace, fulness of joy, or highest usefulness as His servants; and absolutely pledges every attribute of His nature to grant us that blessing, whenever by faith He is "inquired of by us to do it for us." We trusting God to do for us what is pledged in the promise, He must do it for us, or be false to His own word and to His own divine nature. "What then is the creature to do?" I asked again. First of all, the answer was, he is to acquaint himself with the promise, that is, with what it really means, and then go directly to the throne of grace and ask the Father, in the name of Christ, to do for us just what He has pledged to our faith in the promise. When we thus ask, we must "ask in faith, nothing wavering," "counting Him faithful that hath promised," not "staggering at the promise through unbelief," and that on account of its vastness or littleness, and never "limiting the Holy One of Israel." Doubting His promise, we in our hearts "make God a liar." Limiting His promise, that is, expecting to obtain less than what is specified in God's plighted word, we call in question both His power and His grace. Neglecting the promise, we "judge ourselves unworthy of eternal life," and part with our birthright as the sons of God.

But these promises are not only specific, but "exceeding great and precious." The view which I then received of their exceeding greatness and preciousness—that view being of necessity at the time a very limited one—has continued to grow and expand before my mind from that time to the present, and, no doubt, will continue thus to grow and expand to eternity. What strikes the mind as very peculiar about these promises is, not merely their greatness and preciousness, but their *absolute completeness*. In them, every want, demand, and necessity of our mortal and immortal natures is distinctly specified, and to each want a pledge is given to our faith of the specific good which is fully adapted to meet that want in the best possible manner. Negatively, they pledge to our faith a total emancipation from all that would be to us a real evil, and positively all that would be to us a real good, and that the best possible. "No evil shall befall thee, neither shall any plague come nigh thy dwelling." "I pray not that Thou shouldst take them out of the world, but that Thou shouldst keep them from the evil." This is the negative side of the promises. Positively they pledge to the same faith all the possession of which would be to us a real good, and that in its best possible form. "No good thing will He withhold from them that walk uprightly." "He that spared not His own Son, but delivered Him up for us all, how shall He not with Him also freely give us all things?" "Ask, and ye shall receive, that your joy may be full." Such are the promises on their positive side, and they descend to particulars, and specify the evil and the good in all their specific forms, and absolutely pledge to our faith absolute freedom from the one and the full possession of the other. Standing in the presence of the promises, as they shine out in the bright firmament of divine revelation, we can say with absolute assurance, "All things are ours, whether Paul, or Apollos, or Cephas, or the world, or life, or death, or things present, or things to come; all are ours, and we are Christ's, and Christ is God's." Nothing but unbelief in us can prevent our total protection, not against all *seeming*, but against all *real* evil, on the one hand; and our actual possession, not of all *apparent*, but *real* good, on the other; and this not only for life, but for an eternity to come. While the promises present to our faith that which will fully meet each specific want as we apprehend it, they are so worded as to indicate, in every case, that "there is more to follow," and that we are authorised to expect "exceeding abundantly above all that we ask or think."

The apostle now specifies two fundamental purposes for which "the promises were given, and towards which they all in common, tend,—"that by these," that is, by believing in and trusting God's fidelity in all His promises, and by faith seeking and expecting their fulfilment in our experience, "we might be partakers of the divine nature, having escaped the corruption that is in the world through lust." The words, "the divine nature," imply, as all will admit, not only the holiness and blessedness of the divine mind, but also that divine *disposition* or nature in God which induces His holiness and blessedness. For us to become possessed of this "divine nature" implies not only present holiness and blessedness such as God possesses, but a divine disposition in us, a new and divine nature, which induces and prompts us to holiness, just as God's nature prompts Him to the same. In our old or unrenewed state, we not only sinned, but had a nature or dispositions which prompted us to sin. In Christ, we not only obey the divine will, but receive from Him, as the Mediator of the new covenant, a new or "divine nature," which prompts us to purity and obedience, just as our old dispositions prompted us to sin.

When, by faith, we have "obtained the promises," it becomes just as natural in us to obey as it once was to rebel, just as natural and easy to be lovingly quiet and forgiving as it was to be angry and revengeful when injured or provoked,—to bless, as it was to imprecate retribution when reviled,—to return good, as it was to return evil for evil received; —to be "content with such things as we have," as it was to "be careful and troubled about many things;" in short, to bring forth "the fruits of the Spirit"—"love, joy, peace, long-suffering, gentleness, goodness, faith, meekness, temperance," as it once was to do "the works of the flesh."

In illustration of what I now mean, I will state a single example. As an aged coloured woman, of the city of New York, was returning one evening to her home from the place where she had been selling apples during the day, and was carrying on her arm a basket containing the few which she had failed to sell, she was met by a drunken sailor, who thought that a fitting occasion was presented for him to show his temper. He accordingly kicked the basket from her arm, and thereby scattered the apples about the street. He then placed himself bolt-upright before her, and heaped upon her every vile epithet he could think of. Looking the offender in the face with the mildest compassion, the injured woman thus addressed him, and that with a manner of the gentlest meekness: "Young man, I hope God forgives you as freely as I do." The poor creature was startled and confounded, and returning the apples to the basket, he returned it to her arm, and having humbly confessed his wrong, took from his pocket what money he had, and gave that to her. What I desire to have noticed here is the fact that, in consequence of the new and divine nature which God had given that woman, it was as easy and natural for her to feel, and speak, and act, as she did, as it had been, in her old life, to become furiously angry under far less provocation. That woman had no occasion under that provocation to hold back and resist an evil temper; she did as she did in accordance with promptings of her new nature. So it is universally. When the promises are embraced by faith, "God sends the Spirit of His Son into our hearts,"—a spirit which induces in us the same "love of righteousness and hatred of iniquity" as dwelt in Him, and renders it just as natural for us to be "holy, harmless, undefiled, and separate from sinners," as it was for Him—just as natural to do the will and the work of our Father, and to "drink the cup which He giveth us," as it was for Christ. Were this not the case, "the *Spirit*," or disposition, of His Son would not be sent into our hearts.

To "escape the corruption which is in the world through lust," implies that we are not only saved from the actual sins that are in the world, but that the evil propensities and tempers, "the law in our members," which induces sin, are taken from us, and are supplanted by new and divine tendencies which naturally induce the opposite virtues. Nothing less than or diverse from the above exposition can be the meaning of the passage under consideration. To insure all this, as I shall show more fully hereafter, is a main and specific purpose of all the promises. They assure to us, when understood, and embraced by faith, not only deliverance from sinning, but "the death of the old man," or the crucifixion of all those tempers and dispositions which induce sin; and not only actual obedience to the divine will, but "a divine nature," which prompts and constrains obedience in all its forms. It is as much the nature of "the new man," or the promptings of his new and divine tendencies, to be pure in heart and life, as it was that of "the old man" to "obey the law of sin."

CHAPTER II.

THE LIGHT COME, OR THE BRIGHTNESS OF THE DIVINE RISING.

REFLECTING with unspeakable interest and delight upon "the promises," without having then fully apprehended their meaning or obtained them in their fulness, I returned to Oberlin. At a special meeting of the Faculty, it was agreed to hold special religious services on the evenings of the week, as long as the measure should be found expedient. The reason for this determination was the fact that so many of the students and young people in the community were impenitent, and the piety of the membership of the church was so manifestly low. Brother Finney agreed to conduct the meetings for inquiry, this being, in addition to his ordinary duties, about all that he was able to do. The responsibility of doing the preaching was thrown upon me. From the commencement of the meetings, the word of truth had a wonderfully searching power upon all classes. The impenitent, asking what they should do to be saved, and professing Christians pressing the question directly upon us whether there was any "deliverance from the body of this death" under which they were groaning, crowded the inquiry-room. The first Sabbath after the meetings commenced, I delivered a discourse on the text, "Israel is an empty vine: he bringeth forth fruit unto himself." In the discourse I pressed upon professing Christians the fact, that the reason why they were "bringing forth fruit unto themselves," and not unto God—in other words, that the reason, and only reason, of the low state of piety among us—was that individuals were not *'aiming* to do any better than they were doing," and that here was the ground of "the Lord's controversy" with them. Brother Finney, perceiving the searching and convicting power of the truth, arose at the close of the discourse, and remarked, that if there were any self-deceived professors present, they would escape the pressure of the truth upon their consciences by falling back upon their *good desires*. "If we are not living as we should, we *desire* thus to live," they will say. He then showed that in mere desires, that did not induce the serious *aim* or *intent* to do what God requires—that is, did not issue in real obedience—there is no religion at all. "If there are any professors of religion present," he added, "who now see that their hopes are not well founded, let them signify it by rising." To our amazement, quite one-third of the professors present arose, and asked us to tell them "what they should do to be saved." The other portion of the church, with almost one voice, and that from all parts of the assembly, implored us to tell them how they might cease to live at their present "dying rate," and attain to the revealed "liberty of the sons of God."

Myself and associates were now in circumstances in which we had never been before. We had encouraged the people to make inquiries in respect to all the spiritual difficulties and perplexities which pressed upon them. Yet here were questions of fundamental interest put to us, questions which we had never resolved in our own minds, and revealed forms of experience inquired after of which we had no personal knowledge, and about the conditions of attaining which we were as ignorant as the inquirers themselves. The effect upon my mind was the deep impression that the time had come when I *must* know the secret after which I had been so long inquiring. "With strong crying and tears," I carried the subject to "the throne of grace," and entreated the Father of mercies, for Christ's sake, to lead me out of darkness into the light after which I was seeking. On the afternoon of the next day, I arose from my knees in my study in my own house, and went into the room above, a room occupied by one of my associates in the Faculty, and thus addressed him:—"I desire to tell you what I am now seeking after, and have been seeking after these years which are past. I desire to know the *secret* of the piety of Paul, and by that knowledge understand how to make myself the spiritual attainments that he did. His relations to Christ were essentially different from mine. When I attempt to act for Christ, I often find my affections and all the sensibilities of my nature almost cold and dead, and I am necessitated to gird myself up, and force myself forward by dint of my own resolution. The case was utterly different with Paul. At all times, and under all circumstances, as he informs us, 'the love of Christ *constrained* him,' and was 'in his heart as a burning fire shut up in his bones,' always impelling him onward, rendering him 'weary with forbearing' to speak or act for Him 'that loved him, and gave Himself for him.' "What *is* the reason," I asked, "why my love is 'so faint,' and 'so cold,' and so unimpulsive, while that of Paul was such an undying and all-constraining flame?" While thus speaking upon the subject, I suddenly rose from my seat with the joyful exclamation, "I have found it!" and without uttering another word, I returned to my study, and falling again upon my knees, returned most fervent thanksgiving to God, that He had at last clearly revealed to me the divine secret after which I had been so long inquiring.

The reader may be interested and profited by being informed of the vision of divine truth, the vision which then opened upon my mind. As a means of attaining this end, I will cite Eph. iii. 14-19: "For this cause I bow my knees unto the Father of our Lord Jesus Christ, of whom the whole family in heaven and earth is named, that He would grant you, according to the riches of His glory, to be strengthened with might by His Spirit in the inner man; that Christ may dwell in your hearts by faith; that ye, being rooted and grounded in love, may be able to comprehend, with all saints, what is the breadth, and length, and depth, and height, and to know the love of Christ, which passeth knowledge, that ye might be filled with all the fulness of God." While conversing with my associate, I *began* to realise, in experience, what the apostle here prays that all believers may receive and enjoy. In the depth of my inner being, I felt an instantaneous enlargement, expansion, and invigoration of my receptive capacities. There then opened upon my mind a direct apprehension, an open vision, as it were, of the infinite and ineffable love and glory of Christ, a love and glory which filled and occupied the entire compass of my being, and warmed, and quickened, and vitalised all the powers and activities of my mental nature. The rock of the heart was struck with the rod of love divine, and from the cleft thus made there issued forth "rivers of living water," which have ever since been "springing into everlasting life." As I arose from my knees in my study, I sat still in my chair, to "behold the glory of the Lord," to "comprehend the breadth, and length, and depth, and height of the love of Christ, which passeth knowledge," while "the fulness of God" seemed to enter in, and possess and occupy my whole inner being. There I sat, wondering with unutterable wonder that this vision of glory-infinite had never opened upon my mind before. "This," I exclaimed, "is 'life-eternal;' this is 'the brightness of the divine rising;' this is 'the rising of the Sun of Righteousness with healings in His wings;' here is 'the fountain opened for sin and uncleanness;' and here is the 'enduement of power' by which 'he that is feeble among us shall be as David, while the house of David shall be as God, as the angel of the Lord before Him.'" These were the thoughts which passed before my mind as I sat there in the center of that "everlasting light" which had risen upon my waiting spirit. I recognised myself at once, and that without a shadow of doubt, "as complete in Christ," and as able as Paul was to "do all things through Christ which strengtheneth me." The secret of the piety of Paul was now unveiled, and I could, as he had been, be "crucified with Christ," be "crucified to the world, and the world to me," and have "Christ live in me" as He did in him. I understood why "the law of the Spirit of life in Christ Jesus had made him," and might make me, "free from the law of sin and death," and why we are called upon to "reckon ourselves dead indeed unto sin, but alive unto God through Jesus Christ our Lord." The presence of "the love of Christ," His love unveiled to our apprehension by "the Spirit of the Lord," resolves at once all the mysteries of "life and godliness."

CHAPTER III.

SPEAKING TO THE PEOPLE WHEN STANDING IN THE LIGHT.

W<small>HILE</small> I was employed in such meditations, the Professor came down from the upper room, and asked me what subject I intended to preach to the people about the following evening. "I shall preach to them from this text, I replied, 'The love of Christ constraineth us.'" "Are you," he asked with surprise, "intending to preach on that text?" "I am," I replied. "I *know* that I have found at last 'the mystery of the hidden life,' and 'the days of my mourning are ended.'" The Professor has often remarked since that he could never understand the effect produced upon my mind while we were conversing upon that passage in his room. Nor can any one understand it, unless he himself shall receive the apprehension then and there imparted to my mind by the Spirit of God. It was no new exposition of the passage that I then received. I had often, and that most critically, examined it before—had as often reflected upon the diverse relations which Paul and myself sustained to Christ as evinced in the passage, and had obtained all the meaning of it which I now attach to it, or can be derived from it by mere human interpretation. Nor was it any new *doctrine* that I then received. What I did receive, on the other hand, was a direct, immediate, and open *vision* of the glory and love of Christ, that love "which passeth knowledge,"—an inward beholding imparted to the mind by the Spirit of God, a beholding utterly impossible but upon one condition, that "the Spirit shall *take* of the things of Christ, and *show* them unto us." Here we have a full understanding of the meaning of the apostle when he said, "No man can say that Jesus is Lord, but by the Holy Ghost." We can, of course, without any *special* aid of the Spirit, pronounce the words. We can, also, prove doctrinally the incarnation, the divinity, atonement, and lordship of Christ. No man, on the other hand, can pronounce the words referred to, with any proper apprehension of the eternal verity which these words represent, but upon the exclusive condition that "the Holy Ghost" shall open upon his mind a vision or apprehension of the verity itself. Moses, for example, knew enough of the divine character—and so do all—to understand that there was a glory about it which he needed to apprehend, and that he must apprehend this, or he could not, as he desired, "know God, and understand His way, and find grace in His sight." He was also aware that such apprehensions are possible to creatures, but upon the condition that God Himself shall "*show* them His glory," and '*cause* all His goodness to pass before them." Hence the prayer, "I beseech Thee, *show* me Thy glory." I may, as a student of the Bible, obtain a very full exegetical knowledge of its contents, and as a theologian, I may receive a full knowledge of the system of doctrines revealed in the Scriptures, and such forms of knowledge are important, and should not be undervalued. If I would know Christ, and God in Christ, with all kindred truths, as they are in themselves, however, here my dependence is absolute upon the direct and immediate illumination and teaching of the Holy Spirit. Knowledge, in the first form, however clear and extensive, is comparatively "a dead letter," and has very little transforming or vitalising power. In the second form, truth, in all its manifestations, has an all-transforming, quickening, and vitalising power. "Where the Spirit of the Lord is, there is liberty. But we all, with open face beholding as in a glass the glory of the Lord, are changed into the same image, from glory to glory, even as by the Spirit of the Lord." This is the divine illumination promised to all believers, and which they should all seek as the immutable condition of "their knowing God, and Jesus Christ, whom He hath sent," and of their receiving that "eternal life" which comes to the soul through that knowledge. Christ, with the Father in Him, is walking up and down amid the great revelations of His Word, as He did "amid the golden candlesticks," and the Spirit is waiting to show us "the glory of the Lord." When will the prayer of faith became universal—"I beseech thee, show me the *glory* of the Lord"?

As far as the meeting in the evening was concerned, the Spirit of God seemed to have prepared all hearts to receive the new message which God had given me to deliver to the people. After giving forth my text, I remarked to the audience that I had an important confession to make in their hearing. Up to that time I had not been, in the highest sense of the term, a preacher of the gospel. What I had preached had been, as far as it went, the truth of God, and that truth had been so preached as to be instrumental in the conversion of many souls. I had also been sincere in my ministry, and had fully acted up to the light I had. Yet, while my preaching had been efficacious for the end referred to—the conversion of sinners—it had lacked essentially those characteristics requisite to "feed Christ's sheep" and "Christ's lambs;" in other words, to furnish those instructions adapted to "build up believers in the most holy faith," and so to instruct them that they would "grow up in Christ all things," and thus "attain to the measure of the stature of the fulness of Christ." The reason and ground of this deficiency I would now endeavour to make known to the audience. When a sinner had inquired of me what he should do to be saved, I had known perfectly what needed to be done in his case. He needed to be instructed in regard to his sins, his ill-desert on account of sin, and his hopeless ruin in sin. He needed then to be directed to Christ as his only hope and refuge. Having given up his sins, and given himself wholly to Christ to be His servent forever, he must intrust his mortal and immortal interest to the mercy and grace of God in Christ. Under such instruction, the sinner, by "repentance toward God and faith toward our Lord Jesus Christ," obtains pardon, "power to become one of the sons of God," and "peace and joy in believing." But when a believer had come to me and confessed that he was not living as God requires, and asked me how he should escape "the bondage of corruption," and attain to "the liberty of the sons of God," I had instructed him to confess his sins, put them away, renew his purpose of obedience, and go forth with a fixed resolution to do the entire will of God. Now, here was a fundamental mistake. We are not only to be "justified by the faith of Christ," but to be "sanctified also by the faith that is in Him." "Christ is of God made unto us," not only "wisdom and righteousness," that is, justification, but "sanctification and redemption" also.

If you desire a victory over your tempers, your appetites, and all your propensities, take them to Christ, just as you take your sins to Him, and He will give you the victory over the former, just as He gives you pardon from the latter. He is just as able and ready to save you from the power as he is to deliver you from the condemnation of sin. Here is the only cause of your many shortcomings. In the matter of justification, you have trusted Christ, and He has done for you according to your faith. In the matter of sanctification, you have, instead of trusting Christ to "sanctify and cleanse you with the washing of water by the Word," resolved and re-resolved, and, as a consequence, have remained "carnal, sold under sin." So it will be, until you shall cease wholly from man and from yourself, and trust Christ universally. When He shall become the fixed and changeless center about which all your affections, and purposes, and hopes, and confidence, shall revolve, then shall "your righteousness go forth as brightness, and your salvation as a lamp that shineth," and in your love and obedience you shall be "as Mount Zion, which cannot be moved, but which abideth for ever."

The command in the Bible is not Be strong in yourself, or in good resolution, but "Be strong in the Lord, and in the power of His might." Trusting in Christ, you will "always have all-sufficiency in all things, and be abundantly furnished unto every good work." It is not he that resolves, but "he that abideth in Christ, and Christ in him, that bringeth forth much fruit." It is because that "in my ignorance" I talked so much of human ability to do all that is required of us, and in reality trusted in my own resolutions, instead of putting "my hope and trust in the living God" in the matter of holy-living, that I am permitted to speak to you tonight of "the unsearchable riches of Christ," instead of being cast aside as a vessel unfit for its master's use. From this time onward let this be our changeless sentiment—"Let us have *grace* whereby we may serve God acceptably with reverence and godly fear."

I then directed the attention of the audience to the *principle* involved in the words, "The love of Christ constraineth us." The strongest and most enduring principle, I remarked, in rational natures is that of *sympathy*. The action of such natures is strongest, steadiest, and most tireless, when they are brought into the full sympathy with the thoughts, emotions, and purposes of some controlling mind, whom all in common regard with the deepest love and veneration. It is said that during the American Revolution there was a crisis when but one single fact kept our army from disbanding and going home—sympathy with the fixed determination, calm assurance, and deathless patriotism of Washington, their venerated chief. The same principle obtains universally. The design of God is, "in the dispensation of the fulness of times," to "gather together in one all things in Christ, both which are in heaven, and which are on earth, even in Him"—that is, to induce an absolute unity of thought, feeling, sentiment, and fellowship among all holy beings in the universe. This is to be accomplished by bringing all into one common sympathy with "the love of Christ, which passeth knowledge," and that love is to harmonise, vitalise, and constrain all in common to eternity. When you shall come to a comprehension of "the breadth, and length, and depth and height," and shall "know the love of Christ, which passeth knowledge," your whole being will be drawn into sympathy and fellowship with that love; and, to the extent of your capacities, your love will be as full, as pervading, as enduring, and as constraining as is the love and sympathy which controls, and vitalizes all your activities. *Here we have the secret of the piety of Paul.* He *knew* the love of Christ—saw duty, in all its forms, in the light of that love—sympathised with that love, and was *constrained* by it in all his "work and labors of love." He was, consequently, "crucified with Christ," and "Christ lived in him," and "the life which he lived in the flesh" was, as he said, "by the faith of the Son of God, who loved me, and gave Himself for me." Living, dwelling, and acting in the everlasting light, and under the all-constraining influence of that love, it could not but have been to him, at all times and under all circumstances, as "a burning fire shut up in his bones;" and his life could not have been less laborious, less self-denying, less contented, less joyful, less victorious, less "strong in the Lord and in the power of His might," and less fruitful, than it was. "Oh, "the depth of the riches both of the wisdom and knowledge of God!" Oh, "the breadth, and length, and depth, and height of the love of Christ," who has come to us in our darkness, and made manifest unto us this "new and living way"! All that Paul ever experienced in his inner life every one of us may become fully possessed of; because we can know the love of Christ as he knew it.

I then directed the attention of the audience to two distinct and separate points of light in which duty, in all its forms, and in reference to all its objects, may be contemplated. We will consider in illustration, I remarked, the soul, for whose salvation we are called upon to labor. We think of the soul itself; its nature, powers, susceptibilities, its ruin in sin, and its eternal future. Here is an object the contemplation of which ought to move all the activities of our nature. There is another point of view, however, in which this same object may be contemplated. Christ knows the soul, its sins, and the perils and infinitude of its interests, as we cannot know them. "The redemption of the soul," what value does He place upon it? What has He done to redeem it? What is the strength of His desire for its salvation? How much does He love it?

In illustration of the principle under consideration, I now referred to two examples. You attend a funeral service, I remarked. Before you lies the lifeless body of a husband and father. You think of that family as having experienced a great loss. Yet you do not weep. At length the widow and orphans gather around that body. Why do you weep now? Because you see the same object from another standpoint from which you contemplated it before. You now perceive how dear and how valuable the departed was to the heart of that widow and those orphan children.

Years ago, I further stated, the son of an Irish soldier, who had passed through his term of service, and was waiting in London for his papers, was tried and condemned in court for theft. During the trial the father was seen walking to and fro in the most demure and saddened silence. When the sentence was pronounced, he turned to the judge in the most convulsive agony, and exclaimed, "I have carried him many a mile upon my back, your honor." The courtroom instantly became "a Bochim." All suffused with tears, the judge requested the father to tell him about his son. He then informed him that the mother of the child died when it was an infant; that he had nursed the child as its mother would have done; that when he entered the army, he had taken the little one with him, and in all his marches had carried his boy upon his back. While waiting in London to receive his wages and his papers, the lad had been enticed by wicked boys, and had engaged with them in theft.

"And now," exclaimed the father, "I must go home without him." "No, no!" exclaimed the judge and all present. There was no difficulty now in getting signatures to a petition, and advocates for the pardon of the lad. Why did not the spectacle of the child tried and condemned of itself thus move that audience? Why this sudden outburst of feeling? Why this movement for the restoration of the child to the arms of the father? Because the case was now contemplated in the light of a father's love, and in sympathy with that love. To the same principle our Saviour refers in the melting parable of the Prodigal Son.

So, when we shall come to contemplate the soul with all its interests, and duty in all its forms, not only as they are in themselves, but in the light in which Christ views them, of the value which He places upon them, in the light of His "love of righteousness and hatred of iniquity;" of His love to us, to the souls for whom He died, to all rational natures, and to "His Father and our Father, and to His God and our God,"—then we shall no more have occasion to talk and sing about "these cold hearts of ours," about our inability to "fly or go to reach eternal joys," or about "the blessedness we knew when first we saw the Lord." "God will become our everlasting light, and the days of our mourning shall be ended." We shall "mount up on wings as eagles. We shall run and not be weary, and shall walk and not faint." "He that is feeble among us shall be as David, while the house of David shall be as God, as the angel of the Lord before Him." "We shall be in the world as He was in the world." We, abiding in His love, "the works that He did we shall do also, and greater works than these shall we do," because "He has gone to the Father," and shall "endue us with power from on high" for the work to which He has called us. The love of Christ being infinite and unchangeable, when we shall *know* it, and be brought into sympathy with it, we shall be under an influence by which "our love shall be made perfect," and as enduring and constraining as is the love in the everlasting light of which we live and act.

One more topic, I remarked, needed to be elucidated before closing the discourse. Is it possible for us, it may be asked, to "*know* the love of Christ"? and if so, *how* shall we attain to this knowledge? We can attain to this knowledge, I replied, because the Holy Spirit is in the world, and is promised to all believers who seek "the baptism of the Holy Ghost," for the revealed purpose of enabling us to "know the love of Christ, which passeth knowledge." "The Spirit searcheth all things, even the deep things of God;" and when we shall be "filled with the Holy Ghost," as all may be, this "liberty" will be vouchsafed to us—namely, "We all with open face, beholding as in a glass the glory of the Lord, shall be changed into the same image, from glory to glory, even as by the Spirit of the Lord." Yes; when the Holy Spirit shall come, and He is promised, I repeat, to all who seek Him, we shall fully understand in experience what Paul meant when, under the inspiration of the Spirit, he put up the following prayer:—"For this cause I bow my knees unto the Father of our Lord Jesus Christ, of whom the whole family in heaven and earth is named, that He would grant you, according to the riches of His glory, to be strengthened with might by His Spirit in the inner man; that Christ may dwell in your hearts by faith; that ye, being rooted and grounded in love, may be able to comprehend with all saints what is the breadth, and length, and depth, and height; and to know the love of Christ, which passeth knowledge, that ye might be filled with all the fulness of God. Now unto Him that is able to do exceeding abundantly above all that we ask or think, according to the power that worketh in us, unto him be glory in the church by Christ Jesus throughout all ages, world without end. Amen." Let us, then, take our harps down from the willows, never again to tune them to notes of sadness, but that we may "return and come to Zion with songs and everlasting joy upon our hearts," that we "may obtain joy and gladness, and sorrow and sighing flee away."

Such is the exact substance of the first full gospel sermon that I ever preached in my life. It may be considered somewhat remarkable that the doctrine of Christ as our "wisdom, righteousness, sanctification, and redemption," and "the promise of the Spirit," as the great central truths of the gospel, should have been presented to my mind at one and the same time. But so it was. The truths presented in the discourse made manifest to those believers who, with myself, had come to a state of such intense hungering and thirsting after righteousness, "the fountain opened to the house of David, and to the inhabitants of Jerusalem," that is, to all believers, "for sin and for uncleanness." Many descended at once into that fountain, and "washed their garments and made them white" there, finding, at the same time, "the Lord as their everlasting light," and the love of Christ as the same all-vitalizing, all-abiding, and all-constraining power in their hearts as it had been in the heart of Paul. From that time onward nothing was known in our preaching but "Jesus Christ, and Him crucified." Professor Finney especially most heartily indorsed the views presented in the discourse as soon as he was informed of them.

CHAPTER IV.

THE RENEWING OF THE HOLY GHOST.

WITHOUT further statements at the present time of the influence and results of the views under consideration upon others, I will continue the account of my own inner life. The apostle speaks of two distinct stages of Christian experience and moral and spiritual renovation. "According to His mercy hath He saved us, by the *washing* of regeneration and the *renewal* of the Holy Ghost." Prior to regeneration the Spirit convinces the soul of "sin, and of righteousness, and of judgment." So, prior to the period when "Christ manifests Himself" to the believer, and "He and the Father come to him, and make their abode with him," there is commonly a process of heart-searching, in which all our "secret faults," as well as "presumptuous sins," if we have been guilty of the latter, all our evil propensities, tendencies, and habits, with "the depths of Satan" within us, are fully disclosed to the mind. So it was with myself.

A few days after I had received the light of life, as above stated, my thoughts were suddenly turned inward, and my whole inner life and character were made manifest to my mind. My enslavement to my temper and appetites, my pride of character, egotism, self-will, secret ambition, restlessness under disappointments and afflictive providences, and the pain endured in "bearing the cross after Jesus," these, and things like these, were so presented, that I became a loathing to myself; and, but for the prior revelation of the infinitude of Christ's love and grace, together with His absolute power to "save unto the uttermost them that come unto God by Him," the midnight of blank despair would have settled over my mind. As it was, I read in a moment the purpose of the Spirit in the process which was going on. "Christ was manifested to take away my sins," and the preliminary steps to that end were being wisely and lovingly taken. I accordingly, with all earnestness, repeated the prayer of the Psalmist, "Search me, O God, and know my heart; try me, and know my thoughts." "Let the light now shine through all the chambers of imagery within me." Then "sprinkle clean water upon me, and make me clean from all my filthiness, and from all my idols do Thou cleanse me;" and after that, "lead me in the way that is everlasting." It was according to my faith. After the process of searching and self-revelation was completed, the waters of life seemed to flow through every department of my nature, rolling down as the river of life into the Dead Sea of the propensities, and everywhere with the same healing and vitalising efficacy. How often did I exclaim at that time, "There is healing now, and immortal health following the healing"! Truly, Christ is "the way, and the truth, and the life," and "the law of the Spirit of life in Christ Jesus does make free from the law of sin and death."

Let no one, who would know the full power and blessedness of the hidden life, fear or avoid, but rather desire and seek, the searching process under consideration; nor take alarm when the Spirit, instead of showing you at once "the glory of the Lord," and introducing you into the rest of faith, rather shows you your sins, your inward defilements, and sinful tendencies and habits. Seek, on the other hand, to know yourself as God knows you, and this as a means of your being "purified and made white." If we did not know our sins, we should not value the grace and love by which we are saved from our sins. When we have once put our case into the hands of the Great Physician, let us never for a moment distrust His wisdom, power, or fidelity, or become restive, though the healing process may, for the moment, seem severe. Only believe, and we shall "See the glory of the Lord."

CHAPTER V.

FREE IN CHRIST.

As the cleansing process above described went on, I soon became conscious of a power in Christ—a power which I had vainly struggled to acquire during my prior Christian life—*the power of absolute control over all the propensities*. In illustration, I will speak of my temper. Those who have known me most intimately for more than thirty years past, but did not know me before, have often said to me, "You don't seem to have any temper. Nothing whatever appears to provoke your anger. We could be quiet under provocation as you are, provided we had such a temper as you have." The truth upon the subject is, that originally I had one of the worst tempers I ever knew. When reflecting upon the subject when ten or eleven years of age, I said to myself, when alone in my father's pasture, "This temper will ruin me." When I became a Christian, I set about, with all the power of determination possible to me, to subdue and control that temper. All my resolutions, however, under sudden provocations, proved themselves a deceptive trust. When I came, however, to know Christ as my Deliverer, and when "the Son made me free," the first fact of which I became conscious was an absolute control over all the promptings of anger. Not long after, even these promptings disappeared entirely. In my former Christian life, under unexpected provocation, anger would arise, and I would "speak unadvisedly with my lips" before reflection would come to my aid, and then I would set about repairing the injury I had done. Often, as I have said formerly, would I say to myself, "Oh, that I could have time to reflect before speaking!" In my new life, reflection, as I became joyfully conscious, always came in directly between myself and the provocation, and gave me a perfect mastery over it. At length the feeling of anger disappeared, and it became just as natural and easy to be quiet and patient, as it had formerly been to be angry, under provocation. The same held true of my appetites. I had ever been, in the judgment of all who knew me, a very strictly temperate man; yet I was internally conscious that, in forms and particulars unknown to anybody but myself, my appetites did control me, and that my most fixed purposes were powerless to free me from their dominion. Faith in Christ, however, did set me free, and I attained to the state to which Paul refers when, in speaking of divers kinds of food, he says, "I will not be brought under the power of any." I now gratify my appetites as my better judgment dictates, and they do not, even internally, rebel against the dominion to which they are subject.

Finding how absolutely free divine grace had rendered me, relatively to my most despotic propensities, I resolved that, by the same grace, I would be the Lord's freeman in every particular—in other words, that I would have, "by the faith of Christ," and through His power abiding upon and strengthening me, absolute dominion over all my propensities in all their activities. I was well aware that, in regard to things lawful as well as unlawful in themselves, there might be forms and degrees of bondage from which "a believer in Jesus" should be perfectly free. Hence, whenever and wherever I felt an internal and restless cry after any specific gratification, whatever it might be—a cry saying, "I must have this, and I must have that"—I separated myself totally from such objects, until, through prayer and the "power of Christ resting upon me," that cry was subdued, and I felt myself perfectly free to enjoy or to be denied that gratification as providence and the best wisdom given should indicate. I thus found myself standing in "the light of God" and "in the power of His might" above my propensities, one and all of them alike, and rejoicing in God in an absolute "rule over my own spirit." Thus "our old man is crucified with Him, that the body of sin" (our evil propensities, principles, tendencies, and habits) "might be destroyed, that henceforth we should not serve sin."

To all who would enter into "the rest of faith" and continue therein, I present the above facts and suggestions as of infinite moment. Not a few who do enter into, and for a time abide in this rest, fail to continue therein, and thus give occasion to opponents to "speak evil of this way." The reason is, that the propensities, by not being "brought under," and thus "held in subjection," the "old man" not being "crucified with Christ," and "the body of sin not being destroyed" by His sanctifying "power working mightily" in "the inner man," "sin revives" through the renewed activity of "the law in the members." Thus losing their rest, they "cast away their confidence" and return to their old bondage. The rest of the soul in Christ will not be likely at all to continue unless, "through the faith that is in him," all forms of bondage to the propensities are completely broken, and they in all their promptings and activities are brought into complete subjection. For the reason that this liberty is not attained and perfected, Christ may "save us *now*," but not permanently.

I hear instructions given to believers seeking this "rest of faith," instructions which I cannot approve. They are told that Christ will not take away their evil propensities, and prevent their acting within the mind, but will enable believers to resist and hold in subjection such promptings. The apostle, on the other hand, tells us that, for the purpose that henceforth we should not serve sin, "the old man is crucified with Christ," and "the body of sin is destroyed." In express view of this fact, he requires us to "reckon ourselves dead indeed unto sin, but alive unto God, through Jesus Christ our Lord." As long as our lusts are left to "war in our members," there may be expected to be "wars and fightings" in the churches, and lapses and backslidings in all their membership. Christ "takes away our sins" by taking away the evil dispositions within us that prompt us to sin, and in the place of these dispositions giving us "a divine nature," which will prompt us to "love, joy, peace, long-suffering, gentleness, faith, meekness, temperance."

The reader will call to mind here the case of Dr. Hopkins, as stated in a former part of this work. In his case, during a period of more than thirty years, and no doubt to the end of life, he had not only held in subjection, but had experienced not a single prompting of the evil temper which, during his previous life, had had despotic control over him. The reader will also call to mind my own personal testimony on the subject. Similar testimony meets us everywhere. Here, as a fact, is an evil propensity not only held in subjection, but all its evil promptings utterly taken away. If Christ does this—and all admit that He does—in respect to one propensity, why should He not do the same in regard to all? As the Mediator of the new covenant, does He not stand pledged, when "He is inquired of by us to do it for us," to do for us all that is contained in the following "exceeding great and precious promises"? "Then will I sprinkle clean water upon you, and ye shall be clean: from all your filthiness, and from all your idols, will I cleanse you. A new heart also will I give you, and a new spirit will I put within you; and I will take away the stony heart out of your flesh, and I will give you an heart of flesh. And I will put my Spirit within you, and cause you to walk in my statutes, and ye shall keep my judgments, and do them." Such is the express meaning of the new covenant, as expressed in all the Scriptures. I shall have occasion to recur to this subject in subsequent parts of this work. May the reader not fail to understand, and fully to attain, "the glorious liberty of the sons of God"!

CHAPTER VI.

JESUS MANIFESTED TO THE BELIEVERS.

BEFORE introducing the topic of the present discourse, I will request the reader to peruse attentively the following passage, John xiv. 18-23, "I will not leave you comfortless: I will come to you. Yet a little while, and the world seeth me no more; but ye see me: because I live, ye shall live also. At that day ye shall know that I am in my Father, and ye in me, and I in you. He that hath my commandments, and keepeth them, he it is that loveth me; and he that loveth me shall be loved of my Father, and I will love him, and will manifest myself to him. Judas saith unto Him (not Iscariot), Lord, how is it that Thou wilt manifest Thyself unto us, and not unto the world? Jesus answered and said unto him, If a man love me, he will keep my words; and my Father will love him, and we will come unto him, and make our abode with him." The work of the Spirit, from the time when He convinces the sinner of his sins, up to the period in which the "renewing of the Holy Ghost" is completed, is to prepare the way for the consummation referred to in the passage above cited—the consummation in which Christ, with the Father, becomes to the mind a personally manifested and indwelling presence. The language by which this mysterious relation between a human soul and Christ, and God in Him, is expressed in the Scriptures, is quite various and peculiar. God, in referring to this relation between Himself and His people, says, "I will dwell in them, and walk in them." "Your bodies are temples of the Holy Ghost," and "ye are builded for a temple of God through the Spirit." "And truly," says the apostle, "our fellowship is with the Father, and with His Son Jesus Christ." Again, we read of "the communion and fellowship of the Spirit." In the following most memorable passage, our Saviour prays that this union and fellowship may be consummated between Him and all believers:—"Neither pray I for these alone, but for them also which shall believe on me through their word: that they all may be one; as Thou, Father, art in me, and I in Thee, that they also may be one in us: that the world may believe that Thou hast sent me. And the glory which Thou gavest me I have given them; that they may be one, even as we are one: I in them, and Thou in me, that they may be made perfect in one; and that the world may know that Thou hast sent me, and hast loved them, as Thou hast loved me."

The Scriptures also speak of our "dwelling in God, and God in us," and of "Christ dwelling in our hearts by faith." How, it may be asked, can Christ be in us, and we, at the same time, be in Him? An infidel once attempted to embarrass an unlettered but very intelligent coloured man, by putting to him this very question. The reply of the coloured man was amusing, but very impressive and pertinent. "Well, dat are," he replied, "don't trouble me. You take dat are poker and put it in de fire. In a little while de fire will be in de poker, and de poker in de fire. " If we are in Christ, we shall soon be "filled with all the fulness of God," and Christ, with every person of the sacred Trinity, will "make His abode in us." Christ is in us when, as a manifested personal presence, He directly and immediately controls all the powers, susceptibilities, and activities of our being, His manifested love completely moulding our character, drawing our whole hearts, and centering them in Him, and rendering us "holy, harmless, undefiled, and separate from sinners," as He was. We are in Christ when, having "cleansed us from all unrighteousness," He takes us to His heart as the object of His fraternal love, becomes the direct guardian of all our interests, "shows us His glory," and brings us into direct intercommunion with His thoughts, feelings, and purposes of love towards us.

The moment when, and the manner in which, Christ first "manifested Himself" to me, will, I doubt not, be held in remembrance to eternity. I had risen from my knees in my study, and had retired to our bedroom to rest for the night, my wife being already in bed. As I approached the side of the bed, the veil was lifted, and Christ, not as an object of physical, but exclusively mental and spiritual vision, was immediately before me. "With open face I beheld as in a glass His glory," or rather, beheld Christ Himself in His glory, with "the light of His countenance lifted upon me." Then I realised, as I had never done before, not only that He had "given Himself for me," but that "He loved me," and was present to me, to "show me the beauty of my Lord," and, as my eternal Friend and Portion, to abide in me for ever. I did not "fall at His feet as dead," the manifestation being too mildly loving for that. My breathing, however, stopped in an instant, and it was some time before I could recover it again. In deep agitation, my wife asked me what had happened? I replied, that my heart was too full to tell her then; I would endeavour to tell her some other time. All I could say was, that my joy was full.

"The brightness of that rising," reader, has never passed away, but is in the soul as an everlasting and evergrowing light. I *know* now that the words of our Saviour are true: "and this is life eternal, that they might know Thee, the only true God, and Jesus Christ, whom Thou hast sent." I read my inner life now in the words of the promise of God through His inspired prophet:—"The sun shall be no more thy light by day; neither for brightness shall the moon give light unto thee: but the Lord shall be unto thee an everlasting light, and thy God thy glory. Thy sun shall no more go down; neither shall thy moon withdraw itself: for the Lord shall be thine everlasting light, and the days of thy mourning shall be ended." All that the Scriptures record about Christ has a meaning and a life, and a melting and moulding power about it, never experienced before. It is no wonder to me that Paul affirmed, "I can do all things through Christ which strengtheneth me."

If the reading of the above facts and elucidations has not induced the reader, provided he has not yet attained, to say in his heart, "All this, and 'more to follow,' is for *me*, and, 'by the grace of God,' I will seek and walk in this 'everlasting light,'" then, so far as he is concerned, he has read and I have written in vain. "Christ has loved you, and given Himself for you," as He has for me, and is ready to dwell in your heart, as He does in mine. In the words of the aged apostle, I say to you, "That which we have seen and heard declare we unto you, that ye also may have fellowship with us; and truly our fellowship is with the Father, and with His Son Jesus Christ. And these things write we unto you, that your joy might be full."

CHAPTER VII.

THE PROMISE OF THE SPIRIT, OR THE DOCTRINE OF THE BAPTISM OF THE HOLY GHOST.

THERE is, and can be, no subject connected with "the redemption of the soul," no subject about which clearer and more definite information is required at the present time than on the doctrine of "the baptism of the Holy Ghost." In the experiences and elucidations above given, we have been prepared for a direct consideration of this great subject. It should be borne in mind that, in the whole work of human redemption, every Person of the sacred Trinity sustains to sinners and believers relations altogether special and peculiar—relations wholly unlike those which said personalities sustain to other realms and orders of the rational universe. God is a Father to believers in a sense and in relations which pertain to no other beings in existence. No revelation such as the following, as far as we know, is applicable to any other world but this, namely, "There is one God, and one Mediator between God and man, the man Christ Jesus." Equally special and peculiar are the revealed relations of the Holy Spirit to the race on the one hand, and to believers on the other. So peculiar and special are His revealed relations to believers under this, the new dispensation, that inspiration affirms absolutely that "the Holy Ghost was not given" until "after Jesus was glorified." On all these subjects human speculation is wholly out of place. Every ray of light which comes to us on said subjects descends to us directly and exclusively from God Himself through His inspired Word. To understand the doctrine of the Holy Spirit as revealed in the Scriptures, we need to inquire, first of all, into those revealed relations which each person of the Trinity sustains to each of the others, to the universe, and to mankind as sinners and believers.

Of the doctrine itself, I would only say that, on the exclusive authority of revelation, I hold, in common with the teachings of the evangelical faith, that, in opposition to the plurality of heathenism, there is one God or Godhead, and, in opposition to the absolute unity of Mohammedanism and Unitarianism, the same Godhead is clearly revealed to us as a Tri-Unity, represented by the words Father, Son, and Holy Ghost. The grounds of neither this unity on the one hand, nor Tri-personality on the other, are, in any sense or form, revealed in the Scriptures. The two doctrines, the unity on the one hand, and the plurality on the other, are revealed as *facts* of the divine nature, while the *reason* or *ground* of the facts are not revealed at all. We have a mystery, but no absurdity—the seeming contradiction involved in the doctrine arising exclusively from the endeavour of theologians to be "wise above what is written," by their attempts to define the divine unity on the one hand, or tri-personality on the other. What we now have to do with is, the revealed *relations* of the Father, Son, and Holy Ghost. I begin with those of

The Father.

If we will carefully study "what is written" upon the subject, we shall find, that whatever is represented by such words as original, ultimate, and absolute authority, supremacy, and paternity, pertains exclusively to the Father. Each of the other personalities, in all they do, act in absolute subordination to the Father, and exercise no form or degree of authority or power but such as has been *delegated* to them by the Father. As the Creator of the universe, Christ exercised a delegated power, "the Father creating all things by Jesus Christ." As the present Sovereign of the universe, Christ exercises authority delegated to Him by the Father. "All power in heaven and on earth," says our Saviour, "has been given unto me." "The government shall be laid upon His shoulders." The inauguration of Christ as Sovereign of the universe is thus represented by the prophet Daniel: "I saw in the night visions, and, behold, one like the Son of man came with the clouds of heaven, and came to the Ancient of days, and they brought Him near before Him. And there was given Him dominion, and glory, and a kingdom, that all people, nations, and languages, should serve Him: His dominion is an everlasting dominion, which shall not pass away, and His kingdom that which shall not be destroyed." "The Father," says our Saviour again, "judgeth no man, but hath committed all judgment to the Son." As "God manifest in the flesh," our Saviour taught that He was in the world as a *gift* of the Father to our lost race, and as sent by the Father, and that He "came not to do His own will, but the will of Him that sent him," not to do His own work, but to "finish the work which the Father had given Him to do."

The same absolute subordination to the Father obtains in respect to the Holy Spirit. Like the Son, the Spirit comes from the Father, and is sent and given to men by Him. Like the Son, also, the Spirit comes, "not to do His own will, but the will of Him that sent Him." Like the Son, the Spirit "speaks not of Himself; but what He hears that He speaks." "He receives of Christ, and shows them to believers," and "shows them plainly of the Father." In the work of redemption, the Spirit also acts in subordination to the will of Christ as well as of that of the Father. The Father, then, as representing the Godhead in its absolute and universal sovereignty, supremacy, and paternity, is not the exclusive, but, for the most part, the proper object of prayer. We approach Him through the Son. Let us now consider the revealed relations of

The Son.

While the Father represents the Godhead in its absolute supremacy, sovereign authority, and universal paternity, the Son represents the same Godhead in what may be denominated its supreme *executive power, authority,* and *majesty*. The Son is the revealed authoritative executor of the Father's will. The agency of the Father was not direct and immediate in creation. The Father, on the other hand, "created all things by Jesus Christ," "by whom also He" (the Father) "made the worlds." Of the Son, as we read Heb. i. 8-12, the Father thus speaks:—"But unto the Son He saith, Thy throne, O God, is for ever and ever: a sceptre of righteousness is the sceptre of Thy kingdom. Thou hast loved righteousness, and hated iniquity; therefore God, even Thy God, hath anointed Thee with the oil of gladness above Thy fellows. And Thou, Lord, in the beginning hast laid the foundation of the earth and the heavens are the works of Thine hands: They shall perish; but Thou remainest; and they all shall wax old as doth a garment; and as a vesture shalt Thou fold them up, and they shall be changed: but Thou art the same, and Thy years shall not fail." The Father does not directly and immediately govern the universe, but has "laid the government upon the shoulders of the Son," who, as the Supreme executive of the universe, "upholds all things by the word of His power." By Him, also, "all things consist," that is, are sustained, controlled, and governed. As the supreme executive, also, Christ, as the Eternal Word, "was made flesh, and dwelt among us," "bore our sins," "brought in everlasting righteousness," now reigns as the sovereign Lord of all, and will, at the final consummation, sit as "Judge of quick and dead."

A careful study of the Scriptures will also fully evince the great fact that all the *audible* and *visible* manifestations of the Godhead to men were made by Jesus Christ. "He it was that was with the Church in the wilderness," "the Rock" of defence and hope, "which followed the people, being Christ." He it was, consequently, that spake to Moses in the bush, led the people by a pillar of fire out of Egypt, gave the covenant and law from Sinai, and conducted the people through the wilderness. All that we know or can know of God is through Christ, through His works, manifestations, and revelations. When we "see Him we see the Father." In Christ, and only through Him, do we "behold the brightness of the Father's glory, and the express image of His substance." We will now contemplate the revealed relation of

The Holy Spirit.

While the Father represents the Godhead in its high functions as the original source of universal and absolute sovereignty, authority, and paternity, and the Son in those of supreme executive power, and dominion, the Holy Spirit represents the same Godhead in its functions as that invisible divine energy which everywhere acts potentially in nature, and immediately brings about those results which God wills.

The first revelation which we have of the agency of the Spirit, we find in connection with the account of creation in the first chapter of Genesis.

We find that revelation in these words:—"And the Spirit of God moved upon the face of the waters." Had we been present, and witnessed the events here referred to, all that would have been visible to us would have been the simple agitation of the watery elements. The cause of the movement would have been to us wholly invisible. We might, and should, were we infidels, have attributed all these results to the action of mere natural law. The same holds true of the results produced by the Spirit everywhere in the universe of matter and mind. The *results* are manifest; the cause is invisible; and the events appear as they would were they the results of the internal powers of nature itself. When the Spirit, for example, operates upon our minds, in very few instances can we distinguish the thoughts and states induced from those which result from the laws of natural association. Here infidelity comes in, and, in the name of "science, falsely so-called," denies the all-controlling agency of God in nature, attributing all events to natural law. Even theologians, let me add here, are too often accustomed to lead the Church away from God, and in the direction of false science.

Take the all-energising agency of the Spirit of God out of nature, and we are in a blind, cold, and Godless universe, and as really without God in the world as the heathen are.

As a further illustration of the agency of the Spirit, as representing the Godhead in nature, let us, for a moment, contemplate His revealed agency in the miraculous events recorded in the Scriptures. In Matt. xii. 28, Christ affirms that all His miracles were performed by the Spirit. "But if I cast out devils by the Spirit of God, then the kingdom of God is come unto you." This is undeniably uttered as illustrative of the invisible divine agency by which all Christ's miracles and all other miraculous events are produced. Christ, for example, said to the leper, "I will; be thou clean." The Spirit invisibly energised in the system of the individual diseased, and thus induced the cleansing required. Christ stood upon the deck of the vessel amid the night tempest on the Sea of Galilee, and said to the winds and waves, "Peace, be still!" The Spirit invisibly "moved upon the face of the waters," and energised in the atmosphere around, and thus instantly induced the subsidence of the waves and the stillness of the atmosphere which ensued. So in all other instances.

But the Holy Spirit is not only the invisible divine energy which operates in visible nature around us, and induces those events which we behold, but He also operated with the same invisible divine efficiency upon the writers of the Sacred Word, and thus originated

"That dearest of Books, that excels every other,

The old Family Bible, that lays on the stand."

The Bible is what it is, because "all Scripture is given by inspiration of God," and "the holy men" who wrote it "spake as they were moved by the Holy Ghost."

The Holy Spirit is now in the world, and operating upon the minds of men as a convicting and regenerating agency, leading all who will be led to Christ. In the Church, and among all who have received Christ as their "wisdom, righteousness, sanctification, and redemption," the Holy Spirit is present as "the promise of the Father;"—a promised "enduement of power from on high," an indwelling light, by which "we all with open face, beholding as in a glass the glory of the Lord, are changed into the same image, from glory to glory, even as by the Spirit of the Lord," and as an all-strengthening and all-vitalising power, by which we "may be strengthened with might by the Spirit in the inner man, that Christ may dwell in our hearts by faith; that we, being rooted and grounded in love, may be able to comprehend with all saints what is the breadth, and length, and depth, and height, and to know the love of Christ, which passeth knowledge, that we might be filled with all the fulness of God,"—an indwelling and ever-working power, "according to which," or through which, God is "able to do exceeding abundantly above all that we ask or think." Such are the revealed relations and functions of the Holy Spirit—relations and functions as distinct from one another as are the various offices which Christ fulfils distinct from one another. It would be no greater error for us, for example, to confound the office of Christ as "Mediator between God and man" with that of His other function as "Judge of quick and dead," than it would be to confound the office of the Spirit as "the promised enduement of power from on high" with either of His offices in conviction and conversion, or as the invisible divine energy everywhere working potentially in nature.

Essential Errors connected with the Doctrine of the Spirit.

There are three very essential errors connected with the doctrine of the Holy Spirit—errors which require special consideration in this connection. The first that I notice has obtained control over the faith of the Churches in consequence of what has been rightly called "the senseless twaddle of infidelity about the absolute prevalence of law in nature." Under the influence of this error, the influence of the Spirit is supposed to have place only in the kingdom of grace, while the revealed fact that He is omnipresent in universal nature, operating everywhere as the invisible divine energy causing, controlling, and regulating the events which we behold, is practically denied. Hence the error, so deadening to the faith of believers, that prayer has efficacy in the former, and not in the latter kingdom. The Bible, let me say, is one of the most unmeaning and deceptive books that ever was written, if, in respect to revealed objects of prayer, prayer has not the same avail in one kingdom as in the other, and temporal are as distinctly specified as such objects as our spiritual blessings.

But are not all events in the universe around us controlled by fixed and immutable laws? Yes, we answer. Yet these laws work out very different results indeed from what they would do but for the presence, and action, and controlling influence of *finite* spirit in nature. The reciprocal influence of spirit over matter, and of matter over spirit, is no violation of nature's laws, but absolutely accord with those laws. Now, if there is omnipresent in nature an infinite and eternal Spirit invisibly controlling all events, then we should expect that the order of events would be as far different, at least, from what it would be but for His presence and agency, and in consequence of the presence and action of that Spirit, as that order is in consequence of the presence and action of the Spirit of man in nature. Any deduction the opposite of this is as absurd, and contrary to the dictates of true science, as it is to the revealed truth of God. It is, therefore, not only accordant with the express teachings of inspiration, but just as reasonable in itself, for me to expect to receive specific answers to prayer relatively to the temporalities of life—answers through the occurrence of events which would not arise but for my prayers—as it is for me to expect to receive answers to communications sent to friends on the other side of the Atlantic—answers which I should not receive but for the communications which I do send; and it is quite as necessary to our real comfort and well-being to know that God lives and acts in the kingdom of nature, as well as in that of grace, as a Hearer of prayer, as it is to know that our distant friends are alive and ready to answer our communications. Nor will God ever, as He has promised, "dwell in His people, and walk in them," until they recognise the presence and agency of the Eternal Spirit in the world of nature as well as of that of grace, and repose the same confidence in the divine promises relatively to temporal as to spiritual blessings.

Another important error connected with this subject is the too common one of confounding "*the baptism of the Holy Ghost*" with His special functions in *conviction* and *conversion*. In the latter relation He is never called "the Holy Spirit of promise," and is never, more especially, said to be given to "those who obey God," and not to have been given at all until after "Jesus was glorified." In this specific relation He has, in each dispensation alike, been in the world, "striving with men," and "grieved" and "vexed" with their sins, ever since the Fall. In this relation He acts upon the human mind, whether men are willing or unwilling to be "convinced of sin." In the former relation, on the other hand, the Holy Ghost, as promised in the new, was not given at all in the old dispensation: "For the Holy Ghost was not yet given, because Jesus was not yet glorified." In this relation He is given to those, and those only, who obey God, and after they have believed in Jesus. "And we are witnesses of these things; and so is the Holy Ghost, whom God hath given to them that obey Him." "In whom, after that ye believed," or having believed, "ye were sealed by the Holy Spirit of promise." In this relation the Holy Ghost is a gift of grace, a gift promised to those who are already in a state of obedience, and given only to such, and given "after they have believed."

In strict accordance with the above exposition are the express teachings of our Saviour upon this subject: "If ye love me, keep my commandments. And I will pray the Father, and He shall give you another Comforter, that He may abide with you for ever." The special and revealed function of the Spirit in conviction, conversion, and regeneration is to act as a convicting and converting power upon those who are in sin. In His special and revealed function as an "enduement of power from on high," the Spirit has to do with those only who "have believed," who "obey God," and are "keeping Christ's commandments." To confound these two distinct and separate functions of the Spirit is one of the most dangerous errors into which the Church can fall. It has, for centuries past, kept the mass of believers under the darkness of the old dispensation, and shut them out from "all the fulness of God," promised to the faith of all "who obey Him." Pentecostal power will not return to the Churches until the promise of the pentecostal baptism shall be recognised as the common inheritance of all believers.

The only additional error to which I refer is the common one of representing the Spirit, in the influence which He exerts upon the mind, as *confined to the revealed truth of God*. When He would convince of sin, He must, of course, place the facts of our moral states and lives in the clear light of the truth revealed in the Word of God. Hence it is that "the sword of the Spirit is the Word of God." So, when the Spirit would show us "the things of Christ," or impress upon our hearts any truth or promise of God, His illuminations and presentations must be confined to the circle of what is revealed in the Sacred Word. It by no means follows from hence that the influence of the Spirit is confined to the truth. It may be that He may act directly and immediately upon our sensibilities, and thus bring this department of our nature into a state to be affected by the truth such as would otherwise be impossible. For aught that we know, He may thus act upon our propensities, and induce total changes in their tendencies. In a similar manner, He may act upon our *intellectual* capacities, "strengthening us with might in the inner man," and thus enable us to apprehend and comprehend what now lies beyond the reach of our capacities. By acting also upon and through the laws of association, He may suggest trains of thought which would not otherwise occur. The reader has, no doubt, heard of the young woman in Scotland who, on the Sabbath, and in the days of persecution, was on her way to a place of worship, and was met by a company of hostile cavalry, and required by its commander to make known her destination.

At this crisis this promise presented itself to her mind, to wit, "It shall be given you at that hour what you ought to answer;" and she put up a silent prayer that the Spirit of God would put the right words into her mouth. In a moment these words suggested themselves, and she uttered them as suggested "I am going to my Father's house. My Elder Brother has died; His will is to be read to-day, and I have an interest in it." The commander bid her go on her way, expressing the hope that she would find a rich portion left to herself. Who will affirm that those words were not directly and immediately suggested to her mind by the Spirit of God? Yet the words suggested are not found in the Bible. Is not special wisdom for special exigencies specifically promised to those who "lack wisdom" and "ask God" for it? While it is the revealed office of the Spirit to "lead us into all truth"—and He leads us into no form of divine truth but what is revealed—we should greatly err by "limiting the Holy One," and cutting ourselves off from revealed privileges by limiting the influences of the Spirit to the mere use of revealed truth. Let us, on the other hand, carefully inquire after what the Spirit is able to do for us, and what He has promised to our faith, and leave all methods of doing to His own wisdom.

Baptism of the Holy Ghost when Received.

As the agency of the Holy Spirit is always invisible, we become conscious of His presence and workings in ourselves, but through the results which He produces in us. The sinner, for example, becomes conscious of himself, as subject to the Spirit's influences, but through the convictions of sin, and the apprehensions of the way of life and salvation through Christ—convictions and apprehensions which the Spirit induces in the mind. The same holds equally true of the presence and agency of the Spirit, represented by such words as "Ye shall be baptized with the Holy Ghost not many days hence;" "Tarry ye in Jerusalem until ye be endued with power from on high;" "Behold I send the promise of the Father upon you," and "the sealing and earnest of the Spirit in your hearts." We can know that we have received the promised baptism but by becoming conscious in experience of the revealed results which attend or follow that baptism. When, for example, we are conscious of "beholding with open face the glory of the Lord," of being "changed into the same image from glory to glory," of "being strengthened with might in the inner man," of "Christ dwelling in our hearts by faith," of our "becoming rooted and grounded in love," and "able to comprehend the length, and breadth, and depth, and height, and to know the love of Christ, which passeth knowledge," that "our fellowship is with the Father, and with His Son Jesus Christ," and that "the Lord is our everlasting light, and the days of our mourning ended;" we thus know that we have received "the promise of the Spirit," and have been "filled with the Holy Ghost." In waiting for the fulfilment of "the promise of the Spirit," we at length become conscious that "all things are made new," that we have new power over our "propensities, and over all evil principles within and around us, that our powers of apprehension and comprehension are enlarged, that we '*know* the things which are freely given us of God," that the truth of God is in our hearts "as a burning fire shut up in our bones," that our obedience is not forced by dint of our own wills, but sweetly "constrained by the love of Christ," that the spirit of *prophecy* has been given us, and that we are able, as we never were before, to "speak to edification, and exhortation, and comfort," and that "having all sufficiency for all things, we are ready for every good work." In the consciousness of such experiences we know that "Christ has prayed the Father for us, and that He has sent us the Comforter, that He may abide with us for ever," and that Christ Himself has baptized us with the Holy Ghost."

In seeking for this "enduement of power from on high," we must ever bear in mind the revealed conditions on which this crowning blessing of the new dispensation is promised. This condition is definitely specified by our Saviour. "If ye love me, keep my commandments, and I will pray the Father for you, and He shall give you another Comforter, that He may abide with you for ever." "The promise of the Spirit" is fulfilled in the experience of those only who "obey God," "love Christ, and keep His commandments." In seeking for "the promise of the Spirit," we must do so in a state of supreme dedication to Christ, and of absolute subjection to His will.

Here I notice the fundamental mistake of those who suppose that "the baptism of the Holy Ghost" is always given in regeneration. In confirmation of such a conclusion, they cite such passages as these: "If any man have not the Spirit of Christ, he is none of His," and "your bodies are the temples of the Holy Ghost." The inference of such persons is, that none but those who have been "baptized with the holy Ghost" have the "Spirit of Christ" at all, and that the bodies of none but such are "the temples of the Holy Ghost." The Spirit is, first of all, we should bear in mind, in the heart of the sinner as a convicting and converting power. When the sinner has become "a believer in Jesus," the Spirit continues in the heart of the convert to perfect him in the love and obedience which is the necessary condition of his being "baptized with the Holy Ghost." Prior to His crucifixion, Christ told his disciples that the Spirit whom the Father would send as the Comforter was even then in them: "He dwelleth with you, and shall be in you." From the beginning of the world, after the Fall, the Spirit had ever been in the hearts of all saints, and their bodies had been "temples of the Holy Ghost." Yet, as the *great central promise* of the new dispensation, "the Holy Ghost," I repeat, "had never been given until after Jesus was glorified." Those who accept of the work of the Spirit in regeneration and as realised in the common experience of the Church, as the promised "baptism of the Holy Ghost," shut out from themselves "the everlasting light" of the dispensation under which they are permitted to live.

How absurd it is, also, to call the common work of the Spirit among the mass of believers "the baptism of the Holy Ghost," "the promised enduement of power from on high," and "the sealing and earnest of the Spirit in our hearts"! Are these Christians "beholding with open face, as in a glass, the glory of God"? Are they being "changed into the same image from glory to glory, even as by the Spirit of the Lord"? Are they being "filled with all the fulness of God"? Are they "rejoicing with joy unspeakable and full of glory," and "ready for every good word and work"? Is their "joy full"? Is "God their everlasting light," and are "the days of their mourning ended"? These are but examples of the revealed common experience of all who have been "baptized with the Holy Ghost." We should make ourselves ridiculous if we should set up any such pretensions in behalf of the class of believers above referred to.

Let all who are waiting for "the promise of the Spirit," watching for His coming "more than they who watch for the morning," bear this thought with them continually, that Christ is now present to their faith, to do for them all that their present state requires, and that the Spirit is also in them to perfect in them the love and obedience requisite to the reception of "the promise of the Father," that all that is needed is being done in the best possible manner, and that as soon as the way is prepared, they will be "filled with the Holy Ghost." "If the vision tarry, wait for it," and wait for it with the assurance that you "shall be baptized with the Holy Ghost not many days hence." "In due time you will reap, if you faint not.

CHAPTER VIII.

RESULTS OF THE BAPTISM RECEIVED.

The reader may be interested and instructed by receiving some specific account of the effects of the baptism received among us. In regard to myself, I would say, that since that time the Bible in its entireness has been to me a new book. When I became conscious that I was "reading it with new eyes," I read it through and through for the specific purpose of renewing my apprehensions of all its life-imparting revelations. I had, up to that time, been a very careful and critical student of the Bible, making it my fixed habit, unless necessarily prevented, to study critically at least one chapter every day, and that with all the human helps at my command. Now no portions of the Sacred Word appeared more new to me than those which I had most carefully studied, and, in the critical sense, most fully understood. There was "spirit and life" in all I read. While I thus walked up and down amid those great revelations, "the exceeding great and precious promises" beamed down upon me as morning stars in a firmament of everlasting light and love. "I know now," I exclaimed, "that 'all things are mine; whether Paul, or Apollos, or Cephas, or the world, or life, or death, or things present, or things to come, all are mine, and I am Christ's, and Christ is God's.'" The promises render absolutely sure to every believer all this. It is, however, when, and only when, we have received "the anointing," that we do know, or can know, "the things which are freely given us of God," and consequently "that all things are ours."

I will allude here to some specific facts in my experience. I have already alluded to the absolute subjection of the temper, appetites, and other propensities which directly tempt to sin. I have found the promises equally efficacious in respect to tendencies, the action of which tend to weaken our activities or diminish our power, but which cannot be regarded as sinful. I was, for example, from the first, impeded in the discharge of certain functions of my sacred calling by a natural timidity, which rendered me hesitating and fearful in the circumstances referred to. I earnestly besought the Lord, provided I could serve Him more efficiently without it, to "take from me this thorn in the flesh." The next chapter in the Bible that came in my course of reading contained the divine message to Joshua: "Only be strong, and very courageous." The admonition thrilled through every department of my nature, till timidity and fear departed in a moment, and I felt myself girded with a divine courage and strength for "every good word and work." It is by thus trusting in and pleading the promises at a throne of grace that "he that is feeble among us becomes as David, and the house of David as God, as the angel of the Lord before him."

From my earliest memory I had been oppressed with the most terrible fear of dying, and horrified at the idea of being buried. When alone by myself, I would frequently cry out with horror at the thought of being nailed up in a coffin, being let down into the narrow house, and covered up there. Hence the funeral and the burial were to me the most frightful places of which I could conceive. This sentiment oppressed me in all its strength after I became a Christian, and remained until I was "endued with power from on high." I then presented this infirmity at the throne of grace. Soon after this I had in my mind a distinct vision of an open sepulchre, with the body of Christ lying with infinite peacefulness there, angels of God watching at the head and feet of that sacred body. Such a sweetly peaceful scene I had never conceived of before. From that moment I have not only been delivered from all fear and dread of death, the coffin, the grave, the tomb, and the sepulchre, but the thought that, at each setting sun, "I pitch my tent one day nearer" the burying-place, one day "nearer my eternal home than ever before," is one of the sweetest reflections that ever has place in my mind.

> "I would not live always. No; welcome the tomb!
> Since Jesus has lain there, I dread not its gloom."

A few years since, in consequence of necessary but over-exhausting labours, I dropped suddenly and unexpectedly down, and for several weeks lay as near eternity—so it seemed to all—as it was possible for me to lie and return to life again. All expected that each moment might be my last, and once the report went out that I was dead. During all this period I had the most perfect possession of my intellectual faculties, and all the while I seemed to myself to be in the very precinct of heaven. Of a scene of such absolute peace, quietude, and assurance, I had never before had an apprehension. I could only repeat such words as these—

"Safe in the arms of Jesus, safe on His gentle breast,
There, by His love overshadowed, sweetly my soul shall rest."

Like Paul, I then had, not a fear of dying, but "a desire to depart and be with Christ;" and yet, "what I should choose I wot not," not knowing whether God had more need of me for the present on earth or in heaven. I knew well that if "the time of my departure had come," I should not be left to pass alone over the dark river, but that Christ would come to me as I approached the hither bank, would conduct me over, and then "take me to Himself." "Thanks be unto God, who giveth us the victory, through our Lord Jesus Christ." So, all fear being removed,

"I am watching quietly every day;
And the angel answers sweetly in my home,
'Only a few more shadows, and He will come'"

My object in stating such facts is to suggest to believers in Jesus the infinite importance of the fixed habit of carrying to Christ, not only our sins and evil propensities, tendencies, and habits, which tempt to sin, but all natural weaknesses, infirmities, and timidities which disturb our peace, agitate our feelings, or weaken our efforts in the work of Christ. If we should obtain present rest in Christ, and should disregard the admonition to "cast all our cares upon the Lord," inward disturbances would at length break up that rest, and leave us again to "walk in darkness and have no light." When any occurrence induces inward agitation, we should not only resign the event to the divine will, but present the susceptibility through which the agitation is induced to Christ, asking that such a change may be produced in us, that such events shall never more have power to produce any such disturbance, and our request will be granted. A demand, for example, was once made upon me for the payment of a sum of money—a demand which I could not meet without much embarrassment, a demand utterly fraudulent, as myself and the man setting up the claim absolutely knew. In the circumstances, however, I did not then know but that payment might be enforced. The event induced not a little internal agitation. As soon as I became conscious of the fact, and without moving from my seat, I presented this petition to "the throne of grace:"—"Lord, a new susceptibility of my nature has been addressed now, a susceptibility of the existence of which I was not aware before. I ask that this susceptibility shall be so sanctified that such occurrences shall never more have power to produce any inward agitation whatever." In a moment all agitation subsided, and such a change in that susceptibility was induced, that had I been compelled to meet that fraudulent demand, I should have "taken joyfully the spoiling of my goods." The answer to that prayer not only changed that susceptibility relatively to all sudden disturbing causes, but sweetened all my conscious relations to the fulness of divine grace. I have new assurance now, that not only may our wills become absolutely at one with the will of Christ, but that every other department of our nature may be so changed and sanctified that all the activities of our being shall come, with our wills, into the sweetest harmony with the sweet will of God. Outward circumstances will then have no power to induce that internal agitation and care which shall disturb or interrupt the "peace of God" in our hearts. Bear this in mind, however, that you will thus be made new, not only in respect to the action of your will, but of all other departments of your nature, but upon the condition that "God shall be inquired of by you to do this for you."

The Case of Professor Finney

When my associate, then Professor Finney, became aware of the great truth that by being "baptized with the Holy Ghost" we can "be filled with all the fulness of God," he of course sought that baptism with all his heart and with all his soul, and very soon obtained what he sought. After all the services of the sanctuary were passed, "my cup running over" at the time, I called upon him in his study one Sabbath evening. "O my brother!" he exclaimed as I entered, "what visions and manifestations of the glory and love of Christ have opened upon my mind today! Into what 'a large place' have I been brought! Oh, this 'large place'! I keep repeating these words. None others seem so adequately and appropriately to represent my state." After a few words had passed between us, we kneeled in prayer. As soon as he broke silence, he burst forth into rapturous thanksgiving for "the large place" into which the Spirit of God had led him. All his utterances circled round that one expression—'the large place' into which he had been led.

When the Spirit of God "takes of the things of Christ, and shows them unto us," we, "beholding with open face, as in a glass, the glory of the Lord," and beginning to "know the love of Christ, which passeth knowledge," one of the first impressions which the mind receives is "the breadth, and length, and depth, and height" of the vision of glory with which our souls are encircled. What an infinite and boundless range is opened for our immortal faculties to move and revel in, not only for the future of life, but for an eternity to come! What an infinite fulness for all our necessities is everywhere presented! How "complete" we are now conscious of being in Christ! In other words, into what "a large place" have we been brought!

I sometimes illustrate my apprehension of the distinction and contrast in the state of the believer before and after he has received "the anointing" by the following fact. An individual in Scotland was engaged in gathering samphire, a shrub which often grows on the sides of rocky precipices. Shakespeare says of one such man at the cliffs of Dover, "Half way down hangs one that gathers samphire." The man of whom I am speaking had descended, by a rope made fast at the top, about half way down a precipice of a perpendicular height of two or three hundred feet, and getting a standing there on a narrow rocky shelf, was employed in filling the basket at his side with one hand, while with the other he held fast to the rope. In a thoughtless moment the rope slipped from his hand, and went off entirely beyond his reach. He stood fastened to his narrow place in a state of almost total stupefaction, until, as the sun was about to set, he was roused by the cry of his wife and children on the heights above calling for their husband and father. One and only one hope remained. He must leap from the place where he stood, and seize the rope if possible. Succeeding in that single effort, he was saved; failing, he could but die. Committing his soul to God, and after balancing himself for a moment, he took the leap, grasped the rope, and ascended in safety to his agonised family. This fact I am accustomed to employ for three distinct purposes. I use it, in the first place, to illustrate the relation of the sinner seeking salvation—his relation to "the hope set before him in the gospel," the hope upon which he is required to "lay hold." He must as completely renounce all other hopes and dependences but Christ, and as absolutely commit his whole eternity to Christ, as was true of that man in respect to the single hope of life before him when he took that leap, and grasped that rope. So of the believer in every stage of his Christian life. For every advance he would make, he has but one "hope set before him," and that is Christ. Everywhere his self and creature renunciation must be absolute. So of his dedication to, and trust in, Christ, "for grace to help in time of need." The last and leading purpose for which I employ this fact is to illustrate the change from darkness to light, from servitude to freedom, and from confinement to an infinite enlargement of the range of our intellectual, moral, and spiritual faculties, when Jesus "baptizes us with the Holy Ghost." When that man found himself standing in safety on the heights above the cliff where he had been so narrowly confined, when he began in perfect freedom to walk abroad over the hills and through the valleys and plains before and around him, in what "a large place" did he find himself! What a boundless range for all his activities seemed opened before him! So with the believer when he emerges from the confined sphere of the ordinary Christian life into the full light and "liberty of the sons of God." Within what a narrow sphere did his moral and spiritual faculties move! how unvitalising were all the truths he then apprehended, and how obscure and limited were his visions of the glory and love of Christ! But when he emerges out of this narrow obscurity into "the light of God," how marvellous that light appears! What a limitless range is now opened for his thoughts, emotions, and all his moral and spiritual activities! What an infinite fulness is everywhere presented for every demand of his mortal and immortal nature! All his privileges and immunities seem to be enlarged to infinity. "All things are his, and he is Christ's, and Christ is God's." Such is "the large place," reader, into which God, "through the Eternal Spirit," is waiting to lead you, and into which He will lead you, provided you will believe His word, trust His grace, and "with all your heart, and with all your soul," "inquire of Him to do it for you."

Effect upon the Institution

The influence upon the Institution was of no less a marked character. As the theme of all preaching was "repentance toward God, and faith toward our Lord Jesus Christ," and Christ as "our wisdom, righteousness, sanctification, and redemption," a religious influence became visibly the regulating principle not only in the college, but in the village around. We were strangers to the riotous disorders so common in other institutions, and no place where intoxicating drinks were sold existed among us. During the fifteen years in which I remained President of Oberlin College, no year passed without from one to three general revivals, some of the most powerful being in midsummer. I will add here, that during the period of from twenty to thirty years in which I presided as president over colleges, not a single year ever passed without a glorious and marked revival, and all wondered at the permanent spirituality of the converts. My solemn conviction is, that all our institutions and churches should be, and may be, as "watered gardens," ever fresh and green, and ever glorifying God by "bearing much fruit."

To give more specific apprehensions of the results of which I am speaking, I would say that when my associate, Professor Finney, assumed his place as professor of theology in the Institution, he did so with the most earnest and prayerful determination to raise up for the churches a class of holy and sanctified ministers. He consequently met his students weekly for special prayer and exhortation on this subject. In these meetings, all was done that could have been done, by admonition and agonising prayer on the part of the professor and students, to secure the results under consideration. As long as the old regime continued, however, every such meeting, without exception—meetings held under the highest religious influences known in the churches with which we were connected—every such meeting, I say, was closed with singing such a hymn as the following:—

"O for a closer walk with God,
    A calm and heavenly frame,
    A light to shine upon the road
    That leads me to the Lamb.
"Where is the blessedness I knew
    When first I saw the Lord?
Where is the soul refreshing view
    Of Jesus and His Word?
"What peaceful hours I once enjoyed!
    How sweet their memory still!
But they have left an aching void
    The world can never fill."

"Look how we grovel here below;
    Fond of these trifling toys,
Our souls can neither fly nor go
    To reach eternal joys.
"In vain we tune our formal songs;
    In vain we strive to rise;
Hosannas languish on our tongues,
    And our devotion dies."

"Are all our best efforts and most fervent intercessions," I asked myself with the most agonising interest, "to end thus? Must 'the redeemed of the Lord return and come to Zion' with such dirges as these?" I would never join in singing such hymns. There was one verse in one of these hymns, however, in the singing of which I could join most heartily:—

"Dear Lord! and shall we *ever* live
    At this poor dying rate?
Our love so faint, so cold to Thee,
    And Thine to us so great."

"No," I exclaimed, in the secret of my own heart, "we are not doomed to such a dying life as this. 'There is light ahead,' and 'new songs will be put in our mouths' when that light shall come;'" and I knew that "the brightness of that rising was near."

When it was known among us that "Christ had risen indeed," and "had manifested Himself" to not a few, what a change occurred in that prayer-meeting! Infirmities were confessed now "with faith to be healed;" bondage was confessed "with faith to enter into the glorious liberty of the sons of God;" testimonies were given of deliverances, of "joys unspeakable and full of glory," and of our fulness and completeness in Christ—testimonies which must have kindled smiles upon the face of God. And when we bowed in prayer

> "Heaven came down our souls to greet,
> A glory crowned the mercy-seat."

Our meetings now, as invariably as with those dirge songs before, were closed with such hymns as these:—

> "Oh, could I speak the matchless worth,
> Oh, could I sound the glories forth
> That in my Saviour shine,
> I'd soar, and touch the heavenly strings,
> And vie with Gabriel while he sings
> In notes that are divine.
>
> "I'd sing the characters He bears,
> And all the forms of love He wears,
> Exalted on His throne.
> In loftiest songs of sweetest praise,
> I would to everlasting days
> Make all His glories known."

> "Majestic sweetness sits enthroned
> Upon the Saviour's brow:
> His head with radiant glories crowned,
> His lips with grace o'erflow.
> * * * * * * * *
> "Since from His bounty I receive

> Such proofs of love divine,
> Had I a thousand hearts to give,
> Lord, they should all be Thine."

> "Must Jesus bear the cross alone,
> And all the world go free?
> No! there's a cross for every one,
> And there's a cross for me.
> * * * * * * * *
> "The consecrated cross I'll bear,
> Till death shall set me free,
> And then go home my crown to wear;
> For there's a crown for me."

> "Salvation! O the joyful sound!
> 'Tis pleasure to our ears,
> A sovereign balm for every wound,
> A cordial for our fears."

"Well," I said to myself, "this will do. 'The set time to favour Zion has come.' Let 'the light go forth as brightness, and the salvation as a lamp that shineth.' Blessed be God! He *has* 'loosened our bonds,' and as 'His sons and daughters, we are free.'"

I will give an example or two of the testimonies to the power of Christ as a Saviour from "the bondage of corruption," examples among the many of similar interest that I might give. The subject of the first was a young man from Scotland, who was studying as a candidate for the ministry, and in all his conduct was very circumspect and conscientious. Yet he was one of the most unhappy believers I ever knew. His inner life, as we found it, was literally a continued succession of groanings. A Christian lady once said in my presence, that up to a recent period "she had just religion enough to make her as miserable as she could be." This was strictly true of this young man. He almost wearied Professor Finney and myself in his perpetual details of his inward wretchedness, and in his inquiries after deliverance. At length the light, the marvellous light of

God, dawned upon "the midnight of his soul." In giving an account in the prayer-meeting of his great deliverance, he remarked that he could not better illustrate his own case than by first stating a fact of his early life. When in Scotland, he and a number of his young associates went down to the ocean to fish. "The waters were so disturbed that we could do nothing there, and we determined to go to a lake that was located at a long distance up amid the hills above us. The way was long and wearisome under the burning sun that blazed down upon us. At length we came to a moor and searched there for water. What we found was so brackish that we could not drink it, and we were all in great anguish. At length I looked down, and saw a little stream issuing from a fountain that was bubbling up right at my feet. I stooped down and tasted of those waters, and found them perfectly pure, sweet, cool, and refreshing. I drank until my thirst was quenched. So did all my associates, and we went on our way rejoicing. You know, some of you," he continued, "the bondage, and gloom, and groanings of my religious life for years,"—he having been with several of those young men in an institution in the State of New York, then at Lane Seminary, and now at Oberlin. "When in this place I was told that there was liberty in Christ for all who would believe in Him, I grasped at the truth with the earnestness of almost blank despair. As I inquired and inquired, however, without finding 'the living waters,' I began to think that they existed for others and not for me. I did not, however, 'restrain prayer' or cease inquiry. All at once I saw, with unutterable wonder that I had not seen it before—all at once, I say, I saw 'the fountain of the waters of life' rise up just at my feet. As I stooped down and drank, my agonising thirst was for ever quenched. As I continued to drink, however, the volume of those waters increased more and more, until they swelled out into a vast river, upon the surface of which my spirit was born onward and onward, until I was carried out into an ocean of light and love, an ocean the shores of which I have never been able to discern, and the depths of which I have never been able to sound. Here I have been 'comprehending the length, and breadth, and depth, and height,' 'knowing the love of Christ, which passeth knowledge,' and being 'filled with all the fulness of God.' When standing upon the topmost wave of that ocean, I made a vow to God that I would spend my life in making known to saints and sinners this 'great salvation.'" That vow he fully redeemed. To the end of his very useful life his light never grew dim, but brightened more and more, until he took his departure to shine as a fixed star in the firmament of heaven. His graduating address was one of memorable interest on "the baptism of the Holy Ghost."

Another of the theological students, after he had come into the light, came to Professor Finney and remarked to him, that he thought that the time had come when there ought to be something preached to the people on the subject of faith. Professor Finney was at a loss to understand what his pupil meant, that very subject having been the leading theme of all our teachings. In a prayer-meeting not long after this, the whole matter was explained by the young man himself. When he came into the light, his views of truth and his whole internal experience were so entirely new, and so unlike anything which he had experienced before, that he most sincerely supposed that no one among us had had any such experience as his, and that nothing had been preached upon the subject to the people. "Faith, when I came to exercise it," he remarked, "was so unlike my former apprehensions of it, that I really supposed that it had not been preached to us at all. For this reason I went to Professor Finney, and, with perfect sincerity, told him that I thought that the people should be told what faith is. I had no idea but that, as soon my new experience came to be known, Professor Finney, President Mahan, and all of you, would come to me to be taught the secret of this new and divine life. To my surprise and humiliation I found at length, as I compared my own experience with yours, that I had simply emerged into the light in which you had been walking for months," "The sealing and earnest of the Spirit" is to every believer, when the baptism comes upon him, "a new white stone, which no man knoweth but him that receiveth it."

General Influence upon the Churches, and in the Experience of Individuals.

A few facts will distinctly reveal the attitude of all evangelical denominations in the United States—the Methodist excepted—in regard to this subject, when the views of Brother Finney and myself were made known. In a council of Congregational ministers and churches, held in the city of Boston, about thirty years since, to ordain and install a young minister over one of the churches in the city, this question was put to the candidate, namely, "If you should be installed as pastor over this church, would you allow either President Mahan or Professor Finney to preach in your pulpit?" The candidate replied in the affirmative. The council spent about half a day in discussing the question whether, in view of this one fact, no other objections to the candidate existing, the services should proceed any further.

Three years ago last summer, during the sessions of the General Conference for all the Congregational churches in the United States, the Conference meeting at Oberlin, Ohio, my old associate, Brother Finney, was requested by a unanimous vote of the Conference to deliver a special discourse before them on the baptism of the Holy Ghost. At a similar Conference held in New Haven, Connecticut, the past summer, the theme of a special discourse was "the baptism of the Holy Ghost," as received at the Pentecost, as the hope of the Church.

About thirty years since, the authorities of the American Board of Commissioners of Foreign Missions, it being then the organ of the Presbyterian and Congregational Churches of the United States, dismissed from its service two able missionaries in Siam for no other reason than the fact that they had embraced these views. Now, individuals holding these views are as readily employed as any others by this same Board. Near the same period, the Presbytery of Poughkeepsie, by a special order from the Synod of New York, deposed from the ministry two of its members, Messrs Hill and Belden, for no other cause than the one fact that they had embraced the Oberlin error. While the subject was before the Synod, the Moderator of the Presbytery referred to testified that the two brethren on trial were universally regarded as the most useful and godly ministers in their body, and that if Christ should appear in any of their meetings and put the question, "Which of you shall betray me?" the last individual that any one would think of would be either of these brethren. Brother Belden, his associate having died in the faith years ago, has lived to see his name and influence "as ointment poured forth" in this Synod. Dr. Boardman recently stated to me, that when he published his work on "The Higher Life," he did so with the distinct apprehension that he should be deposed from the ministry for what he had done, he being a minister of the Presbyterian Church. An open door, however, is everywhere before him and his works and doctrines, even in that denomination.

An indication of the state of Christian sentiment on this subject is quite manifest by means of the conferences like that at Oxford, which are being held in various parts of the United States, for the specific purpose of promoting personal holiness, conferences attended by ministers and members of all evangelical denominations in common. The following account of one of these conferences—an account given in a recent number of the *Pathway of Power*—will indicate the character and power of such meetings:—

"Among many instances of the special display of the power of God, was one at a recent meeting in Maine, near the borders of Canada, where a great company of Christians assembled for ten days, for purposes very similar to those of the late Oxford meeting. The railway companies reported forty thousand special tickets sold to perhaps twenty or thirty thousand individuals.

"At one of the meetings, the Rev. Dr Steele, whose papers in this periodical have excited so much interest, preached the afternoon sermon about two o'clock. The text was, 'For this cause I bow my knees unto the Father of our Lord Jesus Christ, . . . that He would grant you, according to the riches of His glory, to be strengthened with might by His Spirit in the inner man; that Christ may dwell in your hearts by faith; that ye, being rooted and grounded in love, may be able to comprehend with all saints what is the breadth, and length, and depth, and height; and to *know* the love of Christ which passeth knowledge, that ye might be filled with all the fulness of God.' He dwelt especially on the believer's privilege of being 'filled with all the fulness of God,' and with solemn joy told us of his own experience of the baptism of the Spirit, and of the marvellous possibilities of faith which had opened to his soul since he had realised in power that the Comforter had come: an experience beyond simple consecration and faith's victory over sin; the incoming of the Holy Spirit filling the entire capacities of his being. At the close of this remarkable discourse, the President of the Conference rose and said, 'Our brother, Dr Steele, has something which I have not received. I know that I am all the Lord's, but I want to be *'filled* with the Spirit." We have heard that God is "able to do exceeding abundantly above all that we ask or think, according to the power that worketh in us;" I shall, therefore, now kneel here, and stay upon my knees till what God has done for my brother He also does for me. Let all who desire it do the same.' Above four hundred kneeled, while the thousands in the congregation bowed reverently before the Lord. Then commenced a season of *entirely silent prayer; which continued for three hours*. As the time passed on, the place became, to the spiritual consciousness, awfully glorious. No words can describe the solemn overpowering sense of the presence of God. Any expression in prayer or singing seemed an intrusion, and persons who commenced instinctively stopped. God was Himself speaking to them in their inmost hearts. None dared break the solemn silence of soul before Him. They were now learning what the worship of the whole being to its Creator and God is. As they saw the holiness of God, they gained new views of their own sinfulness in themselves; and with this they saw with equal distinctness the full provision in Christ for all their need.

"At length the tea-bell sounded, and the immense spell bound surrounding crowd slowly and silently left the scene. Many of those who kneeled continued on in silent prayer. Throughout the vicinity, and at the tea-tables, no one seemed able to speak but in subdued tones. The time came for another meeting to be commenced, at another place, but it was found impossible to sing aloud. Nothing could be done but to dismiss the meeting, and join once more the circle of silent prayer. They approached the place softly, as to holy ground, and found a dense mass of people surrounding the spot where these ministers and others still kneeled in silent awful communion with God. Never can the sweet and solemn restfulness of that hour and spot be forgotten.

"When the time for the evening service approached, the President lifted up his hands and said solemnly to the crowd, 'Bow down before the Lord your Maker!' Saints and sinners knelt together. Not another word was said, or hymn sung, but when we gathered in the evening meeting in the immense tent, then we knew what God had done for His people in their waiting before Him. The President said that God had given to him all that he had asked for, and many testified that the words of the prayer for the Ephesians had been answered in their own souls. That evening the conversion of over a hundred persons took place as the result of this wonderful silent meeting before the Lord. . . . .

"'Oh, that salvation were come out of Zion!' is the cry of many a discouraged, down-hearted saint. Remember, dear child of God, that 'salvation' in Scripture is not limited to pardon. It means also deliverance from sin. When, in this more full sense, salvation is in Zion, *'when the Lord bringeth back the captivity of His people,'* delivering them from their bondage to the world, and to partial unbelief, 'Jacob shall rejoice, and Israel shall be glad.'"

I would by no means be understood as intimating that all the changes of religious sentiment above indicated resulted directly from the great baptism at Oberlin. God had for years been preparing the way in all the churches for the reception of the views under consideration, and some outside the Methodist denomination had "entered into rest," before we did. None will question the fact that the movement at Oberlin was one of the main causes of this change.

Facts of Individual Experience.

Before dismissing the topic now under consideration, I will refer to a few facts of individual experience. Dr B., a physician of a very wide practice in one of our large cities, has for quite thirty years been walking in this light. When two Christian gentlemen who had for a long period known him very intimately were once together, one of them put to the other this question, "What do you think of Dr B.?" "When that man dies," was the reply, "he will find the gate of heaven wide open before him. He will go directly in through that gate into the city, and will be at home there." All believers should thus "shine as lights in the world." How is it with you, reader?

A sister in Christ, whom I knew very intimately for upwards of fifteen years prior to her death, was, when I first saw her, so far from Christ that she had merely, as she herself often said, "a name to live."

She immediately sought and obtained "the sealing and earnest of the Spirit." From that time until she was called home, "her sun did not go down, neither did her moon withdraw itself." Her own family, and all who new her most intimately, testified that they never witnessed in her a single un-Christ-like act or utterance. In every circle in which she appeared her single aim was to lead sinners to Christ, or believers "out of darkness into the marvellous light of God," and she had "power with God and with man." At home she was, as a farmer's wife, a model housekeeper, and at home and in the community her influence was "as ointment poured forth." All who knew her will testify to the strictest accuracy of the above statements. At one time her husband employed as a help in his labours a very bigoted but profane Irish Catholic, who had been taught from infancy that out of the Catholic Church salvation is impossible. His attention was soon arrested, however, by the wondrous serenity and sweetness of that woman's spirit and conversation. At the table he would listen with the intensest interest to her conversation upon the love of Christ and the beauty of holiness. He would frequently tarry after meals to speak to the woman on the subject. As he had been listening for some time to her conversation one day, he exclaimed with deep earnestness, "Madame, you will get to heaven before you die." When the membership of the Church shall become such "shining lights" as that, then indeed "will the Gentiles come to her light, and kings to the brightness of her rising." And why, reader, should not you thus shine?

As our writings spread abroad in all directions over the country, we often received letters from persons of whom we had never before heard—letters giving an account of "the rest of faith" into which the writers had entered. In one of these letters a lady from one of the most Eastern States, after detailing the darkness in which she had walked for many years previous, and of the semi-faith which she had had in Christ, and of her prayers and searchings after "the light of life," thus spoke of the love and glory of Christ, which were at length manifested unto her:—"It was all light," she said, "and its essence love." From that hour, as she went on to say, her vision of that light and of that love had never grown dim, and her "joy had been full." Years passed on, when I received a letter from the husband of that woman—a letter giving an account of her subsequent life and death. From the time in which she entered into that light, her light had shined on with a mild, all-attractive, and ever-increasing lustre. In the family, in the church, and community around, all wondered at the deep and undisturbed serenity of her spirit, at the spotless purity of her conversation and example, and at her undying love to Christ and to all who bore His image, and for whom He died. Like her divine Master, she "went about doing good." All who witnessed her last sickness and death felt themselves as near heaven as it is possible for creatures in this world to be.

Another lady from another State gave an account, not only of her former Christian experience and of her entrance into "the everlasting light," but of her inner life for the five years which had transpired since the period last referred to. During these years "the peace of God, which passeth all understanding, had kept her heart and mind by Christ Jesus," and that without interruption. "In no single instance," she remarked, "had she during these years closed her eyes to sleep at night without the absolute assurance that no cloud intervened between her spirit and the face of God." Years after this I received a letter from the husband of this woman also, giving an account of her subsequent life and final departure, an account of which that above given is a perfect transcript.

When Brother Finney came to Oberlin, he brought with him, as their housekeeper, an individual who had been a member of his church in the city of New York. After she had been in his family about a year, he remarked to me that they should be compelled to dismiss the woman, though she was the best help they had ever had. The reason was, that her terrible temper was a constant disturbance to the peace of the family, and was exerting a ruinous influence upon their children. The least temptation would kindle her temper into a blaze, and then it was as violent, and ungovernable, and implacable as a conflagration. During the great revival she became distinctly conscious of her moral and spiritual state, and, "with all her heart and soul," sought deliverance. After she received "the anointing," she continued for several years in the place she then occupied, until she was sent as a missionary teacher among the coloured fugitives in Canada. Such was her influence in her new sphere, that the superintendent of those schools spoke of her in a letter in these words:—"She is a host." Wishing to learn the effect of faith in Christ in such an extreme case as that, I made inquiries of Brother Finney in respect to her spirit and deportment after her "enduement of power from on high." He assured me that, from the time of the change referred to until she left, there had not been the remotest manifestation of that old temper. Her entire spirit, on the other hand, had been ineffably sweet, and neither he, his wife, or any member of their family had noticed a word or act in her which was not in the strictest conformity to Christian character. I give the testimony of Brother Finney in his own words, as nearly as I can recall them, and in no respect exaggerate that testimony. Is not "Christ able to save them to the uttermost that come unto God by Him"?

More than thirty years since, I spent a short period in protracted labours in the city of Lowell, Massachusetts, a great revival resulting from those meetings. The leading member of the Congregational church where I preached was a man of wealth, much intelligence, and of the most unblemished moral and religious reputation; so his pastor assured me. Yet, the religious experience of this individual had taken on a pensive, and often despairing hue. Before I left, he had a long conversation with me, detailing his inward desolation, and expressing the apprehension that he had committed "the unpardonable sin." On inquiry, I found that he was conscious of no form of sin which could be the rational ground of any such apprehension. I assured him that his desire and will to seek and find Jesus was an absolute proof that salvation from doubt and darkness into "the marvellous light of God" was with absolute certainty for him. He had but one thing to do, and that was to look away from all else to Christ, to seek Christ, until he should find himself standing in "the light of God." This my friend promised to do. After I had been in Boston two or three weeks, preaching Christ there, this friend called upon me, and told me that he had come from Lowell for no other purpose but to "tell me what the Lord had done for his soul." All gloom and doubt had departed, and his "cup was running over." I found that once despondent believer in the most perfect enjoyment of "the full assurance of faith," "the full assurance of hope," and "the full assurance of understanding." What, among other considerations, gives me the most absolute assurance that the gospel, as I hold and teach it, is Christ's rock of truth, is the fact that, under its influence, those who are in the deepest darkness emerge into the most enduring and marvellous light, that those who are in the most desponding bondage attain to the most perfect liberty, and that those who are under the heaviest burdens and sorrows find the most enduring rest.

The spiritual writings of the late Professor Upham, of Bodoin College, in the State of Maine, U. S., are "known and read of all men." The manner in which he became such a fruitful writer on such a theme was on this wise. When the peculiar views advocated at Oberlin were spread before the public, he took it for granted that they were wrong, and gave them no examination. Mrs Upham, however, was induced by a lady friend, then residing in the family of the former, to give our writings a careful examination—her husband, in the kindest manner possible, often expressing his utter incredulity in respect to the subject. Mrs. Upham at length became fully convinced, and sought and obtained "the sealing and earnest of the Spirit." The new life to which she had attained, and that in connection with the manifest divineness of the change wrought in her, soon arrested the attention of the husband, and induced him also to inquire, until he was brought fully to accept the views which the wife had embraced. It was the example of the wife, as an epistle of Christ, that rendered the husband "the man of God" and the spiritual writer which he afterwards became. When believers generally shall become such epistles, then will the prayer of our Saviour, in the following words, be fully answered:—"I in them, and Thou in me, that they may be made perfect in one; and that the world may *know* that Thou has sent me, and hast loved them as Thou hast loved me."

The divineness of these views is very strikingly manifest in their perfect adaptation to the conscious moral and spiritual necessities of all classes of believers in common, the most learned and the most ignorant. When I was at Oberlin, for example, there came to the place an elderly coloured woman from a state of servitude in the Southern States. Of course, she could neither read nor write; yet was at once at home with the gospel as we were teaching it; and such was the purity of her life, and the fulness of her knowledge of Christ, as her "wisdom, righteousness, sanctification, and redemption," that not a few even learned persons went to her for instruction in regard to the secret of the divine life which she was leading.

A company of coloured people were once together for conversation and prayer about the higher life. The meeting became quite noisy. One young woman especially leaped, and shouted, and prayed at the top of her voice, and threw her body into almost convulsive contortions. At length an aged coloured saint came up, and laying her hand gently upon her young friend, said, "Honey, dis is not de way. Shoutin' is not de way to obtain de blessin' Why, honey, if you should ebber get de Lamb in your arms and de Dove in your heart, you would feel as if you were in de stable in Bedlehem, and de bressed Mudder had given you de sleepin' Baby to hold." How divine must have been that inner life, and how deeply must a soul have been taught of the Spirit, that could give utterance to such wisdom as that!

At the close of the late war in America, the Confederate States were, for a time, divided out into military districts, over each of which one of our Generals was located, that of Alabama being assigned to General Saxon. As himself and family one day were seated in the verandah of their residence, they saw an aged and infirm coloured woman walking slowly up the path before them. After ascending the steps she bowed to them, with the salutation, "How de ye?" On receiving their expressions in reply, she thus addressed them: "It 'pears dat I shan't live but a little while, and I want to go to de meetins, it does me so much good. Yet it 'pears I habn't any close suitable to go dare, dis ere dress being all the close I has," The dress referred to was a coarse cotton garment, which extended about half way down from her knees to her feet—a garment furnished her when a slave. "Come in and take a seat," said Mrs Saxon, "and my daughters will prepare some dresses for you." "Oh, no," she replied, "it won't do for me to go into dose fine rooms in dare." While the dresses were being prepared, she said to them, with a sweet smile, "I knows you are Christians." "I sometimes hope I am," replied Mrs S., "but I have so many dark hours that I often doubt whether I am a Christian at all." "Oh, honey!"

exclaimed the coloured visitant, "you habn't gibben up de world. Dat is de difficulty. It cost me a great struggle to gib up de world." "What had she to give up?" thought Mrs S. in her own mind. Every individual, reader, has his or her world, and no one gives up that world without a struggle. "But, honey," continued the speaker, "don't you mind dem dark hours. You look right to Jesus, and keep fast hold ob Him, and He will take all dose dark hours from you, and dey will nebber come to you any more. Oh, how lobing Jesus is!" she went on to say. "De bressed Fader said to him: Jesus, my Son, you go down into dat dark and wicked world down dare, and if you find any poor sinners dat want to be sabed, you take from dem dar sins, and den bring dem up here and lay dem in my bosom." Here she began to reel to and fro, her apprehensions of the love of Christ lying with such weight upon her mind as almost to make her stagger. At length she exclaimed, "Won't you sing some of de sweet songs about Jesus?" "Just go into the parlour," replied Mrs S., "and one of our daughters will play upon the piano and sing for you." "Oh, no!" she exclaimed, "it won't do for me to go in dare. But I can hear de music and singing out here." As the music and the songs proceeded, however, she kept drawing nearer and nearer, until she at last looked into the room, and finally entered and kneeled near the instrument. The glow upon her countenance and her frequent ejaculations clearly indicated that her "joy was full." When the garments were ready and were delivered to her, "Tank you, tank you! Jesus bress you!" she exclaimed. When Mrs Saxon told her that, if ever she should again be in want, to call upon them, and they would do what they could for her, "Oh, no!" she replied, "dat will nebber do. I hab got so many tings now, dat I must nebber come again for anyting more. But, honey," she said, addressing Mrs S., "don't you mind dem dark hours. You look right to Jesus, and keep fast hold upon Him, and you will nebber more see dem dark hours." Thus she took her leave. After she had been gone a while, she was seen again coming slowly up the path and the steps of the verandah. Approaching Mrs Saxon, she said, with an ineffable sweetness of voice and manner, "Honey! don't you mind dem dark hours. You look right to Jesus, and keep fast hold ob Him, and you will nebber, nebber again see any of dem dark hours." So she finally passed from sight. General Saxon, in his long account of the transaction—an account published years ago in the *Independent* of New York—says that himself and family felt as if they had been visited by a messenger from heaven—a messenger sent to impart to them higher wisdom in respect to the supreme concern of the divine life than they had ever received before.

I will allude to one other case, taken from the same class as the above. Quite thirty years since, I became acquainted in the city of New York with a coloured woman, whom I never heard designated by any other name than Aunt Dinah. She was then upwards of threescore and ten years of age. Up to her fortieth year she had lived a slave, and had received no religious instruction whatever. On attaining to her freedom she came to the city designated, and was, not long afterwards, converted. As soon as she heard of the views taught at Oberlin, she sought, with all her heart and with all her soul, for "the liberty of the children of God," and entered most fully into all the light and blessedness of the higher life. As her faith, or rather unbelief, did not limit the power, love, and grace of Christ through the Spirit, her whole character and life seemed to be moulded into the divine likeness. All wondered at the beautiful simplicity, symmetry, and completeness of her whole character and life, and at the wondrous wisdom of her conversation. She had very special power in leading believers into the rest of faith, and sinners to Christ. Whenever an impenitent person came under her influence her conversation and prayers were centred in one fixed purpose—his conversion—and very seldom did she fail of her object. Few persons in that city were the means of the conversion of so many individuals as she. Prior to her last sickness, one young man had been with her an object of special effort and prayer, and she earnestly besought the Lord not to call her home until she could be assured of the salvation of that friend. When it was announced to her that he had been converted, she exclaimed, "I am ready now. Let the Master come when He will." What was peculiar about this woman was the fact, that her person was by no means comely, that her dress was always very plain, though neat, while her face was as black as midnight. What gave her free access to all classes, the rich and the poor alike, was the wondrous sanctity of her character and wisdom of her discourse. Nobody repelled her. While, for example, she was once on board a steamboat between New York and Albany, she found that the celebrated statesman, the Hon. De Wit Clinton was among the passengers. Approaching the man and addressing him, while many gathered round, she spoke to him in reverential earnestness in regard to his immortal interests, warning him of the dangers which encircled him in the midst of the pursuits of ambition, the maze of politics, and the floods of worldly cares, and closed with a solemn admonition that he should make the salvation of his soul the first and supreme object of his regard. Mr Clinton listened to her discourse with deepest attention and respect, thanked her for her concern for his eternal welfare, and for her wise admonitions. Such was the respect which her discourse commanded from all. After listening to my preaching, she uniformly met me near the pulpit-stairs, and taking me by the hand, she would say, "My son, 'be thou faithful unto death, and He shall give thee a crown of life.' I solemnly charge you never to cease, while you live, proclaiming this full redemption." There were few persons whose blessing and admonition I more deeply valued than hers. A minister of the gospel, who had been a member of the same church with her while a student of theology in the city, told me that, on returning to the city after years of absence, on meeting his old friend, he thus addressed her: "Well, Aunt Dinah, how are you getting along?" "'The lines,'" she replied, "'have fallen unto me in pleasant places, and I have a goodly heritage.' I do not know what want is. When I feel that I need anything, I look right up to my Father in heaven, who always bends His ear quite down to where I am, and says,' Daughter, what is now thy petition? Tell me.' I always speak directly into His ear, and tell Him just what I need, and I always get what I ask." After her death, as her pastor was passing down Broadway to make arrangements for her funeral, he was met by one of the very wealthy merchants of the city. "I understand," remarked the merchant, "that Aunt Dinah is dead. Have you made arrangements for her funeral?" "I was on that business now," replied the pastor. "I will bear the entire expense of that funeral," replied the merchant. "A grave will be prepared for her in my own family burying-place in Greenwood Cemetery. She will be buried there by the side of a very dear brother of mine. That brother had been an officer in the English army. In this city he providentially became acquainted with Aunt Dinah, and, through her influence and prayers, became a Christian, and died in the Lord. I desire that she shall stand by his side and in the midst of my family in the morning of the resurrection." She thus "made her grave with the rich in her death." It was but seldom that so large a funeral was gathered to pay public respect to departed worth as was gathered at the burial of that woman. Reader, your Christian life ought to be as hallowed as was the one above described.

CHAPTER IX.

TRIALS OF FAITH AND VICTORIES "BY THE BLOOD OF THE LAMB AND THE WORD OF HIS TESTIMONY."

IN the Word of Truth we read, "Thou wilt keep him in perfect peace whose mind is staid on Thee; because he trusteth in Thee." In the same Word we have the following admonition and promise:—"Be careful for nothing; but in everything by prayer and supplication, with thanksgiving, let your requests be made known unto God. And the peace of God, which passeth all understanding, shall keep your hearts and mind through Christ Jesus." "These things," said our Saviour, "have I spoken unto you, that in me ye might have peace. In the world ye shall have tribulation: but be of good cheer; I have overcome the world." In the midst of all earth's tribulations—and none have more of them than believers—"the redeemed of the Lord" are privileged to "return and come to Zion, with songs and everlasting joy upon their heads." Everywhere, and under all circumstances, they are expected to "obtain joy and gladness," while "sorrow and sighing flee away," and "the days of their mourning are ended." In the experience of Paul, all the above declarations and promises were fully verified. Let us listen to his testimony:—"Not that I speak in respect of want; for I have learned, in whatsoever state I am, therewith to be content. I know both how to be abased, and I know how to abound: everywhere and in all things I am instructed both to be full and to be hungry, both to abound and to suffer need. I can do all things through Christ which strengtheneth me." "And He said unto me, My grace is sufficient for thee; for my strength is made perfect in weakness. Most gladly therefore will I rather glory in my infirmities, that the power of Christ may rest upon me. Therefore I take pleasure in infirmities, in reproaches, in necessities, in persecutions, in distresses, for Christ's sake for when I am weak, then am I strong." "As the sufferings of Christ abound in us, so our consolation also aboundeth by Christ. It is the revealed privilege of the saints of God to "glory in tribulation." Paul not only had such an experience, but has also clearly revealed to us the secret by which we may attain to the same experience. "We also believe, and therefore speak." "I live, and yet not I, but Christ liveth in me; and the life which I now live in the flesh, I live by the faith of the Son of God, who loved me, and gave Himself for me." Let us give our special attention to this subject for a few moments.

It is a fixed law of our nature that, when the mind is strongly exercised with some one engrossing subject, other and different objects have no power to reach and disturb the sensibilities and activities of our being. For several years prior to his death, for example, the celebrated President Dwight of Yale College suffered beyond measure from rheumatic and gout affections. As he sat, in excessive agony, before a fire one day, a live-coal fell upon his hand and burned into his flesh without his noticing the fact at all. The reason is obvious. All the sensibilities of his nature were so completely occupied by the causes of pain referred to, that the burning of his flesh even could not reach the sensitive department of his nature. This same principle holds true universally. Now, when "Christ dwells in the heart by faith," and is "formed within, the hope of glory," and "God dwells in us, and walks in us" as His conscious "sons and daughters," all our affections and activities come so completely under the divine control, and all our susceptibilities are so perfectly filled with "the peace of God, which passeth all understanding," that "things seen and temporal" have no power so to reach those susceptibilities as to disturb the fixed content of the mind, which has found its resting-place in the centre of the sweet will of God.

Tertullian and other of the early Christian fathers affirm that the minds of the martyrs, when subjected to the most terrible tortures which their tormentors could inflict, were so completely occupied with the manifested love and glory of Christ, that they did not seem to be affected at all by bodily suffering. When we are out of Christ, all our susceptibilities lie open and exposed to the assaults of worldly tribulations, cares, and perplexities, and we are, of necessity, "like the troubled sea when it cannot rest," and are "weary, tossed with tempests, and not comforted." When we "are in Christ," and "Christ in us," however, "the world, the flesh, and the devil" have no more power over us than they had over Him. His peace is our peace; His rest is our rest; His content is our content; and our "quietness and assurance" are as undisturbed as His was. He overcame the world, that is, destroyed its power to draw the mind into sin or to disturb its rest and peace, through the indwelling presence of the Father in His heart and mind. So we can "overcome the world" by having Christ dwell in us as the Father dwelt in Him. "As the living Father hath sent me, and I live by the Father, so he that eateth me, even he shall live by me."

In the varied conditions and states of our earthly life, we cannot be content with the divine allotments, by resolving upon an acquiescence in the same, nor can we obey the command, "Be careful for nothing," by determining to "take no thought for the morrow;" nor have we any power of will to banish from our hearts the cares which may now pain and agitate us, or to prevent others coming in and disturbing our peace. If, on the other hand, we will, "by prayer and supplication, with thanksgiving, make known our requests unto God," if we will open our hearts, and let Christ and the Father come to us, and "make their abode with us," and if we will wait for "the promise of the Spirit," that "we may know the things which are freely given us of God," then we shall be so "filled with all the fulness of God" that it will be impossible for us to be "careful and troubled" about anything. "The love of Christ," "open visions of His glory," "everlasting consolations and good hope through grace," "the peace of God, which passeth all understanding," "joy in the Holy Ghost," and the repose of our wills in the sweet will of God, will then so completely control all our activities, and occupy all the susceptibilities of our nature, that worldly tribulations and cares will have no power over any department of our mental being, so as to interrupt our joys or disturb the rest into which our immortal spirits have entered. As darkness cannot abide the face of the sun, so "sorrow and sighing," discontent, and fear of what may happen, take their quick departure when "the Sun of Righteousness rises in our hearts with healing in His wings." "If Christ be in you, the body is dead, because of (or in respect to) sin;" that is, all our evil propensities and tendencies, and all internal causes which disturb our peace, lie dead in His presence, and void of power to draw us from our allegiance to Him, or to disquiet our spirits, or shut the peace of God out of our hearts; while "the Spirit is life, because of (or in respect to) righteousness;" that is, all our moral and spiritual activities are quickened into active obedience to the will of God and the law of righteousness. So, also, when Christ is in you, reader, external tribulations will have no more power to approach your sensibilities and disturb the deep rest of your spirits in Him, than the hosts of the Syrians had to break through the fiery circle which surrounded the prophet of God. But if Christ be not in us, the world without, with its tribulations and "fiery trials," and the world within, with its warring lusts, carking cares, and bewildering perplexities, will make our sensitive nature their perpetual prey, and "sin will reign in our mortal bodies."

Permit me here to allude to some experiences of a personal nature, experiences illustrative of the power of Christ to gird the mind with enduring strength, and to "keep the heart and mind in perfect peace" in the midst of the greatest external embarrassments and perplexities. After I had been between two and three years President of Oberlin College, I found myself at the head of an institution endowed with a fund amounting to quite eighty thousand dollars, a larger endowment than any other college in the Western States was then possessed of. I had co-operating with me a very able Faculty of instruction, while our pupils amounted to from five to eight hundred individuals. We had also what was then regarded as a very unusual subscription for the general purposes of the College, a subscription which was rapidly approaching one hundred thousand dollars. No other college west of New England, and very few there, had before it a more quiet or brighter future. I was in the very condition in which, above all others, I would have desired to be. Then each of us felt that he had good reason to say, "I shall die in my nest, and I shall multiply my days as the sand. My root shall spread out by the waters, and the dew shall lie all night upon my branch. My glory shall be fresh in me, and my bow shall be renewed in my hand."

Just at this time a fearful conflagration occurred in the business centre of the city of New York, a conflagration which, in a single night and day, destroyed property amounting to about fifteen millions of dollars. Within that circle of fire lay the business places of the wealthy merchants who held almost every dollar of our endowment funds, and those funds sank with the fortunes of those men. This calamity was immediately followed by a national one, the sudden failure of almost all our banks west of the State of New York, and not a few east of that line; and this was attended with the bankruptcy of a large majority, it is believed, of the men of business throughout the nation, and the utter disarrangement of all our business relations. When we took an account of the pecuniary condition of the College, after the effects of these calamities had become manifest, we found our endowment wholly gone, and of the subscription for general purposes, that not twenty thousand dollars of it would ever be of use to us, while the College was encumbered with a debt amounting to upwards of fifty thousand dollars. No calamity could hardly have fallen more suddenly, and, to all human appearance, no ruin could have been more complete and remediless. "As a snare," the general bankruptcy had fallen upon the nation, and "in one hour" the ruin of the College was apparently consummated, and the life-hopes of no individual appeared to be so hopelessly wrecked as my own.

I shall now speak with perfect freedom of the mental, moral, and spiritual state in which I was preserved, by the "power of Christ resting upon me," in the midst of the circumstances referred to. This I do, leaving it to "Him whom I serve, and whose I am," to judge of motives. To the honour of His dear name, and as illustrative of the power of His sustaining grace, I would say, that the events under consideration never, unless my consciousness utterly misled me, had the power for a single moment to disquiet my spirit, to induce the least motion of internal discontent, to interrupt the onward flow of my peace and joy in God, to induce a moment's despair of the future of the College, or the "batement of one jot of hope" in respect to its ultimate success.

The calamity, as we and the public well knew, had come upon us by no mismanagement on our part. This fact rendered it plain that, in the judgment of God, it was not best that the funds referred to should go for the benefit of the Institution, and my whole being joyfully acquiesced in the divine will upon the subject. In my own mind, I distinctly and specifically reasoned thus—If it is the will of God that the Institution shall die, I have no wish or desire that it shall live. If, on the other hand, God wills that it shall live, and I felt sure that He did thus will, then He will furnish the means to repair these ruins, and perpetuate the life of the College; and this He will do, "not by might, nor by power, but by my Spirit, saith the Lord," God's Spirit moving upon the hearts of those who have the means, and inducing them to give what is requisite to accomplish the divine purpose. With these sentiments in my mind, I commended the great interests before me to the divine care and keeping, and did so with the utmost peace, quietness, and assurance of hope. I cannot now understand how my peace could have been more undisturbed, my joy more full, or my hope more assured, than they were during all that dark period of my own life and of the life of the Institution. During all that period, I can truly say that there was in my inner life a full realisation of all that the following words of the prophet can mean:—"The sun shall be no more thy light by day; neither for brightness shall the moon give light unto thee: but the Lord shall be unto thee an everlasting light, and thy God thy glory. Thy sun shall no more go down; neither shall thy moon withdraw itself: for the Lord shall be thine everlasting light, and the days of thy mourning shall be ended."

The reader may be interested to know what were the dispensations of Providence towards us under the circumstances. As none of my associates were accustomed to agencies, action in this direction at first fell mainly upon me. Knowing that Professor Finney's health and circumstances would not permit him to continue with us unless his salary was promptly paid, and knowing that the large fortune of a mutual friend of his and my own had not suffered in the national calamities, I visited him, and, after full consultation, he agreed to pay regularly the salary under consideration. As far as myself was concerned, I concluded that, by labours in protracted meetings during our vacations among churches who would call for my services, I could secure a large portion of my own salary; and I determined to devote the income thus obtained to that end, and thus relieve the college from the burden of another salary. Thus two of the main pillars of the Institution were securely fixed. Just at this time the late Hon. Gerrit Smith sent us a draft of two thousand dollars on a sound Eastern bank, and, what was more, a deed of some twenty thousand acres of land in Western Virginia. This great gift, prompted by no agency on our part, though the land was not immediately saleable, reassured home and public confidence in the future of the Institution.

At this juncture, also, a wealthy merchant, whose fortune had not suffered at all—William Dawes, Esq.—a merchant living some fifty miles distant from us, visited us; and, after acquainting himself with the facts presented, determined, upon a self-moved agency, to raise some ready means to meet existing exigencies. He soon returned with a reliable subscription of quite two thousand dollars, himself having subscribed five hundred or a thousand dollars of the same. While with us on this second visit, "the Spirit of the Lord God came upon him," and he determined to return home, close up a very lucrative business, move his family to Oberlin, and devote all his energies to the interests of the College. This he did, labouring for us without a salary, and taking nothing but his necessary personal expenses while in our service. Through an agency to England, in company with the Rev. John Keep, he sent over to us from philanthropists here, in addition to all the expenses of the mission, upwards of thirty thousand dollars to help to pay off the debt referred to. Thus all our wants were met, and in a few years all that debt was paid, to the full satisfaction of all parties concerned; and the College was started anew on a line of gradually increasing prosperity which renders its future as cloudless as that of any of our institutions. In Mr Dawes, by a wonderful concurrence of circumstances, God gave us, as it seems, the only man in the world who could instrumentally have saved the College from destruction, and assured for it a permanent prosperity. When I think of such facts, I can only exclaim, "Oh, the depth of the riches both of the wisdom and knowledge of God! How unsearchable are His judgments, and His ways past finding out!"

The reader will call to mind the statement formerly made of the excruciating pain which I had once experienced at the thought, and in view of the fact, of adopting sentiments and assuming positions which would render one the object of deep reprobation, and occasion his separation from the fellowship of those with whom he had in former years been in intimate association, and on terms of open good-will. Few individuals could have had a more sensitive nature in respect to such relations than I had; and the pain which I experienced under such circumstances was but little diminished by the inward assurance that I had parted company with my brethren because I had found truth which they rejected, and was separated from them because I was moving on the line of absolute duty. When passing through the crisis of the College, the crisis above described, in addition to the odium attached to me as representing the only Anti-Slavery College in the United States, and of a principle of liberal education—a principle never before adopted in any other such institution since the world began—that of *the education of mind* irrespective of race, colour, or sex, a principle then generally held in the deepest reprobation,—in addition to all this, I stood before the public as a leading representative and uncompromising advocate of what was generally regarded in all Calvinistic denominations, with whom I had been exclusively associated from childhood up, as the most odious and subversive doctrine known in the churches. As a necessary consequence, my separation and isolation from old associations and fellowships were complete.

The following fact will give the reader a distinct apprehension of the sentiment with which Brother Finney and myself were then regarded. When spending several months in the city of Boston, during one of our vacations, I received an invitation from an influential member of Park Street (Congregational) Church to dine with him in company with his pastor. When I came into the presence of that pastor, I was at once made distinctly conscious that my presence was an offence to him. So marked was the disrespect with which he treated me, and so painful, as I saw, was my presence to him, that, as soon as the formalities of the occasion would permit, I took leave. Between fifteen and twenty years after that, I met that pastor again. As we came into each other's presence, he grasped my hand, saying, "Brother Mahan, I have desired for years to have an opportunity to make a confession to you. You remember the time when I dined with you at the house of Brother F. in Boston. On that occasion your presence was perfectly odious to me, and I felt deeply ashamed to sit, as an invited guest, at the same table with you. I now assure you that I have for years felt as deeply ashamed of my then self as I then did of you. Permit me to say to you, that you are now in my heart as a very highly-esteemed servant of Jesus Christ." The sentiment entertained by that individual on the occasion referred to perfectly represents the regard in which we were then held by the mass of the ministry and membership of the denominations designated. No persons could have been more deeply odious to the churches than we were at that time.

But what was my experience under these circumstances? The exact opposite to what it ever had been before in similar relations. Walking, as I consciously did, in "the light of God," and in the path which Christ had made plain before me, and with His smile consciously resting upon the face of my soul, it was to me a very small matter truly to be "judged of man's judgment." I then clearly understood what the Saviour meant when He said, "Your joy no man taketh from you." I was straitened in my brethren, but they were not straitened in me. I cannot recall a throb of pain, or a feeling of unkindness or bitterness, that had place in my mind during all these years. With Christ in our hearts, and in communion and fellowship with Him, we shall breathe the same Spirit towards the Church and the world that He does. I was under the uninterrupted consciousness that, in the relations then existing, I was called upon, in my interior spirit and visible life, to represent the heart and life of Christ, and consequently that "anger, wrath, malice," must never have place in my heart, words, or acts; that when "reviled, I must bless," and when "persecuted, I must endure it." Nor did I find it difficult to "possess the soul in patience" then. I was conscious of no internal struggle with sentiments or emotions of bitterness. Christ was too near, and my joy in Him was too full, to allow a place in my heart for any such feelings.

One of the special objects which I have in view in recording the above facts is, to bring to light a very common and dangerous error. When individuals, members of "the household of faith," receive injuries and provocations, they too commonly regard themselves as delivered to allow any roots of bitterness whatever to spring up in their hearts, to trouble their spirits, and to defile their character. No, my brother; "you do not well to be angry" when wronged, injured, or provoked by your brethren or the men of the world. Your character, on the other hand, should then and there take on, not the spirit of anger or vengeance, but the divinest form of virtue known in the kingdom of grace—"the ornament of a meek and quiet spirit, which in the sight of God is of great price." "Let no man take thy crown." This you always do when you allow any man to anger you. The final conclusion which I deduce from the experiences above presented is this: We are "complete in Christ," "can do all things through Christ which strengtheneth us," and in all circumstances of our earthly existence can be "more than conquerors through Him that hath loved us."

CHAPTER X.

SUSTAINING AND ANTICIPATORY GRACE.

IN reference to all temptations and "trials of faith" which await believers while journeying towards the heavenly country, this specific promise remains for us: "God is faithful (worthy to be trusted), who will not suffer you to be tempted above that ye are able, but will with the temptation also make a way to escape, that ye may be able to bear it." This promise should be omnipresent to our faith everywhere and under all circumstances, and with a firm and fixed trust for the grace here specifically promised, we should face every temptation which may fall upon us. There is one feature of this subject, however—a form of grace which I do not recollect ever to have heard discourses upon, or known to have been written about—a form of grace which I deem it of special importance that all should be fully instructed about. I refer to what may be called *anticipatory grace*—a form of grace by which we are prepared beforehand for any great and special duties or trials which await us.

I will illustrate my meaning by an allusion to some special events in the experience of Paul. Aside from the visible and audible revelation of Christ to him at the time of his conversion, there are four recorded instances in which Christ revealed Himself to the apostle in a similar form, and in each instance for the specific purpose of preparing him beforehand for his great life-mission, for special and perilous duties, or for great trials and tribulations. The first of these special manifestations occurred when he was in Jerusalem, and was then in the full expectation of devoting his life to the salvation of his countrymen, and was intended to prepare him for a mission of which he had never thought of before, and which was unlike that to which any other individual had ever been called in the history of the race. Without such a manifestation, and the special revelation which accompanied it, Paul never would have become "the apostle of the Gentiles," and never could have been prepared for such a mission.

Of this mission Paul gives the following account: "And it came to pass that, when I was come again to Jerusalem, even while I prayed in the temple, I was in a trance: and saw Him saying unto me, Make haste, and get thee quickly out of Jerusalem: for they will not receive thy testimony concerning me. And I said, Lord, they know that I imprisoned and beat in every synagogue them that believed on Thee: and when the blood of Thy martyr Stephen was shed, I also was standing by, and consenting unto his death, and kept the raiment of them that slew him. And he said unto me, Depart: for I will send thee far hence unto the Gentiles." This revelation was only preparatory for the special one which he subsequently received while at Antioch, and when "the Holy Ghost said, Separate me Barnabas and Saul for the work to which I have called them." With what absolute assurance did the first revelation prepare his mind to go forth in obedience to the second!

The next revelation of the kind occurred during the early part of his ministry at Corinth. He had "fought with the beasts at Ephesus," had been "scourged, imprisoned, and put in the stocks at Philippi," had fled for his life from Thessalonica and Berea, had encountered the derision of the philosophers at Athens, and was then in such "peril from the lying in wait of the Jews "in Corinth, that he would unquestionably have left the city but for the following special vision of Christ which he then had:—"Then spake the Lord to Paul in the night by a vision, Be not afraid, but speak, and hold not thy peace: for I am with thee, and no man shall set on thee to hurt thee: for I have much people in this city." No wonder that, "for a whole year and six months" after he had received that vision, he continued to preach the gospel to that people, and that without fear.

The special vision next vouchsafed was when he was in the castle in Jerusalem, and was then in the midst of the greatest possible perils, with years of gloomy imprisonment in prospect. Of this vision we have the following tenderly impressive account:—"And the night following, the Lord stood by him, and said, Be of good cheer, Paul: for as thou hast testified of me in Jerusalem, so must thou bear witness also at Rome."

Little power, after that, had chains and prison walls to confine the boundless freedom of that soul.

When in the midst of that fearful tempest in which "neither sun nor stars in many days appeared, and no small tempest lay upon them, and all hope that any of them should be saved was taken away," then Christ did not Himself appear, but sent His angel with a special message of cheer, hope, and assurance. Let us read the inspired account of this vision:—"But after long abstinence Paul stood forth in the midst of them, and said, Sirs, ye should have hearkened unto me, and not have loosed from Crete, and to have gained this harm and loss. And now I exhort you to be of good cheer: for there shall be no loss of any man's life among you, but of the ship. For there stood by me this night the angel of God, whose I am, and whom I serve, saying, Fear not, Paul; thou must be brought before Caesar: and lo! God hath given thee all them that sail with thee: Wherefore, sirs, be of good cheer: for I believe God, that it shall be even as it was told me." Thus, by such anticipatory revelations was the apostle prepared for the great exigencies, and trials, and tribulations of his eventful life.

Grace superabundant is provided for and promised to all believers for every "time of need," and special grace for all special necessities. This also we may all expect, that for new and overpowering trials we shall be prepared by anticipatory grace, which will render us more than conquerors when the evil day comes upon us. It does not appear that such grace is now vouchsafed in the specific form in which it was to Paul. Yet we may rest assured that "the Great Shepherd and Bishop of our souls" will not only come to us and walk with us after we have been put into the furnace, but will anticipate our trials of fire by special and gracious preparations. In my own experience there have been periods not a few, periods in which for a long time all providential occurrences combined their influence as very severe trials of faith. During each of these I have been not only sustained by special and all-sufficient grace, but each of them was anticipated by special promises, on which the mind was made to repose, and by special divine influences—promises and influences all tending to one specific result, to prepare the mind for the peculiar trials which were to follow. I will refer to a few facts of the character under consideration.

Prior to the occurrence of the calamitous events in the history of the College, the events above described, this passage was brought home with inexpressible sweetness and power to my heart:—"Hast thou not known, hast thou not heard, that the everlasting God the Lord, the Creator of the ends of the earth, fainteth not, neither is weary? there is no searching of His understanding. He giveth power to the faint, and to them that have no might He increaseth strength. Even the youths shall faint and be weary, and the young men shall utterly fall: but they that wait upon the Lord shall renew their strength; they shall mount up with wings as eagles; they shall run, and not be weary; and they shall walk, and not faint." The portions of the passage most deeply impressed upon my mind were the two following, the first especially:—"He giveth power to the faint; and to them that have no might He increaseth strength." Why these promises were brought home with such power upon my mind and heart I could not tell. They consciously girded me, however, "with everlasting strength" for any providences which God might see fit to send. But when the sudden and crushing avalanche did descend upon us, I then understood fully why its descent had been so specifically provided for by anticipating grace.

The calamities, and the new duties thence arising, found me standing immovably upon a rock of strength, where the former could bring no disquietude, and "endued with power from on high" for the latter. In connection with the quietness and assurance which those promises inspired, and while feeling myself as self-helpless as a feeble worm surrounded with a circle of fire, with what ineffable interest did I read such promises and admonitions as the following:—"Fear not, thou worm Jacob, and ye men of Israel: I will help thee, saith the Lord, and thy Redeemer, the Holy One of Israel." "Fear thou not: for I am with thee: be not dismayed for I am thy God: I will strengthen thee; yea, I will help thee; yea, I will uphold thee with the right hand of my righteousness." I knew well that the Spirit of God would not, with such undying interest and life-imparting power, bring home to my heart these and kindred promises, if He did not intend that I should rest upon them. Then, when the conscious object of the neglect and reprobation of my brethren and former associates, and when consciously regarded by the ministry and churches generally with whom I had been in full fellowship as "a troubler of Israel," how can I express the almost agonising joy with which I would read such passages as the following—"I, even I, am He that comforteth you: who art thou, that thou shouldst be afraid of a man that shall die, and the son of man, which shall be made as grass; and forgettest the Lord thy maker, that hath stretched forth the heavens, and laid the foundations of the earth; and hast feared continually every day because of the fury of the oppressor, as if he were ready to destroy? and where is the fury of the oppressor? The captive exile hasteneth that he may be loosed, and that he should not die in the pit, nor that his bread should fail. But I am the Lord thy God, that divided the sea, whose waves roared: the Lord of Hosts is His name. And I have put my words in thy mouth, and I have covered thee in the shadow of mine hand."

How could calamities disturb my peace or awaken fear when they always found me thus encircled with such "exceeding great and precious promises," God's "horses of fire and chariots of fire"? Why should we fear the descent of an avalanche when it must bring down with it, and that "from God out of heaven," such "everlasting consolations and good hope through grace"? How and why should man's neglect anger and disquiet us when it brings directly to our heart "the smile of the Lord" as "the feast of our souls"? Often, when made most deeply conscious of the intended neglect of brethren with whom I had once "taken sweet counsel, and gone to the house of God in company," have I turned aside and wept for overflowing joy of heart as the above passage would lift its divine form before my mind. I have long ceased to wonder at the words of Paul. Permit me to cite his words once more—"And he said unto me, My grace is sufficient for thee: for my strength is made perfect in weakness. Most gladly therefore will I rather glory in my infirmities, that the power of Christ may rest upon me. Therefore I take pleasure in infirmities, in reproaches, in necessities, in persecutions, in distresses for Christ's sake: for when I am weak, then am I strong."

While the events above referred to were passing, I was called, under circumstances of peculiar embarrassment, to spend our winter vacation of three months in Boston. The church which finally engaged my services had negotiated with Brother Finney to secure his. These negotiations were carried on to within a few days before I left home, he having finally declined to go. In the communications from the church, he was assured that expectation had become so fully centred in him that I, who was a perfect stranger to all but a very few individuals, would be able to do but a very little in the city. Under such circumstances I went there, and, of course, found things as might have been anticipated.

My first evening (week-day) lecture was attended by not more than forty individuals, and these seemed to have come together from a consciousness of duty rather than an expectation of spiritual profit. Weeks before I left home, and while all were expecting that Brother Finney would spend the winter in Boston, my mind became most intensely interested in the declaration of Christ, "The kingdom of heaven is like leaven, which a woman took and hid in three measures of meal, until the whole was leavened." I was led to reflect upon the manner of His ministry, and the principles in conformity to which He laid the foundations of His eternal kingdom. "He went about everywhere doing good," proclaiming the Word of Life, conferring upon all who would receive Him "power to become the sons of God," banding them together as "a little flock," and yet as the sacramental host of God; and as soon as He was glorified, "enduing them with power from on high" for the great world-work to which He had called them. "This," I said, "is the leaven which Christ cast in amid the elements of the world of mind for the world's moral renovation." In view of that fact, my life-mission was made perfectly manifest to my mind. I was to do all I possibly could to induce every mind that I could draw under my influence to "receive, in the love of it, the truth" which Christ had made known to me, and to be "baptized with the Holy Ghost" for the exemplification and propagation of that full redemption in the world and among believers. These believers, "full of faith and of the Holy Ghost," and everywhere, by precept and example, "holding forth the Word of Life," would act as Christ's leaven in the churches until the whole were leavened. Never for a moment, after that passage thus opened upon my mind, did a shadow of doubt cross my mind in respect to the nature of my divinely-designated mission and work, or in respect to the ultimate result. The truth presented thrilled through my whole intellectual, moral, and spiritual being, and endued me with immortal courage and strength for the work before me.

When I arrived in Boston, the facts presented might have rendered me utterly despondent, and induced me to go to some other field, but for the anticipatory grace and preparation above presented. As it was, with that truth in my heart "as a burning fire shut up in my bones," I contemplated these facts with absolute "assurance of hope." Nor was I disappointed in respect to the results. Those few who listened to that first discourse went home to think, to pray, to "speak often one to another" and to their brethren upon the subject; and in a few weeks I found myself addressing, from Sabbath to Sabbath and on the evenings of the week, the most crowded audiences that could be collected anywhere in the city. The immediate result was, that many sinners were converted, and many believers "washed their robes and made them white in the blood of the Lamb," and found God as "their everlasting light," while "the days of their mourning were ended." The permanent result has been, that the leaven thus cast in has remained as a perpetually assimilating and sanctifying power in the churches.

As indicative of these results, I will refer to a single fact. Some two or three years after the above-stated occurrences, Dr Channing inquired of the celebrated seamen's chaplain in the city, Dr Taylor, whether the latter could designate any individuals, or class of individuals, whose inner and visible lives accorded with the revelations of the New Testament in respect to what believers are privileged to become. "There are many such," Dr Taylor replied. At Dr Channing's special request, Dr Taylor designated a lady whom he well knew, and who had for two or three years "walked in the light of God." At Dr C.'s written request, that lady called upon him. As soon as they met, the Doctor said to her, with much feeling, I desire to hear from you about this full redemption of which so much is said in the churches in the city and country." The lady then detailed to him her own personal experience on the subject, telling him how Christ had been presented to her mind; how she had, by faith, received Him; how He had "endued her with power from on high," and what the results had been in her inner and outer life. Dr Channing wept like a child while listening to that narrative, and said, as the lady took her leave, that he should take an opportunity to converse with her again on this subject. Immediately after this the Doctor left the city on his summer vacation, and died while absent. In an address which he delivered just before he died, on the subject of slavery, he made a devout reference to Christ as having made atonement for our sins, as living in the world as "God manifest in the flesh," and as the foundation of all our hopes.

The facts above stated—facts connected with Dr Taylor and the lady referred to—I give as given personally to me by these individuals themselves. The power under which I spoke, of this, I absolutely know, that that power was not my own. All that I can say of it is, that I consciously stood "in the light of God," and spoke "as the Spirit gave me utterance." Nor can I conceive how it was possible for me thus to have spoken but for the anticipatory baptism of light and power which I received before it was determined that I should visit the city at all. When will ministers, and believers universally, recognise their absolute dependence upon the Spirit of God for real Christian thought and utterance? Can any man "say that Jesus is the Christ but by the Holy Ghost"? When will Christians admit the fulness and adequacy of the grace of God in Christ, and of that grace as distributed to us by the Holy Ghost for all our necessities? Are we, or are we not, "complete in Christ"?

While a gracious Providence was thus caring for all my interests, a very singular event occurred an event unlike any other which I have ever experienced, either before or since that time. I had been engaged for some time in excessive labours in New England. The result of these labours was a very depressing and almost shattering effect upon my nervous system. Any sudden calamitous event occurring at that time, or any unexpected intelligence of such an event, might have utterly prostrated my system. I was on my way from Boston, through New York, to the city of Poughkeepsie, where I had an appointment for protracted labours for a considerable period. In the city of New York, intelligence awaited me of an event of the most afflictive and startling character that could have occurred—an event in respect to which I had had no agency or responsibility whatever—an event which I had not the remotest reason to anticipate, and the thought of which had never approached my mind. While sitting in the cars alone by myself, and engaged in quiet meditation, a question in these exact words was directly put to my mind: "How would you feel if, on your arrival in New York, intelligence of"—such an event—"should meet you"? the event being specifically designated. I was never in my life more distinctly conscious that a question was put to me by another mind than my own than I was on that occasion; nor by any facts of experience, or any of the known laws of association, have I been able to account for the fact under consideration on any other supposition.

The first acquaintance that I met with, on my arrival in the city of New York, gave me information of the occurrence of that event. The question put to me in the cars, however, had induced such specific reflections, and moral and spiritual preparations, that the intelligence had no disturbing effect whatever upon my mental or physical system. For myself, I can give but one account of the facts before us. That question was put to me by another mind than my own, and was put for the specific purpose of insuring a needful preparation for the intelligence which I did receive, and this as a means to a higher end, namely, that I might have strength for the accomplishment of the great work which was accomplished through my instrumentality in the city towards which I was journeying. The inference which I drew from such occurrences is this:—Another mind than our own has the care of all our interests as "believers in Jesus," a mind that understands all our needs, and who is "touched with the feeling of our infirmities," a mind whose ever wakeful and watchful presence always encircles us as a "munition of rocks," and who will not fail to anticipate all our great emergencies by needful preparations. I write these things, reader, that, by an entrance into the same rest of faith, your heart with mine may ever inwardly sing—

"Safe in the arms of Jesus,
Safe on His gentle breast."

I refer but to one additional case of the kind now under consideration, and that pertains to the darkest and most trying period of my Christian life. I left Oberlin to take charge of a new university. The basis of the endowment of this institution was a tract of land of two hundred and seventy-five acres, most propitiously located in the immediate vicinity of the city of Cleveland, Ohio. This property, which promised to render the university a better endowed institution by far than any other in any of the Western States, was obtained, and by written covenant was held, by myself and two other individuals in trust, for the purposes named. By the trustees of the university, and by the trustees in trust, a power of attorney was given to one of the latter to lay out this property into city lots, and sell the same for the benefit of the institution. After matters had proceeded for a time, the trusters and community were utterly astounded by the disclosure of the fact, that, under that power of attorney, all this property had been disposed of for private speculation, the house which I had built, and in which my family was residing, being included in the sale, no deed having been yet conveyed to me. By a bogus settlement, against which I recorded a written protest, and for which the trustees afterwards expressed the deepest regret, the ruin of the university was consummated. Standing in the midst of these ruins, with the little property I had put beyond my control, with a large family upon my hands, and with no visible means for their support, I found myself more completely insulated from former associations than I had ever been before, and under the darkest cloud with which I could be overshadowed.

Yet for what I was here called to endure I had been most fully prepared by influences and "enduements of power from on high,"—influences and enduements specifically anticipatory of what did come upon me. Some months prior to my leaving Oberlin my mind had been intensely occupied—I could not conjecture why—with the utterance made by our Saviour in view of His approaching sufferings at Jerusalem, namely, "Verily, verily, I say unto you. Except a corn of wheat fall into the ground and die, it abideth alone; but if it die, it bringeth forth much fruit." Here, I saw, is the immutable condition of fruitfulness in the kingdom of God. What that condition is, is made manifest by the circumstances in which those words were uttered. Christ had distinctly before His mind the entire sufferings and the terrible death which awaited Him. All this He could have avoided had He chosen to do so. "No man took His life from Him; He laid it down of Himself." Had He spoken the word, His persecutors would an have fallen dead before Him. Had He "prayed the Father," "twelve legions of angels" would have appeared for His rescue. That He should surrender Himself to the baptism with which He was to be baptized, that was His Father's will. When Christ, from simple respect to the Father's will, and in view of the eternal fruits thence to result, thus voluntarily "became obedient unto death, even the death of the cross," then "the corn of wheat fell into the ground and died."

So when our wills fall so absolutely into the will of God that we fully and unreservedly consent to do, to be, to become, and to suffer all that God may appoint us, asking nothing and choosing nothing but as He may will for us, then the condition required is perfected on our part, and the promise contained in the words, "If it die, it bringeth forth much fruit," is ours. Under the most distinct, deep, and impressive apprehension of this condition and promise, that black cloud came over me, and for several years shut me in on every side. "Now," I exclaimed, "is the period of my existence when 'the corn of wheat must fall into the ground and die!' While the cloud shall remain, not a murmur, nor sentiment of discontent, must for a moment have place in my mind. Not a wish or choice must be entertained that the 'trial of fire' shall be less severe or less protracted than God wills. Not a movement of anger or ill-will must enter my heart, to whatever injuries or provocations I may be subject. In no single instance must I speak unadvisedly with my lips, and absolute integrity must be maintained, whatever the losses may be which I may suffer thereby." I have no idea but that I should have fallen in that evil day, but for the anticipatory grace and strength which had been previously vouchsafed to me. Had I failed in any particular to fulfil the condition under consideration, I might have been saved from death, but should have failed, I doubt not, of the fruitfulness which has followed, and may yet follow.

Sitting, as I did, under the shadow of that dark cloud, absolutely losing myself in the sweet will of God there, and thus "learning obedience from the things which I suffered," and being—because I was through all that period consciously sustained by a power not my own—"more than a conqueror through Him that hath loved us," I now, as a witness for Christ, have an absolute assurance of the all-sufficiency of divine grace, an assurance otherwise impossible to me. When God at length very unexpectedly took me by the hand, and led me out from under that cloud, and set me again in "a large place," I very soon understood why God had afflicted me. There is one grace—the most valuable of almost all others—one grace in which we can be disciplined and perfected but in "the furnace of affliction." When "patience has had her perfect work" there, then the mind becomes possessed, as it otherwise could not be, of "everlasting consolations and good hope through grace," of "assurances of hope," "assurances of faith," and "assurances of understanding," of divine fellowships and fruitions, and of "fulness of joy." Reader, "despise not thou the chastening (parental discipline) of the Lord, nor faint when thou art rebuked of Him." Remember, also, that they only are blessed, and counted happy, "who *endure* temptation;" that when the hour of trial comes, then and there is the time and place when and where the "corn of wheat must fall into the ground and die."

The final conclusion to which all the above facts and elucidations conduct us is, the absolute assurance with which we may intrust all our mortal and immortal cares and interests to Christ. "Because I live, ye shall live also." When intrusted to Him by an unwavering faith, our well-being is just as safe as His. There is not a condition of existence in which we can be placed in which there is any necessity that we should be anything less than "more than conquerors through Him that hath loved us." When Christ is in us, and we in Him, as He is in the Father, and the Father in Him, we shall be as secure and blessed in Him as He was in the Father, and temptations, in whatever forms they may come upon us, will have no more power over us than they had over Him. "He that abideth in Him sinneth not." In this relation to Christ, into which all may, and all are absolutely bound to enter, we can have nothing less than an "all-sufficiency for all things," and cannot but be "abundantly furnished for every good work," and can do nothing less than "all things through Christ which strengtheneth us." "Great fights of affliction," "divers temptations," "fiery trials," and "resistance unto blood, striving against sin," are eras in "the hidden life," not for inglorious defeats, but for glorious victories and triumphs, "through the blood of the Lamb and the Word of His testimony."

The reason, and the *only reason*, why any believer, the feeblest as well as the strongest, does not "stand in the evil day," is that he *expects* to fall, and hence "casts away his confidence." The reason, and the only reason, why I, as above stated, "remained steadfast and immovable" during the long years in which that dark cloud hung over me, was that I expected Christ would "keep me from falling," and held to Him as with a death-grasp. In my absolute and unlimited consecration of myself to Christ, the "corn of wheat had fallen into the ground;" and now, I said to myself; "the hour is come" for it to remain and die there, and by the grace and power of Christ it shall thus remain and die. During all that dark period my faith heard the voice of Him, for whose sake I regard it as an infinite privilege to suffer all that He wills, calling to me as from heaven, "Hold the fort, for I am coming;" and my whole inner being, with all the "little strength" I had, responded, "By grace I will."

And now, reader, having not only "counted," but found, "Him faithful that hath promised," I say to you, and Christ also authorises me to say, that you need not fall when you are tempted. On the other hand, "the trial of your faith, being much more precious than of gold that perisheth, though it be tried in the fire, *may* be found unto praise and honour and glory at the appearing of Jesus Christ." "If thou wilt believe, thou shalt see the glory of God." "Be strong in the Lord, and in the power of His might;" and at all times, and under all circumstances, expect to be "more than a conqueror through Him that hath loved you." Then shall you be "as Mount Zion, which cannot be moved, but abideth forever."

CHAPTER XI.

THE INTERCESSORY FUNCTIONS OF THE SPIRIT.

In I John ii. 1, Christ is revealed as our "Advocate with the Father." "If any man sin, we have an *Advocate* with the Father, Jesus Christ the Righteous." In John xiv. 16, 26, xv. 26, and xvi. 17, the same original word that is rendered Advocate in the passage above cited, is rendered *Comforter*, and is applied exclusively to the Holy Spirit. In a very important sense, therefore, we have two Advocates with the Father; each to act in His own special sphere—two Advocates, namely, Jesus Christ the Righteous on the one hand, and the Holy Spirit on the other. In Rom. viii. 26, 27, we have a revelation of the nature of this peculiar function of the Holy Spirit. "Likewise the Spirit also helpeth our infirmities: for we know not what we should pray for as we ought; but the Spirit itself maketh intercession for us with groanings which cannot be uttered. And He that searcheth the hearts knoweth what is the mind of the Spirit, because He maketh intercession for the saints according to the will of God." As I have never yet heard this subject satisfactorily explained to my own mind, I will dwell upon it for a few moments. In the promises, two things are absolutely pledged to the faith of the believer—perfect security against all real evil on the one hand, and the possession of all real good on the other.

As examples of the first class of promise; I need only cite the following:—"There shall no evil befall thee, neither shall any plague come nigh thy dwelling." "I pray not that Thou shouldst take them out of the world, but that Thou shouldst keep them from the evil." That prayer is an absolute promise to our faith. Of the other class of promises, the following will suffice:—"No good thing will He withhold from them who walk uprightly." "But my God shall supply all your need, according to his riches in glory, by Christ Jesus." "He that spared not His own Son, but delivered Him up for us all, how shall He not with Him also freely give us all things?" The promises to prayer have but one limit—our capacities to receive. "Ask, and ye shall receive, that your joy may be full." So far the will of God is distinctly and absolutely revealed to us. So far we may ask, knowing assuredly that what we ask is "agreeable to the will of God," and that, "asking in faith," "we shall have the petitions that we desired of Him." And here we have the real meaning of our Saviour in the words, "Ye shall ask what ye will, and it shall be done unto you." What every true believer wills and asks for when he prays is that he may be kept from all that would be to him an evil, and not a good; that he may receive everything which would be to him not an evil, but a good; and that "God will supply all his need," until "his joy is full."

Now, when we come to particulars, and would specify this or that particular object, here come in "our infirmities," and we do not "know what we should pray for as we ought," because we do not know whether particular objects would be to us a good or an evil. Here, also, the Spirit is present to "help our infirmities," and becomes our intercessor for "things which are agreeable to the will of God." What we may not know at all the Spirit knows perfectly, namely, what particular objects would be good, and what objects would be evil to us, and knows, consequently, what objects God wills that we should, or should not, receive at His hands in answer to prayer. The Spirit becomes our Intercessor or Advocate by drawing out our hearts, and working in us to pray "*fervently*," "*earnestly*," and with "groanings which cannot be uttered," for those blessings which are "agreeable to the will of God,"—that is, those blessings which He wills that we should receive when we pray for them.

When the reception of the blessings referred to depends upon human instrumentality, the Spirit not only intercedes with and in us, by inducing in us a spirit of prayer for such blessing, but also moves upon the hearts of those through whom the answer is to come to us, to induce them to do in accordance with our prayers. When the blessing is to come through the operations of nature, the Spirit makes intercession for us as before, and, at the same time, works in nature, our bodies in cases of disease, or in nature around, as the case may be, to produce those changes and arrangements which accord with our petitions. When the Spirit "makes intercession for us" by influencing us to pray for specific spiritual blessings which must come to us directly from God, then the same Spirit, who leads and constrains us thus to pray, answers our prayers by "shedding abroad the love of God in our hearts," "revealing Christ in us," bringing us into "fellowship with the Father and with His Son Jesus Christ," granting "everlasting consolations and good hope through grace," "rendering us strong in weakness," "giving a tongue and wisdom" in proclaiming the truth, filling us with all the fulness of God," and "blessing us with all spiritual blessings in heavenly places in Christ Jesus," just according to the nature of the blessing in respect to which He draws out our hearts in prayer. Let us consider some facts pertaining to answers to prayer in the different relations above indicated.

Agency of the Spirit in Inducing a Spirit of Prayer, and then Securing an Answer through Human Agency.

I have already, in another connection, referred to the case of the building of the second Temple. The building of the first Temple had been, in deed and truth, "by might and by power." Before the work was commenced, the means for its full completion were all furnished, and the civil and military resources of kingdoms were devoted to the accomplishment of the work. The foundations of the second Temple were laid by a small, poor, weak, and despised people, and all this with no visible means to perfect the work begun. Yet the people were commanded to go trustfully forward with the work. The erection of this house was to be, not the work of might nor power, but of God's Spirit. How was the Spirit to do this? Not directly, by a miraculous furnishment of means, but indirectly, through human agency. While the people were to go prayerfully and trustfully forward, the Spirit of God was not only to "help their infirmities" when praying, but to move upon the hearts of kings and princes, and of men who had gold and silver, to induce them, of their own free will, to furnish the means as needed, until "the top-stone of the edifice should be laid with shoutings, Grace, grace unto it!"

When Nehemiah, saddened by the intelligence which he had received in respect to the condition of his countrymen in "the place of his fathers' sepulchres," was inquired of by the King of Persia, the queen sitting by him, in regard to the cause of the sorrow which was too great to be concealed, the sacred writer tells us that "he prayed to the God of heaven" while answering the question put to him. Here we have a striking example of what may be called the double function of the Spirit—inducing prayer in the first instance, and then influencing the heart of the royal sovereign to act in accordance with the prayer previously induced.

Permit me now to adduce some examples in common life and experience—examples illustrative of the same great truth. During one of the pecuniary crises in America, a crisis in which almost all building operations were suspended in the city of New York, a Christian mechanic found himself entirely out of work. The only resource for the support of his family was derived from what was received from a few boarders kept by his wife. This woman had exhausted every possible means to keep up this supply. At length she found herself in this condition: She had been enabled to get a satisfactory breakfast for her boarders and family. Not an article of provision remained in her house, and her money and credit were perfectly exhausted. When her children expressed their apprehensions in regard to the future, she replied that their Father in heaven would give them that day, as He had done in the past, "their daily bread," and retired to her chamber for prayer. Some time after she came down singing for joy of heart, and said to her children, "God will supply the means in time for our next meal. I know He will." Immediately after this, a member of the same church with this woman, the wife of a very wealthy citizen, called, and as soon as they were alone in the parlour, exclaimed with tears, "Sister, you must be in distress about something; do tell me what it is. I have not been able to keep you out of my mind for a moment all this forenoon. I have been impressed with the idea that I should come here and give you money. Here, take my purse and do what you desire with it. But do tell me what has happened to you." When shown the empty cupboard in that house, the visitant exclaimed, "I understand it now. Well, have no concern for the future. As long as my wants are met, yours shall be." And so it was. How manifest is the fact that, while the Spirit directed and helped the one individual to pray, He moved upon the heart of the other to do what was requisite to met the petition presented to a throne of grace!

A city missionary in the city of Brooklyn, New York, having failed to receive his usual stipend during the week, found himself on Saturday evening totally destitute of means to supply his family with food for the approaching Sabbath. The matter was presented at a throne of grace. As the family were about to retire to their beds, in answer to the ring of the bell, the missionary found a wealthy merchant standing at his door. "As I was about to retire to bed," said the merchant, "you was so distinctly and impressively presented to my mind, that I dared not sleep without calling and inquiring whether you have any want that I can meet." Before retiring to rest that night, the family of that missionary sat down to a table bountifully supplied with full provisions for days following, and did retire with the sweet assurance that He who inspires and hears prayer, knows also how to secure the answer, and is equally trustworthy to do so.

The only other case to which I would refer is that of the Rev. David Ingraham, who laid the foundation of the American missions among the freedmen in Jamaica, West Indies. This individual was the first fruit of my ministry after I was settled as pastor. He followed me to Oberlin to study there for the ministry, and early became as "full of faith and of the Holy Ghost" as any person I ever knew. After he had been in the Institution several years, physicians assured him that, on account of the asthma with which he was affected, he must spend the then approaching winter in some warm climate, such as the West Indies, or he must die. Under this conviction, he left the home of his parents in the State of Michigan, and left with means insufficient to pay his passage to the city of New York. Yet he left with a fixed determination, if possible, to get to the place he desired to reach, and did so with a fixed trust that God would furnish the means, if in no other way, from help obtained from a wealthy uncle living in the State of New York.

One of the most interesting and impressive tracts published by the American Tract Society contains an account given by a fellow-passenger, a total stranger to our friend, of the influence exerted by the latter in the vessel in which they passed from Detroit to Buffalo, and on board the packet on the canal for about one hundred and fifty miles. Through the influence of that one young man both those vessels became floating Bethels. Stepping off the packet to spend the Sabbath, our friend spoke twice in one of the churches whose pastor was absent at the time, and on taking leave on Monday morning, received an unsolicited gift of twenty-five dollars from some brethren in Christ. From his uncle he received a similar gift, and then came to the city of New York, where Professor Finney and myself were labouring at the time. I shall never forget the quiet and peaceful aspect of that countenance, or the words he uttered, when that young man met me there. "I have no will or choice of my own," he said: "I am as ready to die here as anywhere else, and now as at any other time, if such is the will of my God. I have a deep conviction, however, that it is His will that I should put forth every possible effort to get to the West Indies. If I shall fail in this, then I shall know that the time has come for me to die, and shall most joyfully accept the will of Him 'whose I am, and whom I serve.'"

Being able to hear of but one vessel which was about to sail to the West Indies, and learning that it was in the harbour at Boston, our friend, having received from Brother Finney and myself what we were able to give him, and taking with him from Brother Finney a letter of introduction to some friends there, left for that city. On visiting the vessel referred to, he was told by the captain most positively that no passengers whatever could be received on board his ship, even the cabin being engaged for goods. Returning to his room, our friend carried his case to a throne of grace, praying that God, by the Holy Spirit, would induce a change of purpose in the mind of that captain. Going down to the harbour the next day, and renewing his request, he received the same positive refusal as before. On returning to his room, "and bowing his knees to the Father of our Lord Jesus Christ," "the Spirit itself made intercession" for our brother "with groanings which cannot be uttered." On the third day he rose from his knees, and went down to the harbour with absolute assurance that then his request would be granted. As soon as he met the captain, the latter asked in the kindest words, "Will you step with me down into the cabin?" As soon as they were seated there, the captain continued, "Are you not, my young friend, out of health, and desirous for that reason to sail to the West Indies?" "Yes, sir." "Well, you can have a place on board my ship." "What will you charge me for the passage, captain?" "Sixteen dollars." The regular price was sixty dollars.

Was that young man wrong in the conclusion that it was the same Spirit that gave him such fervency, faith, and assurance in prayer, that moved also upon the heart of the captain to induce such a change in the spirit and purpose of his mind? Do not the express teachings of the Bible, as well as facts such as we are now considering, teach us most absolutely, that while the Spirit intercedes within our hearts by drawing them out in "effectual fervent prayer," that He also has power to turn the hearts of men as the rivers of water are turned, when answers to prayer depend upon human instrumentality?

The following facts, though not bearing directly upon our present inquiries, will be read with interest. On the voyage, the vessel in which our young friend sailed did indeed become a floating Bethel. On their arrival at Havana, the captain offered to take him, without charge, to all the places whither the vessel was to sail. Finding an opportunity to labour with high wages at his trade, that of a cabinetmaker, in a great manufactory of the kind in the city, our friend determined to stop there, the captain becoming responsible to the authorities for his good conduct. The overseer of the establishment was an American, and was the only individual by whom Mr. Ingraham could be understood, all the hands being slaves. Our friend soon understood, however, that all his fellow-workmen were horridly profane in their language. Whenever such an oath would be uttered, the offender would receive from our friend such a look of surprise, sorrow, and rebuke, that in a few weeks not an oath was heard in the establishment. The last evening which he spent in the city, he spent in prayer and conversation with one of those slaves, who had become an inquirer after the great salvation. Gaining needful information about the English islands, our friend returned to us, received ordination, and, with some associates, went to Jamaica, and there laid the foundation of the missions above referred to.

As an illustration of the character of the converts thus gathered in, I will refer to a single example. One of their early converts was an aged coloured man who had long been a beastly drunkard. Knowing that total abstinence was a necessary condition of saving the man from his former habits, one of the missionaries spoke to him on the subject. "Do Massa Jesus," replied the convert, "no wish me to drink any more liquor?" On being convinced that this was the case, he replied, "Well, since Massa Jesus no wish me to drink any more, me will nebber again taste a drop of liquor." The missionary then referred to the man's servitude to tobacco. "Why," replied the convert, "do Massa Jesus no wish me to use any more tobacco?" On being convinced that this was also true, the convert replied, "Well den, me nebber taste tobacca any more." Meeting the aged convert after this, the missionary found him very happy. "How have you got along without liquor and tobacco?" asked the missionary. "Oh, me nebber tich dem any more." "How do you keep down your appetite?" "Me pray Massa Jesus all de time." Here is wisdom! When will believers learn that "this is the victory that overcomes the world, even our faith"?

The Intercession and Agency of the Spirit relatively to Physical Wants.

If anything is revealed in the Bible, this is revealed there, that prayer has great efficacy relatively to diseases, to rain and sunshine, and events in the physical world around us. "Is any among you afflicted? let him pray. Is any merry? let him sing psalms. Is any sick among you? let him call for the elders of the church; and let them pray over him, anointing him with oil in the name of the Lord: and the prayer of faith shall save the sick, and the Lord shall raise him up; and if he have committed sins, they shall be forgiven him. Confess your faults one to another, and pray one for another, that ye may be healed. The effectual fervent prayer of a righteous man availeth much. Elias was a man subject to like passions as we are, and he prayed earnestly that it might not rain: and it rained not on the earth by the space of three years and six months. And he prayed again, and the heaven gave rain, and the earth brought forth her fruit." Nothing is said here about the subjective influence of prayer in preparing us to receive blessings, or in inducing us to labour diligently to secure them, and thus procure an answer to our own prayers. We are simply informed of what we may expect God to do when we pray to Him. Events, also, in respect to which prayer is affirmed to have great avail on those over which none but God has any control whatever. Such, also, are the teachings of Scripture everywhere on this subject. The individual who repeats the words, "Give us this day our daily bread," and does so, saying in his heart, under the prattle of an infidel philosophy about the laws of nature, that God will do nothing more or less in nature in consequence of our prayers, offers a direct insult to the Almighty. We ask Him, in all such cases, to do for us what we affirm He never will do for us or for anybody else. This dogma, that prayer can have, in our temporal concerns, nothing but a subjective influence, is as unscientific and unreasonable as it is unchristian.

If the Spirit of God is in and over nature, as a free and voluntary determining activity, then, if we are the sons and daughters of the Almighty, it would be, not reason, but unreason, in us not to believe that the Eternal Spirit will determine events around us in accordance with our varying necessities and Spirit inspired prayers. The Spirit is just as able to turn the currents of physical events, as He is to turn the king's heart or the heart of men "as the rivers of water are turned," and no law of nature is violated in one case any more than in the other. It as absolutely accords with the known nature and laws of matter to be influenced and controlled by the free activity of mind, as it does with those of one spirit to be influenced, and even controlled, by the thoughts, feelings, and wills of other spirits. We must deny the living God, or admit and affirm that His free will is the universal law of nature. If God is in and over nature, as a free and rational activity, then it is no more a violation of any law of nature for Him so to direct and control the current of events around us, that He shall be ever manifested to His children as a hearer and answerer of their prayers in respect to their temporal and spiritual interests alike, than it is for an earthly parent to sustain similar relations to his offspring.

If God is not in nature as a Hearer of prayer in the sense now under consideration, then we may say with truth, not only that revelation, but nature itself, as far as rational mind is concerned, is a lie. There is no conviction more intuitive and universal, and no instinct more strictly common to the race, than is the principle of prayer to God in time of need. In times of sudden calamity, and of great and pressing exigencies, it is just as natural to us to pray to God for deliverance and relief, as it is to breathe. Heathen authors of ancient times notice this fact that, in the relations under consideration, all men in common pray, and pray to one and the same God, the Creator and Governor of the universe. Here we have a law of nature, or none such is known to us. The infidelity in the world and the unbelief in the Church, which deny or ignore the "physical value of prayer," is as openly and undeniably opposed to known facts and the deductions of true science as they are to the Bible.

The facts of prayer-cure, "known and read of all men" throughout Christendom, are as absolutely verified as any scientific facts can be, and the deductions based upon the former are as strictly scientific as are those based upon the latter. Take the following fact, stated by Professor Finney under his own name in the *Indpendent* of New York, and, from personal knowledge, affirmed as real by all the people in Oberlin. A woman in that place had, from a complete paralysis of her system, been confined to her bed for upwards of ten years. In that place lives a sister in the Church who has absolute faith in the efficacy of prayer to procure immediate healing of the sick, whenever the Spirit draws out the heart to prayer for such persons. Having had her heart drawn in a very special manner towards this sad case, she went to the sick woman and convinced her from the Bible that she might receive immediate healing in answer to "the prayer of faith." Having gained this end, the visitant invited several of the female members of the Church, individuals of a common faith with her on the subject. She invited, I say, several of her female friends to meet her in that sick-room. While they were all bowed in prayer, and this woman was praying, the sick one rose up as fully recovered as was the mother-in-law of Peter when Christ touched her hand. From that time to the present, that woman has gone out and in before the people of Oberlin, a living and moving demonstration of the truth of the divine testimony, "The prayer of faith shall save the sick, and the Lord shall raise him up."

I now give two cases which were made public through the religious and secular papers of Chicago, and that by eye-witnesses of known intelligence and credibility, no hint ever appearing that the cases were not real. A daughter of a Congregational pastor in Kansas, a child some ten or twelve years of age, had been confined to her bed as a very great sufferer from a rheumatic affection for upwards of three years. One of her limbs had become perfectly helpless by being drawn up and her knee becoming callous. This child having, as she lay upon her bed, read of the healing in Oberlin, said to her mother, "I can be cured as that woman was, and I want you to pray that I may be healed." The mother having expressed doubt, the child found the promises and declarations of the Bible on the subject, and read them to her mother. The physician having prepared a special application, saying it might be of some use, the child refused, affirming that she desired that Christ might have all the honour of her restoration, and the application was laid aside. At length the child called the mother to her bedside, and said, "Mother, I now have faith to be healed. Will you not kneel down at once and pray for me?" The mother did kneel, and, as she testified, prayed as she never was conscious of being able to pray before. While thus employed, the child left her bed, and laying her hand upon the mother, exclaimed, "Wake up, mother! I am cured;" and "she was cured from that very hour." A clergyman who had called a week after this to see, with his own eyes, what had occurred, stated in the public papers, that he found the child out with other children sliding on the ice, and that with limbs as well and strong as theirs.

A physician whose "praise is in all the churches" in the State of Illinois gives this account of his own case—he had been for years afflicted with a disease of the eyes, a disease which utterly baffled the skill of himself and all the physicians around him. At length he went to the city of New York, and had his case examined by a council of the best physicians and oculists of that city. All with one consent pronounced his case a perfectly hopeless one, and affirmed that within three months he would be totally blind, and that for life. On returning home, he stated the facts to his wife and two daughters, all in common with himself having faith in God. To them he observed, that one, and but one, hope remained. God, in answer to "the prayer of faith," might restore his sight. Without further speaking, the wife and daughters retired each to a separate room for prayer. The husband and father knelt where he was, and said, "If thou, Lord, seest it best that I should become blind, I freely consent to be thus afflicted. But if I can better serve Thee with my eyes restored, grant Lord, that I may receive my sight." While thus praying, he distinctly felt each eye touched as with the end of a finger, and knew in himself that a perfect cure was effected. Rising from his knees, he passed into the hall to go to his wife's room to tell her the glad tidings. In the hall, it being totally dark, the lamps not having been lighted up, he met his wife, who threw her arms around him with the exclamation, "Husband, your eyes are cured. I know that God has heard my prayer for that blessing." While she was thus speaking, each daughter came from her room, and throwing her arms around her parents, gave utterance to the same assurance that the mother had done. When the house was lighted up, the eyes of the husband and father were found to be in as sound a state as were those of any individual present, or were those of any individual in the community. So they have remained to this day.

I must here just allude to a statement made to me, many years ago, by Dr Cleveland, then pastor of the First Presbyterian Church in Detroit, Michigan. While I was at his house, a lady of the city, a member of his church, made a call upon her pastor and his family. After she had left, Dr. Cleveland said to me, "That is one of the holiest women I ever knew in my life, and such power in prayer! Her influence is felt throughout the city. Our wicked men of the highest standing are often heard to say, that if 'all Christians were like that woman, we should not be as wicked as we are.'" Her husband, then impenitent, was sick of the cholera years ago. His case utterly baffled the skill of all physicians, until he descended into the lowest state of collapse, a state from which no individual was ever before known to recover. While the physicians and others stood by expecting that each breath would be his last, the wife, looking upon the unconscious face of her husband, said very calmly, "He will not die now." "Why, madam," said one of the physicians, "he is dying, and must be dead in a very few moments." "If that man dies," said the wife, "I am not a Christian. If I have ever had faith at all, I have prayed in faith for his recovery, and if my prayer fails here, I have no hold at all upon God." The man did recover, and no physician, or any other person, could give any account of the fact but this, that in this case, at least, "the prayer of faith did save the sick, and the Lord did raise him up."

For myself I would say, that I have great heaviness and continued sorrow in my heart that the Church, instead of listening to God, has opened her ear to the senseless "twaddle" of infidelity about the fixedness of the laws of nature, until she has experienced a deep eclipse of faith in respect to her solemn duties and high privileges in respect to the subject now under consideration. If you will not believe God's positive testimony here, reader, your faith will be feeble, if you have any at all, everywhere else.

Let us now contemplate the available influence of prayer relatively to events in nature around us. "Ask ye of the Lord rain in the time of the latter rain; so the Lord shall make bright clouds, and give them showers of rain, to every one grass in the field." The command and promise here recorded were inspired by One who understands His own relations to the movements, arrangements, and events of the world around us, and God's relations to us as a Hearer of prayer, quite as well as do those infidel scientists to whose godless teachings our religious instructors, and the flocks they lead, have so lamentably opened their ears. In the New Testament we are positively taught that prayer, relatively to the subject under consideration, and to all our temporal concerns, has all the power that it had in the days of Elias. We are required to "cast all our cares upon the Lord;" and that for this reason, "that He careth for us." To assure us of the universality and particularity of the divine care and superintendence of all our interests, our Saviour tells us, that "the hairs of our head are all numbered," and that not "one of them shall perish," and that God is so omnipresent to us as a Hearer of prayer, and so able and ready to give when we "always pray and do not faint," that "our God shall supply all our need according to His riches in glory by Christ Jesus," and render "our joy full."

Now, suppose that, in our godless unbelief we entertain the sentiment that, mere subjective influence excepted, prayer has no efficacy in respect to our temporal concerns and to the events which are passing in nature around us, we shall, as a necessary result, insulate ourselves from communion and fellowship with our Father in heaven, and put an impenetrable veil between our hearts and the face of our God in all the ordinary relations and concerns of life, and shall, consequently, find God nowhere. What is still worse, we shall become "mockers," and render our "bonds strong," by continuing to utter the words, "'Give us this day our daily bread,' give us rain, and sunshine, and fruitful seasons; heal our diseases, supply all our wants, provide for the widow and orphan, and be the Guardian of all our cares and interests," and all this while we say in our hearts, "God will change nothing and give nothing in answer to our prayers," our words thus becoming nothing but lies in the ear of God. Let me say this to you, reader, that if God shall ever "dwell with you and walk in you," He will do so in the midst of all your temporalities and relations to the world around you and as the ever-trusted Guardian of those temporalities and relations. Separate the superintendence of God from these concernments, and deny to prayer all "physical value," and your heavenly Father will not "lift upon you the light of His countenance," but will "send leanness into your soul."

Permit me to allude to a few facts bearing upon the aspect of the subject now under consideration. Here I would say in general, that I never in my life knew a single individual who had found God as his "everlasting light," and who did not, both theoretically and practically, hold the view of prayer above presented. At one period, when I was a pastor in the city of Cincinnati, Ohio, out of a population of about forty thousand, upwards of twenty-five hundred persons died of one disease, the cholera. When the pestilence was impending over us I preached to my people very earnestly upon the subject, giving them special advice as to means, and urging them to make their own preservation and that of their families the subject of special and believing prayer. We held two separate days of fasting and prayer upon the subject. As the result, not a single individual in my congregation, nor in any family of the same, died of that disease; one man excepted, who openly ridiculed the preaching and measures adopted in respect to the subject, and one little infant, of the real cause of whose death the physician was uncertain. The facts convinced us that it is not "a vain thing to call upon God."

The region of Northern Ohio, the portion of the State which lies immediately south of Lake Erie, is peculiarly subject to excessive rains on the one hand, and desolating droughts on the other. From the time when I became President of Oberlin College I preached much to the Church on the efficacy of prayer in all our temporal concernments, and especially in respect to the evils resulting from excessive rains and drought, and my teachings were most cordially received. Hence it was that, in times of need from the causes under consideration, special prayer was offered and days of fasting and prayer were held. When these fasts became known, we were made the subjects of open ridicule among the population a few miles distant all around us.

In a few years, however, the tone of sentiment among all these people became totally changed. In all periods of drought especially, our people, when they went into the country, would be stopped by this same people, and asked with deep concern whether Christians in Oberlin were praying about the weather, and especially whether we had appointed a day of fasting and prayer in reference to the subject. This one thing we knew, and the people around us knew, that no relation of antecedence and consequence seemed more fixed than that between the ascent of "effectual and fervent prayer" and the descent of the blessing prayed for. One year the drought was so fearful, that but few of the farmers cut any hay at all, and all the late crops failed. The churches of all denominations in two towns lying side by side in Portage County, some sixty miles from Oberlin, came together "with one accord in one place," and spent a day in fasting and fervent prayer to the God of heaven that He would give them rain. Immediately after a thick cloud overshadowed those towns, and poured down upon them all the rain that was needed. What was peculiar in this case was the fact, that the boundaries of that cloud corresponded everywhere with the borders of those two towns. There, and nowhere else in all that region, the rain fell.

The people of all that county were witnesses to the strictest truth of the statement now made.

Christians, several years since, had gathered in Central Ohio for a camp-meeting of ten days' continuance, the special object of the meeting being the promotion of personal holiness among believers in Jesus. At the time when the meetings commenced, excessive rains were falling, and for some time had been falling, all over that part of the State. One half day was spent at the beginning of the meetings in united and earnest prayer that God would give them a clear sky under which they might worship Him. Immediately the sky became cloudless over their heads, and during the remainder of the ten days so continued there, and for miles all around; while outside of that circle, and that in every direction, the rains continued to fall as before. From ten to twenty thousand persons attended that camp-meeting, and all bear witness to the facts as I have stated them, and believe that God's Eternal Spirit has power, not only over the hearts of men, but equally so over the elements of nature around us, and that God is a Hearer of prayer in respect to all our cares and necessities alike.

I will, at the hazard of being regarded as "speaking as a fool," refer to an example of a personal nature. I had an appointment, during a season of afflictive drought, to preach in one of the churches of the city where I live one Sabbath morning. As we came out to our carriage, I said to my wife "There is not the remotest probability that it will rain today. I will, therefore, carry in the robe which we usually take with us," and did so. When I kneeled to pray before that congregation, I had no more expectation that it would rain that day outside than inside that house of God. When I began to pray about the drought, however, a power came upon me which rendered that prayer a wonder to myself and the congregation. The Monday's issue of our daily paper contained this statement: "The preacher in one of our churches prayed very fervently yesterday morning that it might rain, and his congregation were drenched with rain on going home at the close of that service." I can never tell when "the spirit of grace and of supplications," in that form, shall be poured upon me. Nor do I feel under obligation to have such experience whenever I pray. All that I can do, or feel bound to do, is to leave my heart open, and let the Spirit intercede in it as and when He chooses.

This I do say, however, that when the Spirit does thus intercede, I always obtain the specific object for which I pray. Nor can any one pray under the intercessory power of the Spirit without the hearer, as well as himself, marking the peculiarity of the prayer. Hence it is that, for many years past, my students, in times of drought, for example, have been accustomed to say, "We shall have rain now. Did you mark our President's prayer?" Nor were they ever disappointed.

The facts that I have stated above accord fully with the unvarying experience of believers in all ages—believers who have credited God's testimony, and have availed themselves of their revealed privileges at the throne of grace. God is "the rewarder of them that diligently seek Him," and has never said to the seed of Jacob, "Seek ye my face in vain," or taught or required us to pray for what He is not ready to give. It is a fearful thing to "cast off fear, and to restrain prayer before God." We had better not pray at all, however, than to make ourselves "mockers" by approaching the throne of grace with formal requests for blessings which we say in our hearts God will never confer.

A pastor of one of the churches in the city of New York sent to his Sabbath-school, years ago, a tenderly beautiful little poem, containing an account of a visit he had just made to the residence of a poor widow of his church. As he rose in the morning, he felt strangely drawn to visit that lonely habitation. Our Father knows how to meet the wants of His children. On entering, he noticed a very young lad on his knees in prayer in a corner of the room, and heard him say with much fervency, "Our Father which art in heaven, give us this day our daily bread." Rising from his knees, and bowing to the pastor, the child said, "Our mother told us that she had no food for us today, and did not know where to get it. I told her that I could get food for us all. I would ask our Father in heaven for it. I did not think that our Saviour Jesus Christ would have taught us to pray to our heavenly Father to 'give us, day by day, our daily bread,' unless He would give it, if we should ask Him for it. For this reason I told our mother that I would ask our Father to 'give us this day our daily bread,' and He would give it to us." The pastor left that house at once. He soon returned, however, with a bountiful supply for the wants of all that family. The last stanza of the poem reads thus:

> "'I thought God heard me,' said the lad;
> I answered with a nod.
> I could not speak; but much I thought
> Of that child's faith in God."

I can say, without boasting, that I have sounded the depths of the philosophies of all ages, and I have never found in any or all of them a form of wisdom more deep or divine than was manifested by that child. This I also affirm, that that philosopher has been "spoiled by philosophy" whose heart and mind science has not imbued with the identical form of faith in God which dwelt in that child's breast.

Intercessory Functions and Agency of the Spirit in the wide Realm of the Kingdom of Grace.

All evangelical Christians believe that, while the Holy Spirit moves upon our hearts to pray for spiritual blessings in all their forms, He also employs His agency to secure for us the blessings for which we pray. The Spirit, for example, induces in us "the spirit of grace and of supplication" for the salvation of sinners. While He thus intercedes in us for this end, He moves upon the hearts of the persons prayed for, convincing them of sin, and leading them to Christ.

I will give a single example in illustration of the double functions of the Spirit now under consideration. Rev. D. Nash was, prior to the time when he received "the baptism of the Holy Ghost," one of the dullest preachers that ever ascended a pulpit in the United States. Brother Finney once said of him in a public discourse, that that man always, prior to the event referred to, "prayed with his eyes open, and preached with them shut." After his "enduement of power from on high," he became one of the mightiest men in prayer that the world ever knew, and had an almost resistless power in the utterance of divine truth. Wherever he went, "the hearts of the people were moved" by his prayers and preaching "as the trees of the forest are moved by the wind."

At length he was found, upon his knees in his closet, dead before the Lord. He was accustomed, from time to time, to pray with the map of the world before him, and the localities of the various missionary stations marked down on the map. Each station in succession he would make the special object of prayer for a single day or more. In his journal which he kept, his friends found, after his death, such records as the following:—"I think I have had this day," the date being given, "a spirit of prayer for——mission," the name of the mission being also designated. At a subsequent date, a similar record was found in record to another mission, and so on through all the stations. On turning to the pages of the *Missionary Herald*, the organ of the American Board of Commission of Foreign Missions, it was found that revivals of religion did occur in all those missions revivals occurring in the identical order, and commencing at the very date, of the various records above referred to.

Reader, if at a throne of grace you have not princely "power with God and with men," and if you have not wisdom and utterance to speak for Christ to "edification, exhortation, and comfort," it must be that unbelief has, in your mind, limited the sphere of availing prayer to a very narrow circle, or because you have not "received the Holy Ghost since you believed." Had the Spirit been thus given to you, He would be in you as an interceding presence, drawing out your heart in "effectual fervent prayer" for things which accord with the divine will, and God's Word would be in you "as burning fire shut up in your bones." On this subject I need not enlarge, but will close this chapter with some brief reflections.

General Reflections.

1. We can now understand the power which we have in prayer when we are "full of faith and of the Holy Ghost." The Spirit, who understands perfectly all our need, on the one hand, and the good-will of God on the other, will not fail to "make intercession for us," that is, to draw out our hearts in prayer for every blessing requisite to our perfect fulness of joy, or every form of good, temporal and spiritual, which God wills that we should receive and enjoy. All our petitions will come before One whose paternal heart yearns to meet every want of our

mortal and immortal natures, and who has bound Himself; by absolute promise, to suffer "no evil to befall us," and to "withhold no good thing from us," when we thus pray to Him. All our petitions, also, will be presented in the name of Christ, who has absolutely assured us that "whatsoever we shall ask the Father in His name, He will give it us." The Father, therefore, cannot deny our requests without dishonouring His only Son. Finally, in all our petitions, God will hear the voice of His own Spirit "making intercessions for us with groanings which cannot be uttered," and whom He has commissioned to energise with almighty power in the world of nature and the world of grace, to insure for us "the petitions which we desire of Him." "Praying always with all prayer in the Spirit," "nothing will be impossible unto us." These, reader, are the sort of persons we all ought to be. Shall unbelief veil your heart from the face of God, and shut you out from the promise, "Thou shalt call upon me, and I will answer thee, and show thee great and wonderful things that thou knowest not of"?

2. We may also clearly understand why it is that God makes the bestowment of His most precious gifts, temporal and spiritual, conditional upon our prayers for the same. How else, I may inquire, could He be so distinctly and impressively present to our hearts, and known to us as our omnipresent, all-loving, and all-sympathising Father and watchful Guardian of all our interests, the small and the great alike? We call upon Him, and He answers us "in all that we call upon Him for," and that both in respect to ourselves and others, and both in respect to temporal and spiritual interests, concerns, and relations alike, and in every case in which we "cast our cares upon Him," we receive some special and recognisable token of His paternal sympathy and regard. It then becomes omnipresently real to us that God is "our everlasting dwelling-place," and at all times, and under all circumstances, we are the direct objects of His love, sympathy, and care; that "in all our afflictions He is afflicted," while "the angel of His presence saves us;" and that whatever evil "touches us touches the apple of His eye." The main good which we receive through prayer does not consist chiefly in the specific blessings which we obtain, but in the assurance which each answer brings to our hearts that "God is our Father, and we are His

sons and daughters." The former may be but a temporary good, of comparatively little value; the latter brings to us an infinite and eternal good, a blessedness as enduring as the eternal years of God, and as blissful as His everlasting smile. It is thus that, while at "the throne of grace," we "obtain mercy and find grace to help in time of need," and God thus "grants us all things richly to enjoy," all things temporal and spiritual in connection with the specific gifts obtained—

> "Heaven comes down our souls to greet,
> And glory crowns the mercy-seat"

We never can know God as our "everlasting light" until He shall be omnipresent to our hearts as a Hearer and Answerer of prayer, "the Rewarder of them that diligently seek Him" in respect to all our interests, concerns, and relations alike, "we casting ALL our cares upon Him," and that for the revealed reason, "that He careth for us."

3. We notice, finally, the important error of those who limit the operations and power of the Spirit to the revealed truth of God. As our Instructor and Teacher, it is, of course, the revealed office of the Spirit to "lead us into all truth ;" and this function is an infinitely important one. It is nowhere revealed, however, that this is His exclusive function, but it is distinctly revealed that this is not the case.

The same Spirit under whose power Christ, on going out of the wilderness, "came into Galilee," worked also in Christ "in raising Him from the dead." By the same Spirit which "fell upon the disciples at the beginning," God is to "quicken our mortal bodies." The same Spirit which moved Elias to "pray fervently that it might not rain," closed the windows of heaven, so that "it rained not on the earth for the space of three years and six months." The same Spirit which moved him to pray again "that it might rain," caused "the heavens to give rain," and "the earth to bring forth her increase." The same Spirit which moved the Church to "pray day and night for Peter in prison," caused the chains to fall from his limbs, put his keepers to sleep, opened the prison doors, and "the iron gate which led into the city," while the angel of God led the apostle forth in safety.

While the Spirit is in us as the light of God, "leading us into all truth," He may act directly upon other departments of our natures besides our intelligence, and, by acting thus, may change our propensities, and correct evil tendencies within us. While He rests upon us as a baptism of power, He may intercede within for things which accord with the will of God, and may then energise with Omnipotent energy in the world of mind and matter around us, to bring to us from God answers of peace "in all that we call upon Him for." Let us not in any direction "limit the Holy One," but, in reference to all our revealed privileges, "be strong in the faith, giving glory unto God."

CHAPTER XII.

CRUCIFIXION AND SANCTIFICATION OF THE PROPENSITIES.

The forms of expression by which the provisions and promises of the new covenant, of which Christ is our Mediator, are set before us are quite various and peculiar, and require special consideration on the part of all who would understand the secrets of the hidden life. In Jer. xxxi. 31-33, the provisions and promises of this covenant are set forth in the following language:—"Behold, the days come, saith the Lord, that I will make a new Covenant with the house of Israel, and with the house of Judah: not according to the covenant that I made with their fathers in the day that I took them by the hand to bring them out of the land of Egypt; which my covenant they brake, although I was an husband unto them, saith the Lord: but this shall be the covenant that I will make with the house of Israel; After those days, saith the Lord, I will put my law in their inward parts, and write it in their hearts; and will be their God, and they shall be my people." In Ezek. xxxvi. 25-27, these same provisions and promises are expressed in the following words:—'Then will I sprinkle clean water upon you, and ye shall be clean: from all your filthiness, and from all your idols, will I cleanse you. A new heart also will I give you, and a new spirit will I put within you: and I will take away the stony heart out of your flesh, and I will give you an heart of flesh. And I will put my Spirit within you, and cause you to walk in my statutes, and ye shall keep my judgments, and do them."

Under the old dispensation, there was a promise to believers quite analogous to those above presented (Deut. xxx. 6)—"And the Lord thy God will circumcise thine heart, and the heart of thy seed, to love the Lord thy God with all thine heart, and with all thy soul, that thou mayest live." The conditions on which God will do all these things for us are stated with perfect definiteness in the Scriptures. In Ezek. xxxvi. 37, these conditions are thus expressed: "Thus saith the Lord God; I will yet for this be inquired of by the house of Israel to do it for them." Again we read, "Then shall ye seek me, and find me, when ye shall search for me with all your heart." Under the old dispensation, the condition of the promise, as then presented, is thus expressed. The people were to "return unto the Lord, and obey His voice, with all their heart and with all their soul."

Near the close of his life, Moses complains of the people, and charges it upon them as a great crime on their part, that God "had not yet given them an heart to perceive, and eyes to see, and ears to hear, unto that day." In other words, they had not only neglected present obedience, but had not sought of God a "heart to perceive, eyes to see, and ears to hear;" in other words, they had neglected to seek from God *circumcised hearts,* that they might continuously "love the Lord their God, with all their heart and with all their soul." What does God complain of in respect to His Church to-day, and charge upon her as the sin which is the main cause of all her weaknesses, lapses, and backslidings? Is it not this, that she is living in content outside of the provisions and promises of the new covenant, the covenant which, according to the express teachings of the prophet Joel, and, I may add, of all the prophets, includes "the promise of the Spirit"?

Why is it, reader, if such is your state, that God has not "circumcised your heart to love the Lord your God with all your heart and with all your soul"? Why has He not "put His law in your inward parts, and written it in your heart"? Why has He not "sprinkled clean water upon you," and rendered you "clean"? Why has He not "cleansed you from all your filthiness, and from all your idols"? Why has He not "taken the stony heart out of your flesh, and given you a heart of flesh," and "caused you to walk in His statutes," and to "keep His judgments, and do them"? Why has He not "sanctified and cleansed you," so that when your iniquities shall be searched for, there shall be none, and your sins, and they shall not be found"? Why has not God "put His Spirit within you," "endued you with power from on high," and thus "filled you with all the fulness of God"? But one answer can be given to these questions, provided you have not yet thus attained. The Lord your God has not "for this been inquired of by you to do it for you;" you have not "hearkened unto the voice of the Lord your God," obeyed His will, believed His Word, "laid hold of His covenant," and "searched for Him with all your heart and with all your soul." This is your sin, on account of which you "walk in darkness and have no light," groan in "bondage under the law of sin and death," and are shut out from "fellowship with the Father, and with His Son Jesus Christ." If now you will believe God's word, trust His grace, "lay hold of His covenant," "inquire of Him to do these things for you," and "search for Him with all your heart and with all your soul," "He will be found of you," and you will find all His "exceeding great and precious promises" fulfilled in your experience, and He will do exceeding abundantly for you above all that you ask or think." "But if you will not believe, you will not be established."

The Nature of the Blessings Proffered to our Faith in this New Covenant.

It is perfectly evident that two forms of genuine Christian experience are presented to our consideration in the subject before us; that the element of supreme obedience, hearkening to the voice of God, obeying His will, and seeking Him "with all the heart, and with all the soul," characterise each state alike, and that the one is conditional and preparatory to the other. When we "return unto the Lord, and obey His voice with all our heart and with all our soul," we are in one state. When the Lord our God has circumcised our hearts to love the Lord "with all our heart and with all our soul," we must be in another and different state, or the promise is without meaning. We are surely in one state and relation to God when we are "searching for Him with all our hearts," and in another and different state and relation to Him when we have "found Him," He coming to us, and "dwelling in us, and walking in us," as our God, and we having fellowship with Him as "His sons and daughters." When we are "inquiring of God" to do for us what is promised in the new covenant, we are in one state. We are certainly in quite another and different state when God, in fulfilment of the provisions and promises of that covenant, has "put His law in our inward parts, and has written it in our hearts," has "cleansed us from all our filthiness and all our idols," has "taken away the stony heart out of our flesh and given us an heart of flesh," and has "put His Spirit within us" that is, "baptized us with the Holy Ghost." No candid mind will question the truth of the above statements.

But what are the provisions and promises of this new covenant? As far as they include "the promise of the Spirit" the most essential element of the covenant—on this part of the subject I shall not now speak, having said already all that is needful here. What, then, do the words, "take the stony heart out of your flesh, and give you an heart of flesh," mean? What can they mean but a fundamental change and a renewal of our propensities? We are "by nature children of wrath," "prone to evil as the sparks are to fly upward." When God does for us what is provided for and promised to us in the new covenant, we have "a new heart" and "a new spirit," "a divine nature, which impels us to love and obedience, just as our old nature impelled us to sin.

As preparatory to a clear understanding of this subject, let us consider the following statements of the apostle. "Now, the works of the flesh are manifest, which are these adultery, fornication, uncleanness, lasciviousness, idolatry, witchcraft, hatred, variance, emulations, wrath, strife, seditions, heresies, envyings, murders, drunkenness, revellings, and such like. But the fruit of the Spirit is love, joy, peace, long-suffering, gentleness, goodness, faith, meekness, temperance: against such there is no law." Behind all these forms of sin, "works of the flesh," lie certain propensities, dispositions, and tempers, which, when touched by corresponding temptations, set on fire burning and "warring lusts" and evil passions, and these induce the sins and crimes above designated. Suppose, now, that these old propensities, dispositions, and tempers are taken away, and, in this state, new ones of an opposite nature are given; in other words, that "the heart of stone is taken out of our flesh," and in its stead there is "given us heart of flesh." Under our renovated propensities, and new dispositions, tendencies, and tempers, or "divine nature," it becomes just as easy and natural for us to bear "the fruits of the Spirit," as it was, under our old ones, to work "the works of the flesh." Here, then, we perceive clearly what is provided for, and promised to, our faith in the new covenant, what Christ, as the Mediator of that covenant, promises to do for us when He is "inquired of by us to do it for us," and what He will commission the Spirit to work in us when He shall "baptize us with the Holy Ghost"

With the above exposition accords all the teachings of the New Testament upon this subject. The "exceeding great and precious promises" are given us for the revealed purpose that "by these"—that is, by embracing these promises by faith—we "might be partakers of the DIVINE NATURE, having escaped the corruption that is in the world through lust." "By nature"—that is, under the influence of our old nature, or propensities, dispositions, and tempers, we are "children of wrath," and "bring forth fruit unto death." Under the dispositions, tempers, and tendencies of our new or "divine nature," we are just as naturally "children of God," and "have our fruit unto holiness," while "the end is everlasting life." Why are we called upon to "reckon ourselves dead indeed unto sin, but alive unto God through Jesus Christ our Lord"? Because "our old man," our old propensities, dispositions, and tempers, is crucified, "put to death" with Him, that the "body of sin," our old and evil nature, "might be destroyed, that henceforth we should not serve sin." Our old nature, or propensities, dispositions, and tempers, the apostle calls "the body of this death," and thanks God, as we all should, that, "through Jesus Christ our Lord," we are delivered from this "body of sin and death"

One special design of the apostle in the sixth, seventh, and eighth chapters of Romans is to elucidate this great truth. While the old nature remains, fight against its tendencies and promptings as we will, and form what good resolutions we may, "the good which we would we shall not do, but the evil which we would not, that shall we do." The reason, as the apostle affirms, is obvious. "The law in our members will war against the law of our mind, and bring us into captivity to the law of sin which is in our members." From "this law of sin and death" Christ sets us free, putting within us, in place of that law, "the law of the Spirit of life." The same doctrine the apostle obviously teaches in the following passage:—"So, then, they that are in the flesh (under the dominion of their natural propensities) cannot please God. But ye are not in the flesh (under its control), but in the Spirit (under His control), if so be that the Spirit of God dwell in you. Now if any man have not the Spirit of Christ, he is none of His. But if Christ be in you, the body," that is, the body of sin of which the apostle has been exclusively speaking thus far, "is dead, because of sin; but the Spirit," that is, the new nature or spirit which Christ gives, "is life," lives and reigns within us, "because of righteousness."

Now mark the inference which the apostle draws from his previous reasonings "Therefore, brethren, we are debtors, not to the flesh to live after the flesh." In other words, because that, through the Spirit of Christ dwelling in us, "the body of sin," our old and evil propensities, "may be destroyed," and "the old man may be crucified with Him," and we may, "through the law of the Spirit of life in Christ Jesus," be "made free from the law of sin and death," we should indeed cease to "live after the flesh," should be "not in the flesh, but in the Spirit;" and should "reckon ourselves dead indeed unto sin, but alive unto God through Jesus Christ our Lord." Just such teaching runs through all Paul's epistles, and, I may add, as the reader will perceive in the light of these suggestions, through the whole New Testament. Paul, for example, says of himself, "I am Crucified with Christ: nevertheless I live; yet not I, but Christ liveth in me: and the life which I now live in the flesh I live by the faith of the Son of God, who loved me, and gave Himself for me." Again he says, "But God forbid that I should glory, save in the cross of our Lord Jesus Christ, by whom the world is crucified unto me, and I unto the world." To Christians he says, "Ye are dead, and your life is hid with Christ in God." Such language implies more than this, that his old propensities, "the body of sin," "the old man," is yet living and warring in the soul, but, by the grace of Christ, are held in subjection. Mere subjection is not death. What the apostle undeniably intended to teach is this: that his propensities, dispositions, and temper had been so renovated that the world, with its affections and lusts, had no more power over him than they have over the dead. Christ, on the other hand, lived in him, and occupied all his affections, and held undisputed control over all his activities. Some important suggestions and reflections here present themselves.

Forms of Christian Experience before and after we have entered into the Privileges of the New Covenant.

We can now understand clearly the difference in the conditions and relations of the believer before and after the promises of the new covenant have been fulfilled in his experience. An individual, we will suppose, has, through the Spirit, been convicted of sin, and has exercised genuine "repentance toward God, and faith toward our Lord Jesus Christ." As far as his voluntary activities are concerned, he is now in a state of supreme obedience to the will of God. His old propensities, dispositions, temper, and tendencies, however, remain as they were, and remain to war against this new-born purpose of obedience. If the convert is left here, just where the mass of them are left under the teachings they commonly receive—if the convert is left here, what, I ask, will be his future experience? Nothing, I answer, but the loss of his first love, the dying out of his primal joys, and sad falls and lapses, with periods of rejoicing and victories few and far between. It is infinite presumption to expect better results under such circumstances. And this is just what we do witness in the general experience of the Church. Open and gross immoralities excepted, the convert carries with him into the Christian life the same propensities, dispositions, and temper that he had before his conversion, and these, when strongly excited, overcome him as they did before. How absurd for a believer, in such circumstances, to "reckon himself dead indeed unto sin, but alive unto God, through Jesus Christ our Lord."

Suppose, on the other hand, that the convert, instead of being left in this perilous position, is fully taught the provisions and promises of the new covenant, and is led to apprehend Christ as the Mediator of that covenant. The convert now, in the exercise of a strong faith, "inquires of Christ to do this for him." What does Christ do? First of all, "He baptizes the convert with the Holy Ghost," and "endues him with power from on high" for the exigencies of his new life. The Spirit, in the fulfilment of His mission, enters upon the work of universal renovation. He accordingly "takes the heart of stone out of the convert's flesh, and gives him an heart of flesh,"—"gives him a new heart and a new spirit," "writes the law upon his inward parts, and puts it in his heart," "circumcises his heart to love the Lord his God with all his heart and with all his soul," renders him a "partaker of the divine nature," "takes of the things of Christ and shows them unto him," "reveals Christ in him," so that "he beholds with open face the glory of the Lord, and is changed into the same image from glory to glory," and is "filled with all the fulness of God," consummates a vital union between him and Christ, so that Christ is in him, as the Father is in the Son, and thus "blesses him with all spiritual blessings in heavenly places in Christ Jesus," and "abundantly furnishes him for every good work."

This all-cleansing, all-renovating, and all-vitalising process the apostle calls "the renewing of the Holy Ghost." Our salvation is commenced with "the washing of regeneration," and is consummated by "the renewing of the Holy Ghost." Into what new relations does the convert enter when he has passed through the first state, and entered into all the light, and privileges, and enduements of power of the second? He is now "delivered from his enemies," and may "serve God without fear, in righteousness and holiness before Him, all the days of his life." With "the old man crucified," imbued with a new and "divine nature," "filled with the Holy Ghost," and with "the power of Christ resting upon him," he may, with all assurance, "reckon himself dead indeed unto sin, but alive unto God, through Jesus Christ His Lord." When Christ, as "the Mediator of the new covenant," comes to believers, He says to the old propensities, dispositions, tempers, and lusts, the old man which once held them in bondage, "Let my people go, that they may serve me." When that "old man," with his hosts of affections and lusts, pursues after God's people to bring them back into their former bondage, that old tyrant, with all his armed host, is overwhelmed and lost in the Red Sea of Christ's blood. "If the Son shall make you free, ye shall be free indeed." What a melancholy reflection it is that most believers advance no further in the Christian life than "the washing of regeneration," are ignorant of Christ as the Mediator of the new covenant, and, consequently, have no experience of "the renewing of the Holy Ghost"!

Fundamental Misapprehension of the Christian Warfare.

The common idea of the Christian warfare seems to be this—In regeneration, the Christian is brought into a state of voluntary obedience to the will of God, and his sincere purpose is to obey the divine will in all things. His old propensities, dispositions, and tendencies remain, and rise in rebellion against this new law of the mind—this purpose of obedience. The Christian warfare consists in fighting these rebel forces, and holding them in subjection. We shall search in vain for any such idea of this warfare in the New Testament or the Old either. "We wrestle," says the apostle, "not against flesh and blood, but against principalities, against powers, against the rulers of the darkness of this world, against spiritual wickedness in high places." Every believer is "called to be a soldier in the army of the Lord." As the great Captain of our salvation, Christ has organised and disciplined His army to accomplish the purposes for which He was sent into the world, namely, to "make an end of sin, and to bring in everlasting righteousness." Believers are in the world as Christ was in the world. "As Thou hast sent me into the world, even so have I sent them into the world." "Ye have not chosen me, but I have chosen you, and ordained you that ye should go and bring forth fruit, and that your fruit should remain."

Christ was not sent into the world to fight rebel propensities, dispositions, and tendencies in Himself, but to make war upon the sin and evil that is in the world, and thus to bring the world back to God. The proper warfare of every believer is identical with that of Christ. Hence, "the weapons of our warfare," the apostle tells us, "are not carnal, but mighty through God to the pulling down of strongholds; casting down imaginations, and every high thing that exalteth itself against the knowledge of God, and bringing into captivity every thought to the obedience of Christ." Again, the apostle says, "No man that warreth entangleth himself with the affairs of this life; that he may please Him who hath chosen him to be a soldier." That we may, as soldiers of the cross, be perfectly free to serve Christ, and fight His battles against sin and the evils that are in the world, He Himself takes charge of our inward foes, putting them to death, and not suffering them to weaken our energies in His service. In warring upon the powers of sin, we, of course, meet with resistance, and are subject to assaults from our great adversary. Hence our furnishment with divine weapons and armour for defensive as well as offensive purposes. All this furnishment, as presented in the New Testament, has reference to enemies without, and not within the soul. In "fighting against sin," ancient saints "resisted unto blood." Though we may not be, as they were, called upon thus to resist, our warfare is identical with theirs; and in this warfare we, as well as they, are called upon to "endure hardness as good soldiers of Christ." The dogma that the Christian warfare is with foes within, and not with the enemies of God and man without the soul, utterly misleads the mind in respect to the fundamental end and aim of our sacred calling. Christ does not intend that those who serve Him and fight His battles against the kingdom of darkness shall have two enemies to fight at the same time, and the strongest in the citadel of their own souls. In His people, He designs that His reign shall be absolute. Then, indeed, will the sacramental host be "fair as the moon, clear as the sun, and terrible as an army with banners."

With the views now under consideration accord the experience of believers in all generations—believers who know Christ and trust in Him as the Mediator of the new covenant. As a witness for Christ, I would say that, were there a perfect oblivion of the facts of my life prior to the time when I thus knew my Saviour, I should not, from present experiences, ever suspect that these old dispositions, which once tyrannised over me, had ever existed. Those who have known me most intimately for the last twenty or thirty years, and had not known my former life, often, as stated before, say to me, "We could be as quiet under injuries and provocations, and as peaceful and contented under afflictive providences as your are, if we only had your temperament." My reply to all such is: I once had a more fiery temper, and a more easily disquieted and restless spirit than you now have; and you can be as I am if you will inquire of Christ as I did. Of all that I have written about the new covenant, I can truly say, "That which we have seen and heard declare we unto you, that ye also may have fellowship with us: and truly our fellowship is with the Father, and with His Son Jesus Christ. And these things write we unto you, that your joy may be full,"

Entire Sanctification.

We may now attain to a somewhat distinct understanding of the following words of the apostle:—"And the very God of peace sanctify you wholly; and I pray God your whole spirit and soul and body be preserved blameless unto the coming of our Lord Jesus Christ." The original word rendered *wholly*, I would observe, is one of the strongest words known in the Greek or any other language. It is made up of two words, *olos*, or all, and *telos*, everywhere in the New Testament translated *perfect*. The word made up of *pantos*, all, and *telos*, and rendered *uttermost* in the passage "He is able to save unto the *uttermost*," is a word of the same strength of meaning. In the passage above cited, the words "sanctify you wholly," from their original meaning, namely, sanctify you entirely in all respects, and in the connection in which they here stand, can mean nothing less than this—a total renovation and purification of all our propensities, dispositions, temperaments, and activities, mental, moral, spiritual, and physical. The words, "I pray God, your whole spirit and soul and body be preserved blameless," also impart to the phrase "sanctify you wholly" this full breadth of meaning. When we are in this state, we then become partakers of just what is provided for and promised to us in the new covenant. Sanctification, in this form, is also absolutely promised to our faith in connection with the prayer of the apostle under consideration. "Faithful (worthy to be trusted) is He that calleth you, who also will do it."

When thus Sanctified, we are not Free from Temptation.

How often do we hear it said, that if we were once thus sanctified we should never more be tempted! Christ, during His whole life, was thus sanctified; "yet He was tempted in all points like as we are." Our first parents, prior to the fall, were totally free from all evil propensities, dispositions, and temperaments, yet they were tempted and fell. Angels, from their creation, had a divine nature; yet, through temptation, they failed to "keep their first estate." Temptation is incidental to finite natures, it may be, in all conditions of existence. Suppose all our propensities, dispositions, and temperaments are, as they may be, restored to a perfectly normal state. We shall still be subject to tribulation from hunger, thirst, cold, nakedness, disease, the sundering of domestic ties, and from man's inhumanity to man. In "fighting against sin," we shall meet with resistance, and shall need "the shield of faith to quench all the fiery darts of the wicked." "The disciple is not above his master, nor the servant above his lord." Christ was tempted, and so shall we be tempted. With our old nature crucified, and a divine nature given in the stead of the former, with "Christ formed within us the hope of glory," and the power of His Spirit resting upon us, we shall be in very different relations to temptations and "trials of faith" from what we once were. Here we were taken captive when assaulted with temptation; now, in the same circumstances, we are "more than conquerors through Him that loved us."

In what Sense may all Believers accept Christ as their Present Sanctification.

I hear much said, and much is written, about receiving Christ as our present sanctification—much which, as it appears to me, should be received with great caution and self-reflection. When we look to Christ to save us from actual sin, of course we should expect Him to do it now. But when we inquire of Him, as the Mediator of the new covenant, to do for us all that is promised in that covenant, the case is different. Heart-searching may precede the final cleansing, searching for God with all the heart must precede the finding of Him, and waiting and praying may precede, we cannot tell how long, the baptism of power. Here "the vision may tarry;" and if it tarries, we must "wait for it," and watch and pray for its coming with "full assurance of faith," "full assurance of hope," and "full assurance of understanding." The disciples had to tarry for "the promise of the Spirit," and so may we.

Christ, I frequently hear it said, is in us. When we admit the fact that He is thus present in our hearts, then "we enter, at once, into the rest of faith," and become possessed with fulness of joy. I never make such statements myself, and I always listen with regret and apprehension when I hear them made by others. For me to admit that Christ is thus present, and that I am "complete in Him," and to trust Him accordingly, is one thing, and is an essential *condition* of my entering into rest. For Christ to "*manifest* Himself to me," and, with the Father, to "come to me, and make His abode with me," is quite another. Faith on our part does not of itself give us rest. The rest of faith is what Christ gives "after we have believed." "Come unto me, and I will *give* you rest." I believe, for example, that Christ is present "in my mouth and in my heart," and I trust Him to "supply all my needs." If, now, the Spirit should not "take of the things of Christ, and show them unto me," if He should not "enlighten the eyes of my understanding, that I might know the things which are freely given us of the Lord," I should not "enter into rest," nor would "my joy be full." We believe Christ's word, trust His grace, dedicate our whole selves to Him, and yield our wills to His. This is our part of the covenant. Christ now "prays the Father for us," and He gives us "the Comforter," the Holy Ghost "to abide with us for ever." The Spirit "reveals Christ in us," enables us to "behold with open face, as in a glass, the glory of the Lord," and brings us into "fellowship with the Father, and with His Son Jesus Christ." We thus "enter into rest," "the rest of faith," and become possessed with "fulness of joy," while, with ineffable sweetness, our hearts sing—

"Safe in the arms of Jesus,

Safe on His gentle breast"

"He that believeth in me, as the Scripture hath said, out of his belly shall flow rivers of living water. But this He spake of the Spirit, which they that believe on Him should receive: for the Holy Ghost was not yet given, because Jesus was not yet glorified." "The Holy Ghost is now given," and you can have this blessed experience, because that when you shall "inquire of Christ to do it for you," He will "baptize you with the Holy Ghost," and do for you all that is promised in the new covenant.

CHAPTER XIII.

PARENTAL DISCIPLINE OF THE SONS OF GOD.

The Terms Defined.

THE revealed plan of God in regard to His children, while He continues them in the world, is to develop and perfect in them every form of virtue possible to their nature. Every form of such virtue has its specific conditions of growth and development, and we must be subjected to these conditions, or we cannot become possessed of the corresponding virtues. Subjecting believers to these conditions, for the purpose designated, is called in the New Testament the *paideia*, or child-discipline of the sons of God. To this subject the apostle refers with most impressive interest in the twelfth chapter of Hebrews. He there refers particularly, not to afflictions which come upon us in consequence of our own sins, but to the contradictions and tribulations to which we are subject in consequence of our testimony against the sins of others. He calls upon believers to "consider Him who endured such contradictions of sinners" against Himself, lest they, in consequence of meeting with similar trials, "should be wearied and faint in their mind." They, as Christ had done before them, "had not resisted unto blood, striving against sin."

The apostle then goes on to specify God's plan and purpose in permitting His people to be subject to such tribulations, and to afflictions in all their forms, whether they descend upon us in the arrangements of Providence or as reproofs for sin. All in common come upon us for one and the same purpose, child-discipline—the discipline of virtue. Such discipline, therefore, should be patiently endured. Christ "learned obedience from the things which He suffered." So should we. Our parents subjected us to child-discipline, and we gave them reverence. "Shall we not rather be in subjection to the Father of spirits and live? For they verily for a few days chastened us" (subjected us to child-discipline, the literal rendering of the original) "after their own pleasure: but He" (subjects us to such discipline) "for our profit, that we might be partakers of His holiness." Such is the light in which all afflictive providences, from whatever immediate causes they may descend upon us, should by us be regarded—that is, as forms of necessary child-discipline, forms of discipline in virtue, which, when patiently endured, will not fail to "yield the peaceable fruits of righteousness"—"peace, quietness, and assurance for ever." All who do not thus regard and improve such providences, the apostle assures us, "are bastards, and not sons." In all our afflictions we may have, and should have, this life-imparting assurance—namely, we are the sons of God, and He is dealing with us, even when He seems severe, "as sons." With what infinite reason does the apostle bring home the exhortation to our hearts, "Wherefore lift up the hands which hang down, and the feeble knees"!

What it is to Endure Chastening or Child-Discipline

"If ye *endure* chastening" (child-discipline), says the apostle, "God dealeth with you as with sons." "My brethren," says another apostle, "count it all joy when ye fall into divers temptations, knowing that the trial," or discipline, "of your faith worketh patience. But let patience have her perfect work, that ye may be perfect and entire, wanting nothing." Again he says, "Blessed is he that *endureth* temptation; for when he is tried, he shall receive a crown of life, which the Lord hath promised to them that love Him." "Behold, we count them happy which *endure*. Ye have heard of the patience (endurance) of Job, and have seen the end of the Lord"—that is, the blissful consummation to which He conducts those who endure—"how that the Lord is very pitiful, and of tender mercy." All the sacred writers speak thus of God's discipline of His sons and daughters, the words, "temptation," "trials of faith," "fiery trials which are to try you," and "chastening," or child-discipline, being frequently employed by them as synonymous terms.

In reflecting upon this subject, we should ever bear this in mind, that to be merely *subject* to afflictive providences, and to *endure* "chastening," "temptation," "trials of faith," or child-discipline, are very different things. To *endure* is to maintain our fidelity while under discipline—that is, during the time while the pressure of the trial is upon us. He that blesses at the time when he is reviled, remains meek, quiet, and unangered at the time when heavy provocations are heaped upon him—"whose spirit lies down and is still," lies down in quiet submission in the centre of the sweet will of God at the very time when great afflictions press upon him—that "chooses rather to suffer affliction with the people of God than to enjoy the pleasures of sin for a season," "enduring as seeing Him who is invisible,"—and replies to every temptation to sin, "I cannot do this great wickedness, and sin against God,"—these, and these only, "endure chastening," "endure temptation," and "endure hardness as good soldiers of Christ."

Remember this, reader, that if, at the moment when you are under the trial, your faith fails you, you may, by subsequent repentance, escape condemnation, but that you suffered an irreparable loss by missing the golden opportunity then presented to become disciplined in virtues, which would have insured to you an "eternal weight of glory," over and above what you will now receive. At the time when tribulations encircle us, then and there is the time and opportunity for you to "wash your garments, and make them white in the blood of the Lamb."

Special and Peculiar Characteristics of the Child-Discipline of the Son of God.

"No chastening"—that is, no form of child-discipline, says the apostle, "for the present seemeth to be joyous, but grievous." "Wherein," says the apostle Peter, "ye greatly rejoice, though now for a season, if need be, ye are in heaviness through manifold temptations." God is able, we should bear in mind, to keep His people, at all times and under all circumstances, so full of joy and gladness that no providence would "*seem* to be grievous," and they should never be "in heaviness" at all. It is only "if need be"—that is, if the discipline of their virtues require it—that they should ever be possessed of less than perfect fulness of joy. When the discipline of virtue requires, on the other hand, then the Spirit will, for the time, shed no more of the love of God abroad in our hearts, grant us no more of present peace and joy, and suffer to descend upon us just the degree of heaviness, and no more than is requisite, to develop and perfect that virtue in its divinest form. The grace of patience, for example, can be developed and perfected but under the pressure of tribulation. That "patience may have her perfect work," we must have grace to endure, but not the fulness of joy, which would cause the affliction to seem, for the time being, not "grievous," but "joyous."

"Ye have heard of the patience of Job, and have seen the end of the Lord." God designed that this, His servant, should not only be possessed, in a preeminent degree, of this divine virtue, but that he should be to the world, in all coming time, an example of patience, as Abraham is of faith. As a means to this end, Job was, first of all, overwhelmed with unexampled calamities, and this under circumstances which for a time shut him out from the sympathy of all his friends, even the mother of his children being estranged from him. Under these circumstances the man of God was sustained by the most distinct inward assurance of the genuineness of his piety, of the divine approval, and that, after he should be tried, God would lead him out of the furnace, and more than restore to him all that he had lost. To render the discipline perfect for the work intended, however, God withheld, for the time being, the light of His countenance from the afflicted one, and "left him to tread the wine-press alone." This was requisite that "patience might have her perfect work," and that the sufferer might become "perfect and entire, wanting nothing." Suffering having fully accomplished its sacred mission, God more than restored "the light of His countenance" as formerly enjoyed, became to the sufferer, as He never could have been before, "an everlasting light," placed him on high as among "the foremost of the sons of light," and all the world, and heaven too, now regard him as one of the happiest of men.

I will now allude, in further illustration of the great truth before us, to an important fact of my own experience. During the dark period of my life, the period in which I dwelt amid the ruins of the great university which I began to found, I was for the time about as completely isolated from former friendships and associations as was Job when God "chose him in the furnace of affliction." With one or two exceptions, "no man stood with me," but "all forsook me." At the same time, "the light of the divine countenance" was so far withdrawn that all my afflictions pressed with great "heaviness" upon all my susceptibilities, providential disappointments defeating all my plans and efforts for relief. Such were the temptations, trials of faith, and chastening to which I was subject. Such, on the other hand, were the divine helps and strengthening by which I was sustained during all that period. God gave me the most absolute inward assurance that my interior and outward life was fully approved by Him, that these sufferings were for an end of infinite moment to me, and were preparatory to greater fruitfulness in the kingdom of grace than was otherwise possible; that the immutable condition of ensuring this personal good and divine fruitfulness was that "the corn of wheat" must at that very time "fall into the ground and die;" in other words, that until God, in His own time and way, should send deliverance, I must remain in absolute submission and content in the centre of the divine will, entertaining no desire or choice that the pressure of affliction should be less severe or of shorter continuance than God should choose. At times Christ directly manifested Himself to me, not in a manner to fill me with rapture, but to assure me of His deep and abiding sympathy, of the divine results which were being worked out in my interior life, of the fruits that were to follow, and of "the far more exceeding and eternal weight of glory", which lay in reserve in the great hereafter. At other times, the Spirit would open upon my mind a vision of Christ Himself in Gethsemane, in the judgment-hall, or on the cross, and everywhere so meekly submissive to His Father's will, and so patiently enduring when His "soul was exceeding sorrowful, even unto death." Tribulation, affliction, and sorrow, even unto "great heaviness," now became sacred in the mind's regard; and one desire and choice possessed the whole being—namely, to have nothing occur but as God willed. I knew well what Paul meant when he said, "Unto you it is given, in the behalf of Christ, not only to believe on Him, but also to suffer for His sake."

When my will had come into this sweet and absolute acquiescence in the divine will, and was rooted and grounded in that acquiescence; and when all the sensibilities had also become disciplined to similar subjection, so that there was nothing in the heart or soul to dispute the absolute reign of Christ over the whole being, then the *paideia*, "patience, having had her perfect work," had consummated its mission, and "heaviness" and "great tribulation" could do no more for the discipline of virtue. Deliverance accordingly came; and when "the Sun of Righteousness" passed out from that temporary eclipse, and I stood in the broad sunlight of the face of God, I well knew why I had been thus disciplined in the school of sorrow—namely, that I might become possessed of the great and enduring joys, "the everlasting consolations and good hope through grace," amid which I am now permitted to have my present dwelling-place.

Do you ask me, reader, why it is that I affirm, with such absolute assurance, that "we are complete in Him," that "we can do all things through Christ, which strengtheneth us," and that "we may learn in whatever state we are, therewith to be content"? I should refer, as one of the main reasons, to the *paideia* of which I have been speaking, and to other like seasons in which God put me into "the furnace of affliction," subjected me to great "heaviness," but put strength into me to endure, and disciplined my whole being into sweet acquiescence in His holy will, and thus did for me there in that sacred place.

Do you ask me why it is that what the prophet meant in the following wondrous words are so real in my experience? "The sun shall no more be thy light by day, neither for brightness shall the moon give light unto thee, but the Lord shall be unto thee an everlasting light, and thy God thy glory. Thy sun shall no more go down, neither shall thy moon withdraw itself; but the Lord shall be thine everlasting light, and the days of thy mourning shall be ended." I should still, as one of the main reasons, refer you to the *paideia*, in which Christ taught me "obedience from the things which I suffered." The "endurance of temptation" not only disciplines the will to subjection to the will of God, but also capacitates the whole mental being for fellowships, intercommunings, and fruitions, for which nothing else can so fully prepare us.

My object in writing these things, reader, is this—that you "may know your God, understand His way, and find grace in His sight." When you put yourself under the will of God, and do it "with all your heart, and with all your soul," remember this, that you have His absolute word of promise that He "will instruct you, and teach you the way you should go, and guide you by His eye." Do not, therefore, mark out for yourself any particular and specific forms of experience through which you must be led. Let this be your only concern, to keep your hand in the hand of God, and your will in absolute subjection to His. While conscious of this relation to Him, do not be disturbed by any providences which may encircle you, or any "heavinesses which for a time, if need be," may be laid upon you. While you shall "keep the faith," "endure as seeing Him who is invisible;" and "shall cry, My Father, my Father," "not as I will, but as thou wilt," remember this, that God will deal with you but as His son or daughter, all of whose interests are as dear to Him as the apple of His eye. If His parental discipline may sometimes seem severe, bear this in mind, that it is all "for your profit, that you may be a partaker of His holiness." Thus "following on to know the Lord," "your peace," at length, "will be as a river, and your righteousness as the waves of the sea," and your deepest sorrows will be found to be but birth-throes of joys and consolations as great as your mental being can receive, and as enduring as "the eternal years of God."

CHAPTER XIV.

EVERLASTING CONSOLATION, OR OUR HIGHEST JOYS WELLING OUT OF OUR DEEPEST SORROWS.

THE apostle Paul puts up this wonderful prayer in behalf of his converts at Thessalonica:—"Now our Lord Jesus Christ Himself, and God, even our Father, which hath loved us, and hath given us everlasting consolations and good hope through grace, comfort your hearts, and stablish you in every good word and work." One of the most wondrous and memorable characteristics of the hidden life is the fact that our greatest and most enduring joys well out of our deepest sorrows, and those who in heaven stand nearest the eternal throne, and behold with the deepest bliss the face of God, are "they who came out of great tribulation," "endured great fights of affliction," "learned obedience from the things which they suffered," and thus "washed their robes and made them white in the blood of the Lamb." "Ye now, therefore," says our Saviour to His disciples, "have sorrow; but I will see you again, and your heart shall rejoice, and your joy no man taketh from you." The joy which the disciples experienced after the Saviour appeared among them, "as they mourned and wept," was incomparably greater than it could have been but for the great sorrow by which their new-born joy had been preceded, and into which the former blended and was lost. The joy which succeeds, supersedes, and takes up into itself sorrow, is called "consolation;" and because the joy which thus supersedes sorrow in Christian experience is eternally enduring, it is called "everlasting consolation."

Let us see if we cannot attain to some adequate apprehension of this most important subject. Consolation, as I have intimated, is what, for the want of better terms, I would denominate a *blended state of mind*—a state resulting from the blending of two other mutually genial states, sorrow on the one hand, and a genial form of joy on the other; the former sweetly blending into and losing itself in the latter, the new form of joy thus induced becoming a permanent well-spring of life in the mind.

I will give an illustrative fact which occurred in my own family. As I came down from my study and entered our parlour one day, I found our second child, a little daughter about three years of age, alone there, the mother, with the elder daughter, having gone out and left this one in the care of the kitchen-maid. I found this child, from some cause—I never knew what—in a state of mental agony such as I had never witnessed before. Her grief had reached a stage wholly past weeping, and which rendered her utterly unable to speak a single word. As she turned her face to me, there was the look of death in her eyes. Of course I was deeply alarmed. I did not attempt to allay her grief by words. Grief asks our sympathy, not words. I said to her at once, "My dear precious daughter, come to your father and sit here upon his knee, laying your head upon his bosom close to his heart." As she came to me, I took her tenderly up, placed her upon my knee, and pressed her head very gently to my heart. At every sigh I apprehended that the thread of life would break. I spoke not a word; but at each paroxysm I pressed her more closely to my heart, I soon perceived that those sighs became gradually less and less severe. At length they wholly ceased. A little while after, she looked up with a happy smile, and asked me if I recollected a certain event which had given her great pleasure. I entered at once into her new-born joy, enlarging very affectionately and smilingly upon that pleasing event. In a short time we were sweetly conversing together there, the happiest child and the happiest father I ever knew. My manifested sympathy and love had gently drawn from the heart of that child that great sorrow, and had induced in its place a form of joy unlike, and greater than, any she had ever experienced before, and which never could have been generated but in circumstances like those above detailed.

Nor did that joy ever pass away. From that moment onward I became to that child a new being. Whenever it was possible, she would be with me, sitting by me in my study, and walking with me, and seeking every practicable opportunity to exchange words with me. Now and then she would fix her eyes upon me, as if she could not take them away. Some three or four years after the occurrence above stated, while she was sitting with her mother in our parlour in Oberlin, I being absent for the long vacation, she took her pencil and paper, and after studying and writing awhile, handed to her mother a beautiful little poem, a poem that would have honoured a young Tennyson. The measure was peculiar, each stanza being composed of three lines. The subject of the poem was the great void in her heart, the void occasioned by the absence of her father, and her intense desire for his return. When she was on a visit to our house, at the time when she was quite forty years of age, she being herself a parent then, I related to her the incident of her childhood given above, a fact which she had of course forgotten. Then she understood the cause of the mysterious bond which had so linked her being with mine, and rendered her father such a form of sunlight to her heart. Here we have the true idea of *consolation*, a peculiar and special kind of joy, which takes form in the soul only in seasons of special sorrow—a form of sacred joy "that is born, like the rainbow, in tears," but which never, like the rainbow, passes away.

Now, one of the most distinguished and special peculiarities of the gospel, that which separates and peculiarises it from all other religions or any other forms of belief, is the fact that for every form of sorrow with which the heart can be smitten this gospel brings to the believing, trustful, and enduring spirit "everlasting consolation, and good hope through grace," changing such sorrows into forms of joy which are ineffably blissful and eternally enduring. Examine all other religions the earth has ever known, sound the depths of every system of philosophy which unbelief has ever developed, and you will fail utterly to find in any one of them, or in all of them together, a single ray or element of consolation, a single element of power to bring joy and gladness to a broken heart or a wounded spirit. "I do wish," said a widowed daughter of a very wealthy citizen of the city of New York, as the family had returned one Sabbath from their place of worship, their minister being a celebrated preacher of the Broad Church,—"I do wish that our pastor would say something to bring consolation to a bereaved heart such as I have." "Why," said a friend of ours who had accompanied the family to their place of worship that day, "the God your pastor preaches is a mere force, utterly void of all feeling or emotion of any kind, and is, therefore, wholly void, and incapable of any kind of sympathy with human joy or sorrow." The next time my friend visited that family, he found them worshipping in an Evangelical congregation, where an incarnate Saviour is preached, a Saviour who has been anointed by the Eternal Father to "bind up the broken-hearted." What absolutely evinces the gospel as, like the New Jerusalem, coming down to us from "God out of heaven," is this power to bring to every sin-blighted and sorrow-smitten heart such "everlasting consolations and good hope through grace."

All the world have read with admiration and wonder the beauteous scene which transpired at the house of Simon the leper, the scene in which Mary, the sister of Lazarus, anointed both the head and feet of Jesus with precious ointment. Having been informed by our Saviour of His approaching death, she had purchased the ointment, and had "kept it against the day of His burying." Seeing Jesus sitting with her brother at the feast, her love and gratitude induced her to change her purpose, and to anoint that sacred body "beforehand to the burying." What so deeply moved the gratitude of that sister, and brought such "everlasting consolation" to her heart, was not the mere fact that her brother had been raised from the dead, but the melting scene which preceded that event. Let us read it. "Then when Mary was come where Jesus was, and saw Him, she fell down at His feet, saying unto him, Lord, if Thou hadst been here, my brother had not died. When Jesus therefore saw her weeping, and the Jews also weeping which came with her, He groaned in the spirit and was troubled. And said, Where have ye laid him? They said unto Him, Lord, come and see. Jesus wept. Then said the Jews, Behold how He loved him!" All heaven must have looked with silent, if not with tearful, wonder at that spectacle. It was not the mere fact, I repeat, of the resurrection of that brother, but the ineffable compassion, sympathy, and love, manifested in connection with the bestowment of the gift that ever after made such eternal sunlight in the hearts of that brother and his two sisters. In the event, the sisters received a temporary good of great value. In the love revealed in the manner of the gift "everlasting consolations and good hope through grace" came to their hearts. As the perfections and glory of Christ shall unfold more and more, through eternal ages, before their mind, the fact represented in the words, "Jesus wept," will be a central light through which that glory shall be seen. So it will be with all the universe. In like manner, when the sanctified mind is smitten with any form or degree of sorrow whatever, let the Spirit unveil to that mind the face of Christ looking with ineffable love upon the face of that soul, and all its sorrow will sweetly blend into a form of joy and consolation eternally enduring. Just such power has Christ over all our sorrows.

Let us now turn our thoughts to another scene. "But Mary stood without at the sepulchre weeping: and as she wept, she stooped down, and looked into the sepulchre, and seeth two angels in white sitting, the one at the head, and the other at the feet, where the body of Jesus had lain. And they say unto her, Woman, why weepest thou? She saith unto them, Because they have taken away my Lord, and I know not where they have laid Him. And when she had thus said, she turned herself back, and saw Jesus standing, and knew not that it was Jesus. Jesus saith unto her, Woman, why weepest thou? whom seekest thou? She, supposing Him to be the gardener, saith unto him, Sir, if thou have borne Him hence, tell me where thou hast laid Him, and I will take Him away. Jesus saith unto her, Mary. She turned herself, and saith unto Him, Rabboni; which is to say Master."

I have often enquired with myself as to the tone and manner in which that name was then uttered, and have asked myself "How shall I utter it when I read the passage?" On some former occasion, perhaps at the time when He restored her to her right mind, or immediately after that event, He must have uttered her name in a tone and manner which thrilled through her whole being, and made the utterance one of the memorable facts of her existence. No wonder that when Jesus now pronounced that name with the same tone and manner as on that, to her, eternally memorable occasion, no wonder, I say, that she instantly exclaimed "Rabboni." She intuitively apprehended that no being but Christ could thus pronounce that name. As she heard that name thus pronounced, how instantly did the deep midnight of her soul change into eternal sunlight! how instantly did her great sorrow blend and lose itself in "everlasting consolation and good hope through grace"! But for that great sorrow, Christ could not have become to her what He afterwards was, and ever will be to eternity. The new-born joy which then filled her whole being is in her yet, and there it will remain, deepening and expanding for ever and ever. The word "Mary," as Jesus then pronounced it, will ever cause her heart-strings to vibrate with a music that "will make melody in the ear of God."

Few people seem at all to understand the full meaning of the apostle John in the words, "Then were the disciples glad when they saw the Lord." The last evening which He spent with them before He suffered, He thus spoke of the sorrow which then filled their hearts:—"A woman when she is in travail hath sorrow, because her hour is come but as soon as she is delivered of the child, she remembereth no more the anguish, for joy that a man is born into the world. And ye now therefore have sorrow: but I will see you again and your heart shall rejoice, and your joy no man taketh from you." After their hearts were filled, and even burdened, with "joy unspeakable and full of glory" at the reappearing of Christ in their midst, John, calling to mind the words of our Saviour, the words above cited, says, "Then," that is, just as Christ said it should be, 'WERE the disciples glad when they saw the Lord." Jesus said, "I will see you again, and your heart shall rejoice," and so we found it. Jesus also said, "Your joy no man taketh from you," and "neither tribulation, nor distress, nor persecution, nor famine, nor peril, nor sword, nor death, nor life, nor angels, nor principalities, nor powers, nor things present, nor things to come, nor height, nor depth, nor any other creature," hath been able, nor ever will be able, to take that joy out of their hearts. So it ever is. The joy which wells out of sorrow in the true believer's heart can take on but one form, that of "everlasting consolation and good hope through grace."

I must refer to one additional illustration taken from Scripture—the manifestation of Christ to John when the Saviour appeared in glory to the apostle at the opening of the vision of the Apocalypse. The following passage presents the fact to which I refer:—"And when I saw Him, I fell at His feet as dead. And He laid His right hand upon me, saying unto me, Fear not; I am the First and the Last: and I am He that liveth, and was dead; and behold, I am alive for ever more, Amen; and have the keys of hell and of death." The beauty and impressiveness of the original is almost wholly darkened by the above translation. The object of our Saviour in the words addressed to John was to allay his dread, and impart to him such an assurance that he could calmly receive the message which Christ was to send to the Churches through His disciple. The words, "Fear not; I am the First and the Last," would have tended but to deepen and perfect the death-terror which Christ's appearance had induced. Literally rendered, the passage reads thus:—"Fear not; it is I, the First and the Last: and I am alive; and I was dead, and behold I am alive for ever more, Amen: and have the keys of hell and of death." The original words which I have translated "It is I," had been, in the exact form here repeated, twice uttered in the hearing of John, and that under circumstances of most memorable and tenderly impressive interest: first when our Saviour came "walking upon the water," during the night-tempest on the Sea of Galilee, and allayed their fears by saying, "It is I; be not afraid;" and secondly, when He first appeared in their midst after His resurrection, and again allayed their fears by saying to them, "Be not affrighted; handle me, and see that it is I myself." Now, when Christ so gently laid His right hand upon the apostle, who was almost dead with terror, and so tenderly repeated those ever-memorable words in his ears, at the same time recalling those wonderful memories which had made such melody in the apostle's mind, how adapted all this was to revive his spirits, put strength into him, and to "assure his heart" in the presence of his glorified Redeemer! It is no wonder that, from that moment onward, all dread and terror of Christ departed for ever from the heart of the apostle, and he became possessed with but one sentiment in view of every form of the coming of his Lord: "Even so, come, Lord Jesus, come quickly. Amen."

My object in presenting such facts is to assure the reader of this great truth, that when we are in Christ, He will turn all our sorrows into everlasting joy and gladness, gird us with immortal strength in all our weaknesses, impart to us in our darkest hours the everlasting light of God, and in all our necessities do for us "exceeding abundantly above all that we ask or think."

I will now allude to a case which came to my knowledge since my present sojourn in this city. While in attendance at a meeting for the promotion of personal holiness, a lady, giving me her hand, inquired if I did not recollect her? My reply was, that I did recollect her countenance, but could not designate her name, or the circumstances in which we had met. "Do you not recollect that, when you were in London, some twenty-five years ago, a Mrs N., a lady friend of yours from America, introduced you to the family of a Mr M.?" "I well recollect that family," I replied. "I often spoke of it in my own country, and have inquired after it since my late arrival in London." "I am Mrs M. My husband is also present, and will rejoice to take you by the hand. You will recollect how great was my peace and joy in believing when you first saw us. I had been greatly blessed in reading your work on 'Christian Perfection.'" Mrs M., an influential member of one of the churches of the Establishment in this city, was among the happiest believers I ever met with. "Well," she continued, "the joy that then dwelt in my heart has never departed nor grown less, but has increased more and more. Do you remember our children?" "I recollect that you had children about you then, but that is all." "Well, our eldest, our only son, grew to be twenty-three years of age. Christ called for him then, and we gave him up. Our daughter, next in age, grew to twenty-five. Christ asked for her also, and we replied, 'As Thou wilt, Lord only give us more of Thyself.' We had one lamb left, 'a little one,' a daughter ten and a half years of age. Christ called for her too, and our reply was, 'The cup which our Father giveth us, shall we not drink it?' Thus 'we were written childless.' But it is all the same. Our light has never gone out or grown dim, but shineth more and more as the perfect day dawns on." This, I said in my heart, is the consolation. Surely "we can do all things through Christ which strengtheneth us." With what unspeakable interest have I listened to the rich testimony for Christ which that husband and wife have given in conferences which I have attended!

A poor slave, after he had been, for no reason for which slaves are usually beaten, scourged till he barely had the breath of life in him, crept away to his lonely hut, and lay groaning there. The Spirit of God soon brought heaven so near to the sufferer's mind, and made his sufferings appear so momentary to him, that he sat up and began to sing for joy of heart—

> "My suffering time will soon be o'er;
> I soon shall weep and sigh no more.
> My ransomed soul shall soar away,
> And sing God's praise in endless day."

The master, who had been listening outside, now rushed in, and implored the forgiveness and prayers of the sufferer. From that moment suffering and toil were other things than they had been to that slave's mind—the suffering and toil appearing so short, and the glory to follow so infinite and endless, that the former had no power to disturb his peace. This, I repeat, is the consolation. So were "the sufferings of this present time" to the mind of Paul. God's Spirit made them appear to him as they are in themselves, and as they are in their endless consequences, to all who "*endure* temptation," and "learn obedience from the things which they suffer." Over such minds afflictions have no power but to discipline and perfect virtue, and induce new forms of "everlasting consolations and good hope through grace." They consequently "glory in tribulation."

The reader may be inclined to ask, How is it possible that pain, suffering, and sorrow can induce such joyful experiences? Take a single case in illustration. Many years since, a young man of a very wealthy family in Charleston, S.C., came to the city of New York and submitted his case to a council of physicians. As the result of the examination, he was informed that his case was indeed a sad one, that a hard substance was forming about one of the orifices of his heart, and would soon close it up and cause his death. In answer to the inquiry whether the substance could be removed by a surgical operation, he was told that the event was possible, but that the probabilities appeared as a hundred to one against him. "But death is certain if this tumour is not removed?" "Yes." "Then I take the risk," replied the youth. The surgeons refused to do anything about it until they had sent to the parents a written statement of the perils of the operation, and had received from them a written request to undertake it. When the operation was commenced, the young man was told that if at any time the operators should stop cutting his flesh, he might know that death must ensue. At length, contrary to all prior calculations, a suspension for a few moments became necessary. No one spoke or whispered. What a moment of suspense to the young man! Was it death? At length the experience of an acute pain indicated that the operation had been recommenced. "That pain," said the young man afterwards, the operation proving a success,—"that pain was to me the most blissful feeling I ever experienced in my life." The reason is manifest. The pain stood connected in his mind with a promise of life, and the absence of pain with the assurance of death. Now the Spirit of God can so connect with every pain and affliction and form of sorrow we may experience a promise of life eternal, that suffering shall seem blissful rather than distressing, while the promise shall induce forms of fulness of joy eternally enduring. This is the consolation reserved for the believer in all "the sufferings of this present time."

As far as my own case is concerned, I would say, that sorrow and suffering, bereavement, disappointment, and "hope deferred," seem to have but one mission—to develop, refine, and enlarge the susceptibilities, and to new capacitate the mind for the reception of new and higher forms of blessedness than were before possible. Each special form of sorrow is attended with some special and correlative manifestation of the character, love, or grace of Christ, a manifestation which ever after remains in the mind as a source of everlasting consolation and "joy unspeakable and full of glory." Among the aspects of Christ's character and grace—aspects which induce the fullest and most abiding blessedness—are those which the Spirit has unveiled to the mind when some great sorrow lay upon the heart. Hence it is that afflictions, tribulations, and great heavinesses become almost sacred in the mind's regard, followed as they all are, and that so soon, with such "everlasting consolations and good hope through grace." The mind does not desire or pray for such providences. When they are sent, however—

"As clouds of glory do they come,

From God, who is our home."

Since that great *paideia*, that sacred heaven-descended *paideia*, sorrow and affliction sustain different relations to the mind from what they ever did before. They have power to melt the soul, but not so to affect the sensibilities as to produce mental pain or agony. Simultaneously with the sorrow comes the joy of the Lord, with such fullness that the former blends into the latter without paining the soul at all. Under the severest bodily suffering the mind lies in perfect quietness and assurance.

I may refer in illustration to one scene. During the late war in the United States, our only son entered the army. On occasion of the first great battle where he was present, he rose from a sick-bed, and, contrary to the absolute prohibition of his physician, as first lieutenant led his company into the scene, and remained with them during the day, leading fifty-six men into the battle, and sixteen out of it. In the next great battle into which, as captain, he led his company, he himself received a fatal injury, from which he died some six months afterwards. And such a death. He seemed to "see the heavens opened, and the Son of Man standing on the right hand of God," the Son of Man holding out to the dying one "a crown of life." From the grave of our son, the wife of my youth went home with me to die, she having fatally overtaxed her strength in caring for him during the last months of his sickness. A blooming daughter, twenty-two years of age, whose being had ever been strangely linked with that mother and brother, drooped under the bereavement, and, despite all our efforts to sustain and save her, "dropped into the lap of God," her death being not so rapturous, but as peaceful, as that of her brother. Under these bereavements my whole soul was melted and flowed out like water. At the same time, the peace of God was so full, pervading, and so ineffable in my heart, that I could not tell what was the chief cause of my tears—the great sorrow on the one hand, or the unspeakable joy of the Lord on the other.

Such, reader, is the real experience of those who are in the world and in Christ while here. If they have sorrow—and "in the world they will have tribulation"—their sorrows are but momentary birth-throes of joys ineffable and eternally enduring. The deepest shades with which earth's tribulations can darken their horizon are but the shadows which the Sun of Righteousness casts before Him when He is about to rise in our hearts "with healings in His wings." When walking with God—

BY ASA MAHAN.

"Take this thought with you as you go abroad,
That shade is the creation of light,
And light is the shadow of God."

CHAPTER XV.

SPIRITUAL DISCERNING AND ENLIGHTENMENT.

"THE things of God," we are taught in the Sacred Word, "knoweth no man, but the Spirit of God." "The things of God," when revealed to us, are called "the things of the Spirit of God," because "God hath revealed them unto us by His Spirit." Now, of "the things of the Spirit of God," that is, of "the things which God hath revealed to us *by* His Spirit," the Scriptures contain the exclusive and all authoritative record. Outside of the Sacred Word, we have no authoritative record or standard of revealed truth. "The things which are revealed" in "this dearest of Books, that excels every other," "belong unto us and to our children." "Things of God" not herein revealed, those excepted "which are clearly seen, being understood by the things which are made," are "secret things which belong unto God." One of the most important questions which any believer can put to himself is this, How may I know "the things of the Spirit of God," "the things which are freely given us of God"?

There are two classes of individuals who, as the apostle informs us, do not, and cannot, know these things—"the natural man," the man who, in the pride of self-sufficiency, relies upon his own unaided powers of inquiry, and, consequently, repudiates as folly the idea of being taught of God, and as foolishness "the things revealed by the Spirit of God;" and the believer who is yet under the influence of a carnal spirit, of carnal principles, and carnal apprehensions. "He that is spiritual," on the other hand, does know "the things of God," the things which "God has revealed to us by His Spirit." The reason why he knows these things is the fact that the Spirit so "strengtheneth him with might in the inner man," and so "enlightens the eyes of his understanding," that he "discerns" or apprehends these things as they are in themselves. "The natural man cannot know them, because they are spiritually discerned;" that is, they are, and must be, as the immutable condition of our apprehending them, presented to the mind by the Spirit.

Let us see if we cannot understand, clearly and distinctly, the real relations of the three individuals under consideration to the revealed truth of God—the three individuals, namely, "the natural man," the believer who is yet carnal or a babe in Christ, and "the spiritual man." We will take as the basis of our elucidation the account which we find in 2 Kings vi. 15-17:—"And when the servant of the man of God was risen early, and gone forth, behold, an host compassed the city both with horses and chariots. And his servant said unto him, Alas, my master! how shall we do? And he answered, Fear not: for they that be with us are more than they that be with them. And Elisha prayed, and said, Lord, I pray thee, open his eyes, that he may see. And the Lord opened the eyes of the young man; and he saw: and, behold, the mountain was full of horses and chariots of fire round about Elisha." Let us suppose that, at the time when these events transpired, there had been present with the prophet, in addition to his servant, two other individuals, corresponding to "the natural man" on the one hand, and the unspiritual believer on the other, and that to these the prophet had stated the facts just as his servant afterwards saw them. How would his utterances have affected these three individuals, the eyes of the servant, and his only, being opened to see what was before and around them?

The natural man would have promptly replied thus, "I don't believe a word of it. I see the hosts of the Syrians; but I don't see, and nobody can see, 'the chariots of fire' or 'the horses of fire' to which this man refers. It is all superstition and delusion." "But the natural man receiveth not the things of the Spirit of God for they are foolishness unto him: neither can he know them because they are spiritually discerned."

The unspiritual believer, on the other hand, would say, "What the prophet says is unquestionably true, and it gives me a degree of inward joy and peace to think so. Yet I cannot make his statements *seem* real. I *see* the hosts of the Syrians; but do not see 'the chariots of fire' or 'the horses of fire.' Hence it is that I cannot wholly expel the sentiment of fear and apprehension from my mind. I wish I could feel as the prophet and his servant do; but I cannot do it."

Ask the servant, now that "his eyes have been opened," if he believes what the prophet has uttered, and his reply would be, "I *know* that what he says is true. Why, the mountain is full of horses and chariots of fire round about Elisha. I see them as plainly as I see the hosts of the Syrians, and 'they that be with us are more than they that be with them.'" The conscious security and peace of the prophet and of his servant could not but be absolute.

Let us now apply the above illustration to the three classes of individuals under consideration, "the natural man," the believer who is yet carnal, and "the spiritual man. " In the same sense in which all could have understood the statements which we have supposed the prophet to have made, all of common intelligence can understand the Bible. Without special divine illumination, learned men may understand the facts and doctrines of this Book, and systematise the same, just as they can determine and interpret the teachings of any other book. Some of the ablest commentaries upon the Scriptures that have ever appeared have been composed by individuals who utterly repudiate the inspiration of these writings. Individuals of the same class have also correctly stated and systematised the doctrines of Scripture, and have proved beyond dispute that the Bible does, in fact, teach all the doctrines and principles of the evangelical faith. Nor are correct interpretations of the Scriptures or true presentations of its doctrines to be undervalued, and last of all will they be undervalued by really spiritually- minded believers.

In what sense, then, is it true that neither the "natural man," nor the believer who is yet carnal, or "a babe in Christ," can "know the things of the Spirit of God"? In what sense is it true that these things are "spiritually discerned"?—that is, can be apprehended as they are but by special illumination of the Spirit? A ready answer to these questions can now be given. The servant of the prophet, had the latter stated the facts to the former, could have understood that there was a celestial host with "horses and chariots of fire round about Elisha." Until the eyes of that servant were opened, however, and he saw that host for himself, he could by no possibility have formed real apprehensions of that host. So I may correctly understand what inspiration affirms of "the things of the Spirit of God." I can apprehend the things themselves, and know them as they are, but upon the condition that, by the Spirit of God, "the eyes of my understanding are enlightened," so that I see these things, that is, mentally apprehend them, as they are in themselves.

Moses, for example, knew well that the glory of God was infinite. He was equally well aware; however, that no finite mind could know that glory—that is, could apprehend it as it is—but upon the exclusive condition that God Himself should *show* His glory to the creature. Hence the prayer of that man of God, "I beseech Thee *show* me Thy glory." To all eternity an impenetrable veil would have remained between that man and the divine glory, had not God fulfilled in the experience of His servant the promise, "I will cause all my goodness to pass before thee."

The same great truth is implied in the prayer of the psalmist, "Open *Thou* mine eyes, and I shall behold wondrous things out of Thy law." The psalmist well knew that wondrous things were revealed in the Word of God. He was equally aware of the fact that he could behold these things but upon the condition that God Himself should open the eyes of his understanding to apprehend them, just as the eyes of the servant were opened to behold the flaming hosts that were "round about Elisha." So of all the eternal verities revealed to our faith in the Scriptures. We can understand what is written about these realities. The realities themselves, however, we can apprehend as they are but upon the condition that the Spirit of God shall Himself "take of these things and show them unto us," we thus "beholding with open face as in a glass" (as we behold our own selves in a mirror) "the glory of the Lord," "the love of Christ," and all "the things which are freely given us of God."

We have before us, we will suppose, to use another illustration, a correct map and a full and true delineation of the entire scenery of the Alps. Careful study will enable us to understand fully the map and the writings in our possession. We afterwards visit that scenery and behold it with open vision. On comparing the apprehensions obtained by reading and study with those received through a direct beholding of the scenery itself, we should find that the former apprehensions very imperfectly represent the latter. Suppose now that, while we are studying the documents and map referred to, God should enable us to form the same apprehensions of that scenery that we do when beholding it with direct and open vision. He would then do for us relatively to this scenery what the Spirit does relatively to the eternal verities revealed in the Scriptures. In the study of the Scriptures the Spirit of God so "enlightens the eyes of the understanding" of "the spiritual man," that he beholds, as with direct and open vision, "the wondrous things" of which he reads.

The relations of the three individuals under consideration to "the things of the Spirit of God," now admit of a ready explanation. "The natural man" does not apprehend these things for two reasons. They are "foolishness unto him" in the first place, and he does not endeavour to understand them. Then, in the next place, "they are spiritually discerned," and he "has not the Spirit of God."

The believer who is "yet carnal" may understand and believe what is written about these things. Of the things themselves, however, he has no divinely-illumined apprehensions. He believes them to be eternal verities. Yet they do not *seem* real to him, and he cannot make them *seem* thus. According to the Scriptures, Christ is at the door calling and knocking for admittance. The man understands what is written, and confesses that it must be so of a truth. To him, however, Christ does not seem to be thus near, thus loving, and ready to save and to bless; but afar off in heaven, afar off where He cannot be found. The love of Christ to us, according to the Scriptures "passeth knowledge." The man understands what is written, and admits its truth. To his mind, however, it is not, and he cannot make it seem, a present and heart-moving and transforming reality that "Christ loved him, and gave Himself for him," and loves him now.

To "the spiritual man," on the other hand, nothing seems so real, and of such ready and all-impressive apprehension, as "the things of the Spirit of God." He not only understands and believes what is written about the love of Christ, but inwardly "beholds with open face" Christ Himself as a personal presence in the actual exercise of a love towards the believer "that passeth knowledge." The Spirit "takes of the things of Christ," and shows them to this individual, and "shows him plainly of the Father." Such a believer, consequently, "knows the things which are freely given us of God." To his mind "the things of the Spirit of God,"—"things unseen and eternal," "revealed to us by the Spirit of God,"—are realities as palpable as was the fiery host round about Elisha to the servant of the prophet after "the Lord had opened the eyes of that servant." In the same sense in which the Spirit of God opened the eyes of that servant to behold the "horses and chariots of fire" referred to, does the same Spirit "enlighten the eyes of the understanding" of "the spiritual man" to "behold the glory of the Lord," to "comprehend the breadth, and depth, and length, and height, and to know the love of Christ, which passeth knowledge."

We are now prepared to understand clearly the meaning of the apostle in the following passage:—"He that is spiritual judgeth all things, yet he himself is judged of no man." The obvious meaning of the passage is this: "The spiritual man" understands, and appreciates as they are, the views and experiences of all other men, not, like himself, under divine illumination. Those who have not received this illumination, however, cannot judge the spiritual man—that is, understand his views and experiences—because they have never become possessed of such views and experiences. They can, if they will, know that he has views and experiences which they have not, and which they imperiously need to possess, and they may and can inquire of God, as he did, that the Lord may open the eyes of their understanding, as He did those of his, that they may thus "know God, and Jesus Christ whom He hath sent," as he knows them; that they with him may "have fellowship with the Father, and with His Son Jesus Christ," and, like him, "be filled with all the fulness of God." All these things they may inquire after, and "will know if they follow on to know the Lord." Until they do thus inquire, and God, by His Spirit, "shall give them light," they will walk in darkness, while he "has the light of life," and his divine and blissful views and experiences will be veiled even from their apprehensions.

I am here reminded of a very melancholy fact which we often meet with among professing Christians. I refer to those who persistently shut themselves out from "the liberty of the sons of God," and veil from their hearts "the light of God," in which it is their blood-bought privilege to walk. Before I speak particularly of this class, however, let me refer to another class who are in darkness, but are seeking "the light of life." By special request, I once, for example, visited the room of a theological student who was spiritually in "a horror of great darkness." Before him lay an open Bible, with his eyes resting upon some of its most soul-moving revelations. "President Mahan," he said, "what is here revealed is all real to you. No wonder, therefore, that you are one of the happiest of men. To me, however, they don't seem real at all. I read that 'Christ tasted death for every man,' and Paul says of Him, 'He loved me, and gave Himself for me.' It don't seem to me that I have any interest at all in Christ's death, or that He has any love for me whatever. I can understand Job when he cried out, 'Oh, that I knew where I might find Him! that I might come near even to His seat. Behold, I go forward, but He is not there; and backward, but I cannot perceive Him: on the left hand, where He doth work, but I cannot behold Him: He hideth Himself on the right hand that I cannot see Him.' Is there any hope for me?"

As I took my seat by the side of that young man, I said to him, "My brother, you are now in the most hopeful condition possible. If you will 'only believe,' your next step will be upon the pinnacle of the delectable mountains, where 'the Lord shall be to you for an everlasting light, and your God your glory.' 'Only believe,' and you will find the darkness around you to be that which precedes the brightness of the divine rising."

"But how shall I believe, when nothing seems real to me?"

"God says, in His own Word, does He not, that 'Christ did taste death for every man,' and consequently for you; that He loves the world, and consequently loves you; that if you will 'confess your sins,' He 'will forgive you your sins, and cleanse you from all unrighteousness;' that He 'will give the Holy Spirit to them that ask Him,' and that none that 'follow Christ shall walk in darkness, but shall have the light of life.'"

"I know that God says these things, and I suppose they are realities in themselves. To me, however, they are not realities, and I cannot make them appear so."

"Cease for ever now all efforts to make these realities seem real to your mind. Admit them to be such, and that on the simple testimony of God. Confess your sins to God, trusting Christ, for the reason that He says He will do it when you thus confess, to 'take away your sins.' Having done this, and having surrendered your whole being to the divine will, ask your Father in heaven, simply because He has promised to do so to all who ask, to give you the Holy Spirit of promise, that you may realise and 'know the things which are freely given you of God.' Do this, my young brother, and your darkness will soon pass away, and you will wonder, with unutterable wonder, at the marvellous light of God which shall shine upon you."

I have, during the last forty years, met with very many individuals, as that young man was, in the deepest spiritual darkness, and have never yet met with one who has followed such simple counsels, and who did not soon find him self "sitting in heavenly places in Christ Jesus," and "rejoicing there with joy unspeakable, and full of glory."

I will here give a single example in illustration of the above statements. Several months since, I met at the house of a mutual friend in this city a physician and his wife, both from my own country, and both influential members of a leading Presbyterian church in the city of New York. Mrs S. was in a very peculiar and self-dissatisfied state of mind. She had read, as she stated, the productions of the leading writers on the higher life, had honestly endeavoured to follow the directions given therein, and had supposed that she had attained to the state of which such authors and teachers speak; yet she had found herself mistaken. What was called salvation from sin, she had found to be nothing but the substitution of one form of sin for another still more hateful in the sight of God—spiritual pride. She had, accordingly, repudiated wholly this whole doctrine of the higher life. Such had been her spiritual darkness, however, that when they were in Rome she had inquired of the highest authorities there whether there was for her any way out into "the light of God." Their answers were, of course, wholly unsatisfactory and she was in a state of almost utter hopelessness in regard to any escape from "the bondage of corruption into the glorious liberty of the sons of God," of which the Bible says so much. I assured her that the Bible was a lie throughout, or this liberty, in all its fulness, was in reserve for her. Christ had prayed for her that she might be one with Him, as He is one with the Father, and that the Father might, consequently, love her as He loves His only begotten Son; and that prayer would be fulfilled in her experience, provided she would "lay hold on the hope set before her."

The oneness with Christ referred to is called in the Bible "the union and fellowship of the Spirit." We "are builded for an habitation of God through the Spirit." It is through the Spirit that "God dwells in us and walks in us," and "reveals His Son in us." We must be "strengthened with might by the Spirit in the inner man," or Christ cannot "dwell in our hearts by faith," and be "formed within us the hope of glory." "Where the Spirit of the Lord is, there is liberty;" and there is, and can be, this liberty nowhere else. Such, and only such, do or can behold "with open face, as in a glass, the glory of the Lord." "In that day," the day when "the Comforter shall come unto you," says our Saviour, "ye shall know that I am in the Father, and ye in me, and I in you." "The promise of the Spirit" is before you. If you desire this vital union with Christ, and with the Father through Him, having committed your whole being to Christ, ask Him, and trust Him, first of all, "to pray the Father for you, that He may "give you the Comforter," that "He may abide with you forever," and, as God is true, He will "endue you with power from on high," and "fill you with His Spirit," as He did "the disciples at the beginning;" and then, as they were, you "shall be filled with all the fulness of God."

"The mistake, as it seems to me," I remarked, "of very many who teach the doctrine of the higher life, is the fact that they do not set forth, as the immutable condition of entering into and continuing in that life, that we must receive 'the promise of the Spirit in our hearts.'" I then told her how that, having sought and obtained "the promise of the Father," I had for forty years "walked with God," and known Him as my "everlasting light." "Among 'the sons and daughters of the Lord,'" I remarked, "I am no specially privileged believer. What I have obtained and enjoyed, you may obtain and enjoy."

Such is the substance of my statements to this individual. After a season of prayer we separated, she with a fixed "purpose of heart" never to rest until she had obtained the promised baptism, and I with a fervent inward prayer that God would grant her what she desired, and, through the power of His indwelling Spirit, "do for her exceeding abundantly above all that she might ask or think." The following extracts from this lady's letter, received by the wife of the mutual friend referred to, will indicate the results of that conversation:—"Within three days of our return," she says, "the Doctor's father was brought down to our house very feeble, and suffering with heart disease. For five weeks I nursed him night and day. . . . . December 6, he went home. . . . . Before I had any time to rest, I came here (Philadelphia) to my mother to spend Christmas, and to help to cheer her through this, to her, sad part of the year; for a year ago, last night, my own father entered into glory. Two more peaceful death-beds than the two I have stood beside this year could never be, and heaven seems nearer and more real from the lessons I have been taught by them." Out of sorrow into "everlasting consolations and good hope through grace" is the fixed order of true Christian experience. . . . . "Never shall I forget," she goes on to say, "that Sabbath evening which I spent with Dr. Mahan. I wonder if he is yet in London? If so, will you give my love to him, and tell him Jesus has been making plain to me what I so vainly tried to comprehend during that conversation. Never in my life have I seen what a soul-union there might be between the believer and his Saviour as the Lord has shown me of late. 'One with Christ' does not seem too strong language now. I am so glad that I am one of the weak foolish ones of the earth; for I have not had the trouble which I should have in trying to come to an intellectual comprehension of *how* this could be. I cannot tell the 'how' even now but I do know that Christ has taken me in a sense He never did before, and is keeping me very close to Himself. Oh, how my very heart goes out for you to know this great treasure, my dear sister! It seems as though, if I could cross the ocean that divides us and sit by your side, I could show you *from the Word* how much more Jesus has for us than either you or I imagined last September. I begin to have a little taste of that 'love which passeth knowledge,' and it makes my heart bound and ache with the longing I have that others should know it too. . . . . I owe so much to you for your kindness in regard to Dr Mahan. I have never been *satisfied* since the talk we had in your parlour. I saw, and you did also, that he had a secret we did not possess."

She then states that she soon became conscious of the defects I had stated in the very common teachings in regard to the higher life, and then adds,—"A strong faith is not enough; there must be a *filling with love.* I do not know how to express it except as a conscious 'oneness with Christ.' I cannot tell you as I would like to of this dear Jesus; but if you look into your Bible, you will find what I mean on almost every page of the Acts and Epistles. Now that I really believe every promise, just as I would promises from any reliable, loving friend, the whole thing seems plain and unmistakable. I did not intend to write as I have done when I began, but what was in my heart has dropped off from my pen." All who thus seek, find; and of all who do thus seek and find, "there is not a weak nor sickly one among them." All in common are "more than conquerors through Him that hath loved them."

How do individuals shut themselves out from this "everlasting light," and from all this "glorious liberty of the sons of God"? When they are spoken to about "the promise of the Spirit," and of "the glory which follows" this "enduement of power from on high," their reply is, "that all Christians receive the promised 'baptism of the Holy Ghost,' at the time of their conversion, and no such promise as you speak of is in reserve for us now." While they reply thus, they will not deny that they are in darkness, and walk in darkness, and have lost "the blessedness they knew when first they saw the Lord." Whatever the past may have been, do they not now need to be "baptized with the Holy Ghost"? They admit that they "can neither fly nor go to reach eternal joys." Do they not need the "enduement of power," by which they can "mount up on wings as eagles," and "run and not be weary, and walk and not faint"? Still their reply is, "All believers were 'baptized with the Holy Ghost' at the time of their conversion, and they now 'have the Spirit of Christ,' and their 'bodies are the temples of the Holy Ghost.'"

But does not Christ make prior obedience the express condition of the reception of "the Comforter," and does not the Bible as expressly teach that God "gives the Holy Ghost to them that *obey* Him"? Does not inspiration speak expressly of two classes of converted persons,—of the one class as "spiritual," and the other as "yet carnal,"—the one as made, and the other as not yet made, "perfect in love,—the one as having, and the other as not having, "fellowship with the Father and with His Son Jesus Christ,—the one as having received, and the other as not having received, the Holy Ghost since they believed—and of the "joy" of the one class as being, and of the other as not being, "full"? Still the reply is, "All believers do receive 'the baptism of the Holy Ghost' at the time of their conversion, and no such promise as you speak of is in reserve for us." Thus individuals plead and argue for their blindness, and darkness, and feebleness, their bondage under the law of sin and death, and their barrenness of spiritual joy and power, as if they were certain that "life eternal" is to be found in these things and nowhere else. How can they find the light of life when they thus turn away from God's "exceeding great and precious promises," and will not accept the testimony of God, on the one hand, and that of those who have believed, and "have entered into rest," on the other!

CHAPTER XVI.

THE LETTER AND THE SPIRIT, AND THE FLESH AND THE SPIRIT.

THE sacred writers speak of "the letter and the Spirit" on the one hand, and of "the flesh and the Spirit" on the other. Paul, affirming himself and associates to have been made by God Himself "able ministers of the New Testament, not of the letter, but of the Spirit," says that "the letter killeth, but the Spirit giveth life." On the distinction between "the flesh and the Spirit" our Saviour thus speaks: "It is the Spirit that quickeneth; the flesh profiteth nothing: the words that I speak unto you, they are spirit and they are life." Let us see if we cannot understand this great subject.

Our Saviour, having spoken of Himself in distinction from natural food, flesh, and from the manna, as "the living bread which came down from heaven," told the people that that bread was His "flesh, which He would give for the life of the world." When the Jews strove among themselves, saying, "How can this man give us His flesh to eat"? Jesus assured them that they "must eat the flesh of the Son of Man, and drink His blood," or they could "have no life in them."

At such utterances even some of His disciples took offence, they, in common with other Jews, understanding His words in their literal sense. Christ now informs His disciples that soon He should "ascend up where He was before," and where, consequently, they could not approach His body; that could they do this, and even in the literal or fleshly sense, "eat His flesh and drink His blood," they would thus receive from Him no profit at all. That the words which He had employed symbolised a great and all-vitalising spiritual truth, a fixed relation which must obtain between Him personally and their spirits, or "they could have no life in them;" and that when, and only when, they should apprehend and believe in Him in that relation, would they understand the real import of the words He had employed.

He Himself was to their spirits what food was to their bodies. When they should apprehend and know Him in this relation, they would receive eternal life through Him, just as their natural lives were sustained by the food which they ate. As symbolising this all-vitalising relation, "His words were spirit, and they were life." As, in the literal sense, "eating His flesh and drinking His blood" would "profit them nothing," so His words, not understood and received in their true spiritual import, would be of no benefit to them. The immutable condition of our knowing Christ in this all-vitalising relation is, as our Saviour affirms in this connection, that we are "taught of God," that is, by the Spirit of God, and thus "drawn to Him by the Father." This knowledge we can by no possibility receive but through the illumination of the Spirit in His special office as the promised Comforter.

The same distinction the apostle Paul represents by the terms "letter" and "spirit." When we apprehend the real meaning of the language of Scripture, we are in "the letter." When we have a direct, immediate, and all-transforming apprehension of the realities symbolised by that language, then we are in "the Spirit." While we are in "the letter," truth is to us as "a dead letter," and exerts very little, and commonly no vitalising power at all. When in "the Spirit," every truth apprehended has a life-imparting power over our whole moral and spiritual nature. "The letter killeth, but the Spirit giveth life." Here again we apprehend the special functions of the Comforter. "Now the Lord is that Spirit: and where the Spirit of the Lord is, there is liberty. But we all with open face beholding as in a glass the glory of the Lord, are changed into the same image, from glory to glory, even as by the Spirit of the Lord." Such is the revealed distinction between "the flesh and the Spirit" on the one hand, and "the letter and the Spirit" on the other.

In illustration of the above distinctions, permit me to adduce a fact which occurred in my own family. When my elder children were small about me, and when I had begun to experience the life-imparting power of an apprehension of "the glory of the Lord" upon my own inner life, I made this a specific and special object of prayer, that I might be enabled to get the character of Christ before the minds of my children, so that, as the beauty, and grace, and perfection of the Lord should take form in their apprehensions, their spirit, and character, and life should be drawn and moulded into conformity to His. After I had been praying thus for some time, I found myself in our family circle, at the time of evening prayer, in circumstances most favourable to the end for which I had been praying. I accordingly remarked to my children, that I would read and talk to them about Jesus Christ, and particularly of His love to children. As I began to read the wonderful account pertaining to this subject, our little son, just upwards of three years of age, came to me, and putting his elbows upon my knee, looked me intently in the face. As I read on, and commented upon what I read, "Oh!" he exclaimed, while the most affectionate wonder sat upon his countenance. Such exclamations were repeated as every new feature of Christ's character lifted its divine form before that child's mind. Perceiving that I was beginning to receive what I had been praying for, I remarked, that the next evening we would read and talk again about the dear Jesus. On this occasion our little son was at my knee as before, and listened with the same expressions of wonder and surprise. From that time onward for a long period, these apprehensions of Christ remained, and visibly moulded his whole moral being. Often would he come into my study, and say to me, "Pa, won't you talk to me about the dear Jesus?" As I would speak to him upon the subject, "Oh!" he would exclaim. As I would tell him how happy it made me to think about Christ, "It makes me happy too," he would reply. When I think of the wonderful death of that son, I have, to account for the fact, to go back to the event in his childhood-life above presented.

I spoke formerly of the peaceful death of a daughter. At her funeral, her pastor remarked, that he had never in his life received such benefit in visiting a sick-room as he had in visiting that of that young woman. The reason was, that she had known not about Christ, but Christ Himself as her life. How did these dear ones thus know Christ? Because "the Spirit took of the things of Christ and showed them unto them." Communications from my home in my own country have just brought me intelligence of the death of another beloved daughter. She also "died in the Lord," and when I would account for the manner of her death, I must refer back to the knowledge of Christ which she received when a little child.

To show early spiritual discernment may arise in the minds of the very young, I will refer to a single fact given in the religious papers by one of our female teachers years ago. In the school taught by this young lady was a little boy of wondrous brightness of intellect and purity of mind, a child so young as to be unable to speak many of his words plainly, and so sprightly, that he was the sunbeam of the school. At the close of the school each day, he would come to his instructress and ask; "Teacer, is I a good boy to-day?" At the close of the school one day, the teacher read the account of Christ's blessing children, and told her school how He loved little children. After dismissing the school, and while seated at her table adjusting her papers, with no thought that any one but herself was in the room, this little child put his hand gently upon her shoulder, and with the deepest interest said, "Teacer, who *is* Quist et loved little children?" "I had an appointment after school, and was in a hurry to be gone, and, as Christians too often do, neglected the present opportunity, and put this child off by promising to tell him about Christ the next day. The next day I was startled at not hearing the ringing voice of that child among my scholars, and all day my conscience smote me on account of that neglected opportunity. As soon as my school was dismissed, I started for the house of the child's father, who was not a Christian man. On the way I was met by the child's sister, who came running, and saying, 'Do hasten to our house; my little brother is very sick, and is constantly calling for his teacher, to tell him who is Christ that loved little children.' As I stood by his side, he said to me, 'Teacer, who is Quist et loved little children?' I attempted now to convey to his mind the knowledge he desired. The fever was on him, however, and his mind wandered, so that he could not understand what I told him. At the father's request we kneeled in prayer, and I prayed that God by His Spirit would impart the knowledge which I was now unable to communicate. As we rose from out knees, the little one exclaimed, 'Do, do, tell me who is Quist et loved little children?'—'Will not somebody tell me who is Quist et loved little children'? 'Won't you pray again for the child?' said the weeping father. Then I prayed as I never did before in my life. As we rose from prayer and looked upon the form before us, his countenance suddenly brightened, and extending his hands, he exclaimed, 'There, there is Quist et loved little children!' and his spirit departed to the everlasting arms of the divine Lover of little children."

The lessons which such facts as the above teach us are to my mind such as these: that it is the Spirit, and He only, that can "reveal Christ in us," so that we shall know, not merely about Him, but Christ Himself; in His personal beauty, glory, and perfection; that the Spirit can make this revelation even to our children; that religious instruction in all its forms, in the family, the Sabbath-school, and everywhere else, is blindly directed when the fixed aim of such instruction is not to communicate this knowledge of Christ; and that when the Spirit does "take of the things of Christ and show them unto us," and imparts to the mind a direct and open vision, or "beholding" of Christ Himself in His personal beauty, glory, and perfection, one fixed desire will possess the mind, the desire to *know* Him, to be like Him, and for ever to "abide in His love."

I also take from such facts as the above my apprehension of the entrance of our babes and little children into the kingdom of light. I think that the Spirit of God will, first of all, impart to the minds of such little ones direct and immediate apprehensions of Christ in His personal beauty, glory, and love—love to such little ones—and that the opening of this vision upon their minds will be the beginning and starting point of their intellectual, moral, and spiritual development and growth for an eternity to come.

Some fifteen or sixteen years after the death of our infant son, "I had a vision in my sleep,"—a vision the remembrance of which no earthly considerations would induce me to part with. I supposed myself to have left the body, and to be in the precincts of the celestial city. I was slowly advancing towards the eternal throne, which was just visible in the distance. If the blessedness of the soul in heaven can be more perfect than mine was then, I can form no conception of what that blessedness can be. "The glory of the Lord did lighten the place, and the Lamb was the light thereof." Infinite quietude and bliss was all about me, and every capacity of my nature was filled with the light, and peace, and blessedness of God. As I was thus slowly advancing towards the throne, there appeared directly before me a youth in all the freshness and bloom of immortality—a youth who approached very near, and, with intense inquiry, looked me in the face. Suddenly his whole countenance lighted up with a smile of joyful recognition: "It is my father come at last." Thus may we expect to meet our little ones who have gone before us, provided we ourselves shall be permitted to "pass through the gates into the city." The effect of that smile of recognition upon me was such that I suddenly awoke. Since I had the vision, however, heaven has appeared more like home to me than it could otherwise have done. I have wandered from my subject, namely, being not in "the flesh," nor in "the letter," but in "the Spirit."

Reader, do you desire to possess this all-renovating and all vitalising knowledge? Go to your Father in heaven and say unto Him that you desire to "know Him, the only true God, and Jesus Christ whom He hath sent," and that, as a means to this end, you ask that He will "baptize you with the Holy Ghost," that the Spirit may "take of the things of Christ and show them unto you," and "show you plainly of the Father," and thus "lead you into all truth." Do this, and you will "receive the promise of the Father," and, having thus received, you will "behold with open face as in a glass the glory of the Lord," will "know the love of Christ, which passeth knowledge," will be "made perfect in love," and will be "filled with all the fulness of God." Neglect to do this, and you will ever remain in "the flesh" and in "the letter," and all this, while you might have walked in the light as God is in the light."

CHAPTER XVII.

"CHRIST IN US, AND CHRIST FOR US."

WE sometimes meet with utterances which, on account of their wonderful adaptation and comprehensiveness, obtain a permanent and influential place in our minds. Such an utterance we met with, when in Edinburgh twenty-five years ago last summer. "Some months since," said a gentleman to us, "I had occasion when in Aberdeen to call upon an Italian artist. After completing my business arrangements, the artist inquired of me in respect to the state of religion in the Protestant Churches. On being told that it was very low, the stranger replied that it was so in the Catholic Church, of which he was a member. 'My house,' he added, 'is the home of our Catholic priests. I not unfrequently find them so vulgar and vile in their conversation that I rise up and drive them out of my residence.' This the man said with tears, and then added, 'The sum of the gospel, sir, is this—*Christ in us, and Christ for us.*'" This, I said, is an utterance to be held in perpetual remembrance, as it fully represents all the relations which do exist, or can exist, between Christ and the believer.

When we think of all our necessities as creatures, and above all, as sinners, Christ appears as our security in respect to them all. There is not one of them that He has overlooked, and not one for the supply of which He has not made full and abundant provision. We think of our sins, and of the infinitude of our guilt as sinners, and even here Christ, "who is our life," appears for us as having "borne our sins in His own body on the tree," and as our "Advocate with the Father," "making intercession for the transgressors." "Sinners may hope," since "Christ has died, yea, rather, has risen again, who is even at the right hand of God, who also maketh intercession for us." We think of our hopeless ruin and bondage under "the law of sin and death," of the number and strength of the evil principles and propensities by which we have been so long held in abject and powerless servitude, and of the resistless powers wielded by our great enemy in the world around us to perfect and perpetuate our bondage. Here again Christ is for us, to take away our sins, to break the power of all evil principles and propensities, to render us "more than conquerors" in every conflict "with the world, the flesh, and the devil," to "sprinkle clean water upon us that we may be clean," to "cleanse us from all our filthiness, and from all our idols," to "wash us, and make us whiter than snow," that we may be "without spot or wrinkle, or any such thing," that we may "be holy and without blemish."

In respect to the temptations that beset us, Christ is with us and for us, never to "suffer us to be tempted above that we are able, but with the temptation to make a way of escape, that we may be able to bear it." Yes, Christ is ever with us and for us, as "able to save unto the uttermost them that come unto God by Him." In reference to our many and great infirmities, He is for us to "render God's strength perfect in our weakness," so that "when we are weak we shall be strong." In regard to our cares great and small, our tribulations and "fiery trials," our afflictions and sorrows, Christ is for us, to "teach us in every state in which we are therewith to be content," to "keep us in perfect peace," to fill us with "everlasting consolation and good hope through grace," to enable us to "learn obedience from the things which we suffer," and to cause "our light afflictions, which are but for a moment, to work out for us a far more exceeding and eternal weight of glory. When we approach "a throne of grace, that we may obtain mercy, and find grace to help in time of need," He is for us there, interceding with the Father, that He will "do for us exceeding abundantly above all that we ask or think."

We have a mission and a work appointed for us here. "As Thou has sent me into the world, even so have I sent them into the world." "He that believeth on me, the works that I do shall he do also." "Ye have not chosen me, but I have chosen you, and ordained you, that ye should go and bring forth fruit, and that your fruit should remain." When we reflect upon our own insufficiency, and on the magnitude of the work assigned us, we naturally cry out, "Who is sufficient for these things?" When we think again, and call to mind the fact that Christ is with us and for us in "all our work and labour of love," we rest in the assurance that we, having in Christ "all-sufficiency for all things, shall be abundantly furnished unto every good work." In regard to what awaits us after death, Christ is for us here also, preparing, amid the many mansions in His Father's house, "a place for us," and ready, when we have "finished the work which He has given us to do," to "come to us, and take us to Himself; that where He is, there we may be also." And, finally, at the eternal judgment, He will be for us then and there, not to condemn, but to justify us, and to "welcome us, as the blessed of His Father," to "inherit the kingdom prepared for us from the foundation of the world." Then, reader, take this thought with you when you go forth to meet coming events, that whatever necessity may come upon you, Christ is for you for the supply of that want, and with the supply to bring to your heart the assurance that "no evil shall befall you," and that "no good thing shall He withhold from you."

But, reader, in all the relations in which Christ is for us, He is for us as a means to a still higher end, that He may be in us, and live, and dwell, and reign within us for ever and ever. The heart of the creature is the home of God, the proper dwelling-place of every person of the sacred Trinity. Sin has banished God from His own house, and rendered it the abode of every foul and unclean thing. Christ has come, and is for us, for the cleansing of this, His own sanctuary, and to rebuild it "for an habitation of God through the Spirit." Christ will never "see of the travail of His soul and be satisfied," in respect to you or me, until He shall take up "His abode in us," and shall dwell in us as the father dwells in Him.

With what impressive language is this great truth of an indwelling Christ expressed in the Bible!—as, for example—"Christ in you the hope of glory;" "That Christ may dwell in your hearts by faith;" "Till Christ be formed in you;" "Abide in me, and I in you;" "I in them, and Thou in me;" "Christ liveth in me;" and "I will dwell in them and walk in them;" "We will come unto him, and make our abode with him;" and "In whom ye also are builded for an habitation of God through the Spirit." When Christ shall be "formed within us," and shall be "in us the hope of glory," His indwelling will be attended with that of each of the other

Persons of the Trinity, and He will bring with Him, when He shall enter the sanctuary of our hearts, "all the fulness of God," and we shall be filled with the same. Then shall we "behold with open face, as in a glass, the glory of the Lord," and shall be "changed into the same image from glory to glory," and shall become possessed, in our measure, of every virtue and grace, and form of moral beauty and perfection, which adorn the character of Christ. Then shall we "comprehend the breadth, and length, and depth, and height, and shall know the love of Christ, which passeth knowledge," and in "knowing and believing the love that God hath unto us, our love will be made perfect." Then shall "our fellowship be with the Father, and with His Son Jesus Christ," and "God shall become our everlasting light, and the days of our mourning shall be ended."

Then, I remark again, shall we fully understand and know all that our Saviour meant in the following utterances:—"Neither pray I for these alone, but for them also which shall believe on me through their word; that they all may be one; as Thou, Father, art in me, and I in Thee, that they also may be one in us that the world may believe that Thou hast sent me. And the glory which Thou gavest me I have given them; that they may be one, even as we are one: I in them, and Thou in me, that they may be made perfect in one; and that the world may know that Thou hast sent me, and hast loved them, as Thou hast loved me." When Christ shall be in you, reader, I would add still further, prayer will be to you a new service. "Moses spake to God face to face, as a man speaketh with his friend." So you, in prayer, will address God not merely as your "Father in heaven," but as directly and immediately before and within you, with a present Christ before and in you to intercede for you, and you will know that "God hears you, and that you have the petitions that you desired of Him."

You will literally "read your Bible with new eyes." The great realities of which it speaks will be as mentally visible to you as to the servant of the prophet, after the Lord had opened his eyes, was the celestial host "round about Elisha." Nothing will be more real to you than Christ as a personal presence directly and immediately before you, and "in you the hope of glory;" nothing will be beheld with such open-faced distinctness and impressiveness as "the glory of the Lord; nothing will be so comprehensible as "the love of Christ which passeth knowledge;" and nothing so receivable as "all the fulness of God." This is very strong language. But what else do the words of Christ permit us to write? "We will come to him, and make our abode with him." "I in them, and Thou in me, that they may be made perfect in one." "I will dwell in them, and will walk in them, and be their God, and they shall be my sons and daughters."

If any one should ask us to explain in what sense, and in what form, Christ dwells and lives in believers, I would reply, that those who have not had an experimental knowledge of that indwelling can have no more apprehensions of it than we can now have of heaven, and of what we shall be when we are there. We know that in heaven our "bodies will be fashioned after the likeness of Christ's glorified body," and that we shall be morally and spiritually "like Him, because we shall see Him as He is." So we know also that when "Christ shall be in us, and we in Him," our union, fellowship, and intercommunion with Him, and His with us, will be the same in kind as mutually obtain between Christ and the Father. "*As* Thou, Father, art in me, and I in Thee, that they also maybe one in us." "I in them, and Thou in me, that they may be made perfect in one." In that union we know still further that Christ will so completely control and determine our mental and moral states and activities, and so completely transform our whole moral characters after His own image, that the Father will love us as He does Christ. "That the love wherewith Thou hast loved me may be in them, and I in them," "That the world may know that Thou hast sent me, and hast loved them, as Thou hast loved me."

In this indwelling of Christ in us, our love to Him will, in our measure, be rendered as perfect as His is to us. "Herein is our love made perfect." When Christ is in us, He will render our content under all the allotments of Providence as perfect, our submission to the divine will as absolute, and our peace and joy as constant and full as were His. "That they might have my joy fulfilled in themselves." When Christ shall thus dwell in a number of believers, their "fellowship one with another" will be the same in kind as that which exists between Christ and the Father.

"That they all may be one, as Thou, Father, art in me, and I in thee." The final result will be this: The world, seeing "how believers love one another," perceiving them, all in common, "walking in the light of God," "kept in perfect peace," and "rejoicing with joy unspeakable, and full of glory," will "believe" and "know" that "the Father has sent Christ into the world," and "has loved believers as He has loved Christ." "I in them, and Thou in me, that they may be made perfect in one, and that the world may know that Thou hast sent me, and hast loved them as Thou hast loved me." Thus we can designate some of the results of the union between Christ and believers—the union represented by the words, "I in them, and Thou in me;" and this is all the explanation we can give of the subject.

If any one should inquire after the *conditions* on which our experience can accord with the union, fellowship, and intercommunion represented by the words, "I in them, and Thou in me," a twofold answer must be given to such an inquiry. We must, in the first place, through faith in Christ, in the varied relations in which He is for us, as a Saviour from sin, be brought into a state of full present consecration to Christ, and obedience to His commandments. On this subject the words of our Saviour are perfectly plain and explicit. "He that hath my commandments, and keepeth them, he it is that loveth me: and he that loveth me shall be loved of my Father, and I will love him, and will manifest myself to him. Judas saith unto Him (not Iscariot), Lord, how is it that Thou wilt manifest Thyself unto us, and not unto the world? Jesus answered and said unto him, If a man love me, he will keep my words: and my Father will love him, and we will come unto him, and make our abode with him." Before Christ will "manifest Himself unto us," and before "He and the Father will come unto us, and make their abode with us," we must first "love Christ" and "keep His words." With loving hearts and obedient spirits, with these, and these only, will Christ and the Father make their abode.

Before this indwelling can arise, even then another condition must be fulfilled, namely, "the Comforter" must be sent to us, to enlarge our capacities to receive Christ and the Father, and to "enlighten the eyes of our understanding," that we may "behold the glory of the Lord," and "comprehend the breadth, and length, and depth, and height, and know the love of Christ, which passeth knowledge." "If ye love me," says our Saviour, "keep my commandments; and I will pray the Father for you, and He shall give you another Comforter, that He may abide with you for ever, even the Spirit of truth." "At that day," the Saviour adds, the day when the Comforter shall come unto you, "ye shall know that I am in my Father, and ye in me, and I in you." Christ and the Father can dwell in us but upon the condition that the Spirit shall first "strengthen us with might in the inner man;" shall "take of the things of Christ, and show them unto us," and shall "show us plainly of the Father." Christ and the Father are, at all times, very near to us. We shall never find them, however, until the Spirit shall open our eyes to "behold with open face, as in a glass, the glory of the Lord." "In whom ye also are builded for an habitation of God THROUGH the Spirit." It is "the Spirit whom Christ sends unto us from the Father" that brings us into "fellowship with the Father, and with His Son Jesus Christ." Hence this fellowship is called "the communion and fellowship of the Spirit." It is when, and only when, we have "received the promise of the Spirit," and are thus "filled with the Holy Ghost," that we can "know the love of Christ," "behold the glory of the Lord," and "God become our everlasting light, and the days of our mourning be ended."

Read often and ponder deeply, reader, the words of inspiration:—"He that believeth on me, as the Scripture hath said, out of his belly shall flow rivers of living water. But this spake He of the Spirit, which they that believe on Him should receive: for the Holy Ghost was not yet given, because that Jesus was not yet glorified." Remember this, that this promise can be fulfilled in your experience but upon the condition that you shall love and obey Christ, as the disciples did, and "the Holy Ghost shall fall upon you as He did upon them at the beginning." Then, and only then, "will Christ be in you the hope of glory."

A question of very great practical importance here presents itself; a question which each believer should, with deep and solemn interest, put to his own heart and conscience, namely, In what relations, and to what extent, do I really and truly *know* my Saviour? "This," He tells us, "is life eternal, that they might know Thee, the only true God, and Jesus Christ, whom Thou hast sent." "This is life eternal" is ours in possession, in exact accordance with the extent and limits of the knowledge referred to.

In regard to the mass of professing Christians, it is no slander to affirm that they in reality know no more of Christ as a manifested indwelling presence than they do of heaven. In the relations in which Christ is for us, their real knowledge of Him is circumscribed almost wholly within the sphere of our justification, the sphere in which "we have redemption through His blood, the forgiveness of sins." As a consequence, as soon as the freshness of the consciousness of "sins forgiven" has passed away, their primal joys fade out, leaving in the centre of the heart "an aching void the world can never fill." As long as these circumscribed views of the relations in which Christ is for us continue, that void will not only remain unfilled, but new and higher joys will not well out in the soul, none of the conditions of Christ's manifesting Himself to, and living in, the believer being fulfilled. What a fearful error it is to teach such believers that they have received "the promised baptism of the Holy Ghost;" that they are "in Christ, and Christ in them;" that "their bodies are the temples of the Holy Ghost;" that "God dwells in them and walks in them;" and that they are "beholding with open face, as in a glass, the glory of the Lord," and are being "changed into the same image, from glory to glory, even as by the Spirit of the Lord,"—all of which is absolutely affirmed of all who have received "the promise of the Spirit."

Must we suppose that all that such language really imports is what is realised in the common experience of the mass of professing Christians, whom Christian charity requires us to regard as converted persons? "He that believeth on me," says our Saviour, "as the Scripture hath said, out of his belly shall flow rivers of living water." Does this mean nothing more than the experience of which we are speaking? All this, as the Saviour absolutely affirms, is, and shall be, true of all who shall receive "the promise of the Spirit." "But this He spake of the Spirit, which they that believe on Him should receive; for the Holy Ghost was not yet given, because Jesus was not yet glorified." If what Christ then promised has not been made real in your experience, reader, you do yourself infinite wrong if you entertain the idea that you have been "baptized with the Holy Ghost."

We also understand the conditions of the possibility of our receiving what the inspiration means in the following wonderful words, namely, "Now unto Him that is able to do exceeding abundantly above all that we ask or think, according to," or through, "the power (of the Holy Ghost) that worketh in us, unto Him be glory in the Church by Christ Jesus throughout all ages, world without end. Amen." Before we can come into such relations to Christ, relations in which what is here referred to can become real in our experience, we must pass through the process to which the apostle refers in the preceding parts of the epistle, and especially in the verses which immediately precede that under consideration.

First of all, we must be sealed with the Holy Spirit of promise," and "the eyes of our understanding must thus be enlightened, that we may know what is the hope of His calling, and what the riches of the glory of His inheritance in the saints." Then we must "be strengthened with might by the Spirit in the inner man," and this as a means to this end, "that Christ may dwell in our hearts by faith," "that we," by such indwelling, "being rooted and grounded in love, may be able to comprehend with all saints what is the breadth, and length, and depth, and height, and to know the love of Christ, which passeth knowledge, that we may be filled with all the fulness of God." When we shall have received "the promise of the Father," "the baptism of the Holy Ghost," and when the Spirit shall have led us on through all these enlightenments and experiences, then we shall have been brought into such relations to and fellowships "with the Father and with His Son Jesus Christ," that all that "we ask or think" will fall infinitely short of what the Spirit will ever after evince Himself as able to do for us. On no other conditions are the experiences and fulnesses under consideration possible to us, and they are, in all their "lengths, and breadths, and depths, and heights," possible to all who will "follow on to know the Lord," as He has made known to us the way.

CHAPTER XVIII.

RELIGIOUS JOY.

IN the Scriptures we are told that "the joy of the Lord is our strength," that "the fruit of righteousness shall be peace, and the effect of righteousness quietness and assurance for ever." Religious joy is also positively required of us in the Word of God. "Rejoice in the Lord always, and again I say, rejoice." We are required and admonished by our Saviour to "ask and receive, until our joy is full." One of His special petitions to "His Father and our Father," to "His God and our God," was that we "might have His joy fulfilled in ourselves." What He promises to all that come unto Him, however burdened they may be, is that He "will give them rest," and that "they shall find rest unto their souls." "Peace," says our Lord, "I leave with you; my peace I give unto you." "These things," says the inspired writer, "write I unto you, that your joy may be full." The angels of God heralded the advent of Christ on earth as "glad tidings of great joy." While all the world "weep for sorrow of heart," all believers in Jesus are expected to "sing for joy of heart." Among the revealed "fruits of the Spirit" are "joy, peace." All the promises come to us " heavily laden" with "the peace of God which passeth all understanding," "joy unspeakable and full of glory," and everlasting consolations and good hope through grace."

Peace and joy, ever full and eternally enduring, are also represented as one of the special and peculiar characteristics of the new dispensation, that under which we now live. "And the ransomed of the Lord shall return, and come to Zion with songs and everlasting joy upon their heads: they shall obtain joy and gladness, and sorrow and sighing shall flee away." "Thy sun shall no more go down, neither shall thy moon withdraw itself: for the Lord shall be their *everlasting* light, and the days of thy mourning shall be ended." Such being the revealed facts of the case, we should not undervalue or avoid to seek religious joy as a supreme good of our immortal natures. Every believer owes it to his

God and Saviour, to himself, to the Church, and to the world, to verify in his inward experience and visible life the truth that "the fruit of righteousness is peace, and the effect of righteousness quietness and assurance for ever," and that "whosoever believeth in Christ, as the Scripture hath said, out of his belly do flow rivers of living water," "the Spirit now being given, because Jesus has been glorified."

If you, reader, affirm yourself "a believer in Jesus," and your experience and life do not accord with the above revelations, then your testimony and influence before the Church and the world are not for the truth, but against the truth. How and why the ministry and the churches do and can expect "that the Gentiles shall come to the light of Zion, and kings to the brightness of her rising," while the sacramental host is moving on very much as a funeral procession, singing their dirge songs, and testifying one to another of the loss of the blessedness each knew "when first he saw the Lord," of his utter impotence to "fly or go to reach eternal joys," is a mystery to me. Neither you nor I have a right to testify before the Church and world that you have found Christ, unless you can also testify that in Christ you have found God as "the everlasting light" of your soul. If you have not yet thus found Christ, He is yet to be found by you, and "you will seek Him and find Him" when, and only when, "you shall search for Him with all your heart." Be assured of this, reader, that if "your peace is not as a river, and your righteousness as the waves of the sea," and "the peace of God" and "joy of the Holy Ghost" do not abide in your heart, your "heart is not right with God," and your relations to Him must be newly and rightly adjusted, or your immortal interests are imperilled.

When I, for example, became conscious that my primal Christian joy had faded out, leaving "an aching void" within, that God was not "my everlasting light," nor "the days of my mourning ended," and that my faith in Christ did not induce in my heart "joy unspeakable and full of glory," and that "the peace of God, which passeth all understanding, did not keep my heart and mind through Christ Jesus," I said to myself, as I have before stated, "I know that I have missed my way, and that my inner life is not rightly adjusted relatively to Christ and His salvation. I know that I have essentially erred somewhere, and I will never rest, and will give my God no rest, until the error is discovered and corrected. I will never rest, nor faint in prayer, until I am conscious in myself of all the forms of moral purification, 'fruits of the Spirit,' 'rest of faith,' 'fulness of joy,' and immortal fruitions revealed in the Scriptures as the blood bought privileges and immunities of the sons of God." It was because I thus reasoned and acted, and did not, as most believers do, content myself to "walk in darkness and have no light," that I was, at length, "led out of darkness into light," the marvellous light of God; and for these forty years, have had such divine fellowships, such endurances, such victories of faith, such enduring peace, quietness, assurance, and fulness of joy. All this, reader, is in reserve for you. You will become possessed of it, however, on this condition, that, with all sincerity, earnestness, and tireless perseverance, "God shall for this be inquired of by you to do it for you." If you do not value "the joy of the Lord" sufficiently to induce you to "search for it as for hid treasures," to inquire after it, pray for it, and rest not until you possess it, you, in all probability, will never find it in this world or the next. Nothing but the love and joy of the Lord in your heart, and filling it, will keep the world and "its affections and lusts" out of your heart. If the "peace of God, which passeth all understanding, does not keep your heart and mind by Christ Jesus," care and trouble, and discontent and worldly vexations, and fearful lookings for what may come upon you, will occupy them. You must "obtain joy and gladness," or "sorrow and sighing will not flee away."

When you are told not to make any efforts to banish your cares or sorrows, or to induce religious peace and joy, you receive wise and healthful advice. The tempest of trouble and care and discontent dies within us, and the calmness of peace and holy joy reigns in our hearts, not at the bidding of our wills, but at the bidding of Christ. The rest which we cannot induce in ourselves, Christ gives us when we come unto Him for it. "God," and not we ourselves, "keeps us in perfect peace when we stay ourselves upon Him, because we trust in Him." Pardon, sanctification, and peace are all in common and alike "gifts of God through Jesus Christ our Lord," and are available to us, each on the same condition, namely, that "God for this be inquired of by us to do it for us."

When inquirers are told, however, as they frequently are, not to think anything about their feelings, nor to give themselves any concern about them one way or the other, then advice is given which divine wisdom admonishes us not to heed. Moses prayed not unwisely, nor undirected by the Spirit of God, when he sent up the following petition: "Oh, satisfy us early with Thy mercy, that we may rejoice and be glad all our days. Make us glad according to the days wherein Thou has afflicted us, and the years wherein we have seen evil." Nor was David undirected by the Spirit when he thus prayed, "Make me to hear joy and gladness, that the bones which Thou hast broken may rejoice. Restore unto me the joy of thy salvation; and uphold me with Thy free Spirit. Then will I teach transgressors Thy ways, and sinners shall be converted unto Thee."

If Christ has been anointed to "bind up the broken-hearted," and to "set at liberty them that are bruised," broken hearts and bruised spirits should be taken to Him for healing. When He says to us, "Ask and ye shall receive, that your joy may be full," He specifically directs us to make religious joy a special object of thought and prayer. When the presence and love of Christ, and the power of His Spirit, fail to move and to melt our sensibilities, kindle emotion, and to stir up the great deep of the soul, then is a time for special heart-searching and prayer. "Who is among you that feareth the Lord, that obeyeth the voice of His servant, that walketh in darkness, and hath no light? Let him trust in the name of the Lord, and stay himself upon his God."

When I was once sitting in a circle of Christian friends, prayer was proposed, in which all were to lead in succession, one after the other. The prayer of a lady in that circle I shall never forget. It was to this effect, and nearly in these words: "Lord, when Thou didst take from me my only child, and all hope of its place being supplied by another, I said to Thee that Thou hadst made a great vacancy in my soul, a void which nothing but Thyself could fill, and that I trusted Thee so to fill that void with Thine own fulness, that I should never more feel the absence of that child. I told Thee that I must now have far more of Thyself than I had ever had before. I bless Thee that that prayer was heard, and that Thou didst so occupy my whole being with Thy manifested presence and love, that the absence of that dear one occasions no sense of loneliness at all. I joy to think of it now as in Thine everlasting arms, where I expect myself soon to be."

The special form of the prayer was occasioned, I doubt not, by the peculiar tone of the conversation immediately preceding, the burden of which was the power of Christ to take away our sorrows as well as our sins, to perfect our joys as well as our virtues and graces, and to meet fully every want of our being as it arises. The lesson which we learn from such examples, as well as from the express teachings of the Word of God, is the great truth that our emotions, as well as our moral states, should be the objects of reflection, faith, and prayer. The divine direction is this:—"Be careful for nothing; but in everything by prayer and supplication, with thanksgiving, let your requests be made known unto God. And the peace of God, which passeth all understanding, shall keep your hearts and minds by Christ Jesus." The promises pertaining to our peace are as really the objects of faith and prayer as those pertaining to our justification or sanctification. We should not, of course, expect that our emotive states shall be always of an ecstatic character, heaven having its seasons of silence as well as of singing and shouting. We should expect, however, to be "*kept* in perfect peace," and should trust God to render our "peace as a river," as well our "righteousness as the waves of the sea." When "the peace of God, which passeth all understanding," does not "keep our hearts and minds by Christ Jesus," and "our joy is not full," we should conclude that our faith, prayer, or obedience "has been hindered."

Paul considered religious joy as an immutable condition of his "making full proof of his ministry." Let us carefully weigh his words:— "Blessed be God, even the Father of our Lord Jesus Christ, the Father of mercies, and the God of all comfort, who comforteth us in all our tribulation, that we may be able to comfort them which are in any trouble, by the comfort wherewith we ourselves are comforted of God. For as the sufferings of Christ abound in us, so our consolation also aboundeth by Christ." When God shall become "the everlasting light" of

His people, and "the days of their mourning shall be ended," then, as inspiration informs us, "will the Gentiles come to their light, and kings to the brightness of their rising." That which peculiarises the gospel, and distinguishes it from all other religions and forms of belief; is its sovereign power to "take away sin," and to bring in its stead "everlasting righteousness," on the one hand, and, on the other, to "take away" sorrow in all its forms, and to induce in its place "everlasting consolations and good hope through grace." You must know this gospel, reader, not only in theory, but in full experience, as possessed of these two forms of sovereign power, or you fail essentially in fundamental qualifications to serve Christ effectively in any department of your divine and holy calling as a believer in Jesus.

CHAPTER XIX.

MISCELLANEOUS TOPICS AND SUGGESTIONS.

THERE are certain general questions of a miscellaneous character—questions which require special consideration before I close this treatise. I place them together, not because they are naturally connected, but because neither would demand a separate chapter.

Section I.—Giving Testimony in respect to Facts of Personal Experience.

In many minds there is a strong prejudice against public testimony to facts of personal Christian experience. Such testimony, it is said, reveals pride of heart in the first instance, and tends to increase the evil in the next. Perhaps those who entertain such sentiments need a word of caution and admonition here. We should be very careful about impugning motives, "judging a brother, and setting at naught a brother." Let us for a moment contemplate the impeachment under consideration. I have been sick, apparently unto death, we will suppose, and have found a sovereign remedy in the use of a certain medicine, and have found by observation that the same medicine has had the same efficacy in all similar cases to which it has been applied. To commend the use of the medicine on the part of all who need it as I did, I state the fact of its efficacy in my own case and that of others. Is there good ground to impeach motives, and affirm a tendency to promote pride, on account of such testimony?

I become conscious of a spiritual necessity, a disease of the mind—a want for which no remedy exists in myself; or in any finite objects in the universe around. I look to Christ as the great Physician of the soul, and that all-overshadowing want is perfectly met. As a means of commending this "precious faith" to all others, I tell them of "the great things which God hath done for me," how, when I sought unto Him, "He had mercy on me." I tell them, also, how it is that "the peace of God, which passeth all understanding, keeps the hearts and minds, by Christ Jesus," of all who, "by prayer and supplication, with thanksgiving, make known their requests unto God." Why is the motive to be impeached in such case any more than in that first presented? Why is a tendency to induce pride affirmed in one case any more than in the other?

Those who object to such testimony do, in fact, condemn the example of Christ, of the prophets, apostles, and all the sacred writers. Why did Christ testify to the fact of the saving power that resided in Him, and that the Father always heard when the Son prayed to Him? That men might "believe that Jesus is the Christ, and, believing, might have life through His name." Why did He direct the demoniac of Gadara to "go home to his kindred and friends and tell them how great things the Lord had done for him, and how He had mercy on him?" That, hearing, "they might believe, and that, believing, they might have life through His name.

Let us see if we cannot find an example of inspired wisdom—an example bearing directly upon the subject before us. "I waited patiently for the Lord, and He inclined unto me, and heard my cry. He brought me up also out of an horrible pit, out of the miry clay, and set my feet upon a rock, and established my goings. And He hath put a new song in my mouth, even praise unto our God. Many shall see it, and fear, and shall trust in the Lord." "That which we have seen and heard," says the apostle John, "declare we unto you, that ye also may have fellowship with us; and truly our fellowship is with the Father and with His Son Jesus Christ." "These things write we unto you, that your joy may be full." Here is personal testimony to the fact of the highest attainment that can be made by a creature of God, "fellowship with the Father, and with His Son Jesus Christ."

The reasons which justify such professions are obvious. The testimony was true, in the first instance, and was requisite to induce all believers to seek and attain the same divine fellowship and fulness of joy of which the apostle was possessed. Paul gives this testimony to his own attainments through the faith of Christ: "I am crucified with Christ" —"By whom I am crucified to the world, and the world to me" "I thank my God, whom I serve with a pure conscience" I have learned, in whatsoever state I am, therewith to be content," and "I can do all things through Christ, which strengtheneth me." His motive in giving such testimony to his own personal attainments is undeniable—that "we may believe, and therefore speak," as he did. Those who question the propriety, expediency, and necessity of such testimony, have not, it is quite evident, taken their views on this subject from the Word of God. All depends upon the validity of the testimony, and the motive which prompted it. If I, for example, in what I have written of my own inner life, have consciously misstated facts, or "have sought my own glory," then Christ will put me to shame before Him at His coming. But if my single purpose has been to make known to you, reader, facts as they are, and to secure in you a full understanding and appreciation of your privileges and immunities as one of "the sons or daughters of the Lord, the Almighty," and as "a believer in Jesus," then I may reasonably expect the everlasting "smile of the Lord as the feast of my soul," on account of what I have written. "These things I have written, that your joy might be full."

Section II.—Proposed Remedies for Pride of Heart.

Pride of heart on the one hand, and subjection to appetite on the other, constitute the primal sins of human nature, and are the main sources of sin in all its forms. "Ye shall be as gods, knowing good and evil." "And when the woman saw that the tree was good for food, and that it was pleasant to the eyes, and a tree to be desired to make one wise, she took of the fruit thereof, and did eat, and gave also unto her husband with her, and he did eat." If the grace of Christ were not adequate to save us from these primal sins, our salvation would be an impossibility. The remedy which the gospel prescribes for pride, for example, is very simple and of ready application—namely, that we consider the spirit of pride, in all its forms and manifestations, as morally criminal in itself, and a great sin before God; that we sincerely repent of, and confess it as such; that we look to Christ to be saved from the penalty, and delivered from the spirit and power of the sin, and to perfect us in the opposite virtues, meekness and humbleness of mind.

In the Scriptures, permit me to add here, self-ignorance is never represented as an element of humility, or as promotive of the same; nor is self-knowledge prohibited, or referred to as an element of pride, or as conducive to the same. On all subjects in common, believers are represented as "children of the light and of the day," and as living and acting "according to knowledge." While we are prohibited "thinking of ourselves more highly than we ought to think"—that is, to think ourselves better than we really are—we are positively required "to think soberly according as God hath dealt to every man the measure of faith" that is, to understand our moral states, gifts, and adaptations as they are. Nothing is more particularly required of us than self-knowledge in the widest acceptation of the term. Nor does pride, according to the Bible, consist in our holding in high regard the virtues of which we, as believers in Jesus, become possessed. When our characters, through faith in Christ, take on "the ornament of a meek and quiet spirit," they take on adornings "which, in the sight of God, are of great price," adornings on account of which "Christ is glorified in us," and "God is not ashamed to be called our God." "Our rejoicing is this, the testimony of our consciences, that, in simplicity and godly sincerity, not with fleshly wisdom, but by the grace of God, we have our conversation in the world." When our Saviour uttered these words, "Whosoever shall do the will of my Father which is in heaven, the same is my brother, and sister, and mother," He intended to impress our minds with the conviction of the infinite importance and worth of such obedience.

It is equally manifest, also, that just *commendation* for moral excellence, in all its forms and manifestations, meets with the divine approval. In the Sermon on the Mount, our Saviour told the young converts before Him that they were "the salt of the earth," and "the light of the world." In the presence of Mary and the company assembled at the house of Simon, the Saviour affirmed that "she had done a good work upon Him," and that what she had done should "in all the world, wherever His gospel should be preached, be told as a memorial of her." "O woman! great is thy faith." "I have not found so great faith, no not in Israel." Such was the conduct of our Saviour everywhere, and such also are the examples and teachings of the Bible throughout. One of its most striking peculiarities, that which most especially manifests the divine integrity of its writers, is the fact that men and things are set before us, with their good and bad qualities, just as they are. Commending goodness and good men is as absolutely required of us as is testifying against sin and bad men.

Nor, let me add once more, is the fact that we receive with gratitude and joy the approbation of our own consciences, and the approval and manifested favour of God, and of all the good in heaven and on earth, any evidence at all of pride in us. All this is the revealed reward of righteousness, and it would be no reward at all if we did not enjoy it. The perfection of Christian character, and the best evidence of true humbleness of mind, is a just and righteous appreciation and treatment of all objects of thought, both in relation to ourselves and others. Pride, on the other hand, makes self its centre, and the exaltation of self its supreme aim, and thus becomes the source and fountain of envy, detraction, defamation, self-boasting, and flattery, when commending others will secure personal ends. You meet an individual who always keeps himself; and only the bright sides of his character, before you. You know very well that pride is at the bottom of such representations. You meet with another individual, who manifests a just regard for persons and things, speaks of them as they are, and of himself but as a means of doing good. Here is "the honest man," and here too is the truly humble man.

The reader will naturally infer from the above, that I do not approve of not a few of the representations we have in respect to pride and its remedies and preventions. In a very important article, one written by an individual who has great wisdom in teaching the essentials of the life of faith, I find the following statement and advice, which, of course, I do not approve:—

"Years ago I came across this sentence in an old book: 'Never indulge at the close of an action in any self-reflective acts of any kind, whether of self-congratulation or of self-despair. Forget the things that are behind the moment they are past, leaving them with God.' It has been of unspeakable value to me. When the temptation comes, as it always does, to indulge in these reflections, either of one sort or the other, I turn from them at once, and positively refuse to think about my work at all, leaving it with the Lord to overrule the mistakes, and to bless it as He chooses."

In another Book, "that dearest of Books, that excels every other," we find this precept: "Let every man prove" (determine the real character of) "his own work, and then shall he have rejoicing in himself alone, and not in another." If we have spoken or acted in any form for Christ, we are required absolutely to reflect upon what we have done, and know its character as it is. If we have spoken or acted well, we should thank God for the grace given to us. If not well, we should humble ourselves before the Lord, and seek grace and wisdom for the future. The whole life of the believer should be one of self-reflective activity. We should know what we have done, what we are doing, and what we ought to do in the future.

It is quite common with individuals to suppose it conducive to humility, and a sure preventive of pride, for Christians to hold a low estimate, of the Christian virtues of which they may be possessed. Because the prophet confessed that all "the righteousnesses" of a "disobedient and gainsaying people," were "as filthy rags," not a few believers suppose that humility requires that they employ the same language to represent the divine virtues with which Christ has adorned their character. If Christ, reader, has saved you from your sins, and has adorned your character and life with any form of Christian virtue—and you are not His at all unless He has done so—you do injustice to truth and to the honour of your Saviour when, in such confessions as the above, you represent Him as having put upon you a mass of "filthy rags." If, on the other hand, you do not place an infinite value upon those virtues, and do not seek to be perfected in the same, you will be certain to lose what you have received.

Not a few individuals fail utterly to distinguish between flattery, which is a grievous sin, and a just appreciation and commendation of excellence wherever, and in whomsoever, it appears. A flatterer is one who idolises self and particular individuals, and appreciates excellence nowhere else, or who, for personal gain, and irrespective of truth, praises all he meets, and generally decries them behind their backs. Such an individual is "a spot in our feasts of charity," and "a cloud without water" everywhere. Christian integrity, on the other hand, judges and speaks truthfully of all men, and approves and commends goodness, and reprobates and reproves wrong, wherever they appear. The personal commendation of such persons has no tendency to promote pride, but everywhere conduces to "love and good works." Christ helped the special gifts of James and John by naming them "sons of thunder," and of Peter by naming him "a rock," and rendered permanent the integrity of Nathaniel by calling him an "Israelite indeed, in whom is no guile." Just commendation is one of the divinely-appointed means by which we are to "support the weak, comfort the feeble-minded," and encourage the timid. Should any desire to understand what kind of encouragement and commendation young converts should receive "for their work and labour of love," let them read the Epistles to the Thessalonians. Take the following as an example:—"And ye became followers of us and of the Lord, having received the Word in much affliction, with joy of the Holy Ghost: so that ye were ensamples to all that believe in Macedonia and Achaia. For from you sounded out the Word of the Lord, not only in Macedonia and Achaia, but also in every place your faith to God-ward is spread abroad; so that we need not to speak anything." How such commendations tended to strengthen and encourage those converts to persevere and endure unto the end! Not a few of my pupils remind me, when I meet them, of the life-benefits which they received from words of encouragement and commendation at particular crises of their student-lives. The prejudice which exists in the Churches against true and just commendation of virtuous deeds and manifestations has no foundation in Scripture teaching or example.

Section III.—Confessing Sin.

If you, reader, have sinned against God, by doing what you ought not, or omitting to do what you ought, if you are living below your known and acknowledged privileges, "an evil thing and a bitter" is written against you in the book of God. Careless and general confessions, my brother, will not meet your case. Your humiliation must be deep and unfeigned, or those sins will stand against you at the eternal judgment. If, with "repentance toward God, and faith toward our Lord

Jesus Christ," you shall "confess your sins," you will be "forgiven and cleansed from all unrighteousness." If you fail to do this, your expectation of being "saved from death" will be "as the giving up of the ghost." God will not accept at our hands, as the condition of pardon, any general, formal, and unheart-felt confessions of sin. "Except ye repent, ye shall all likewise perish." Are you thus, my brother, really and truly repenting of the sins which you admit to characterise your daily life? I refer to such as admit this to be the fact in their case.

We are now prepared to understand and appreciate one of the most offensive and alarming features of ordinary religious service. In such services, the Church publicly acknowledges herself, and that before God and the world, guilty of sins of the most inexcusable and aggravating character, of "doing many things which ought not to be done, and of leaving undone many things which ought to be done." Yet those sins are confessed with a manner and spirit which clearly indicate that said sins are very little, if at all, cared about, and the absence of all serious intention to abandon them. No custom whatever can have a stronger tendency to "sear the conscience," harden the heart, and "render our bands strong." In all such confessions, we say to men of the world, If you are anxious about your sins, you concern yourselves about that of which we have very little regard. By such confessions, young disciples are schooled into hardened indifference to their covenant vows. Yet, perhaps most professing Christians seem quite satisfied with a prayer, however cold and formal it may be, if it contains a confession of daily sin, and greatly dissatisfied with one, however fervent, if it wants such confession. For one, I never gratify such a prejudice, and, as I view the subject, I should peril my immortal interests by so doing. That of sinners I am one of the chief, I well know, and confess this fact most sincerely. Hence I am always at home in the utterance of the Lord's Prayer. Sins of "this present time" I publicly confess when my conscience convicts me of the same, when such sins are publicly known, and I am conscious of unfeigned repentance for what I confess. Secret sins, when convicted of them, I adjust between conscience and God. I do not feel authorised, but prohibited by the Word of God, to make confession before a congregation that all believers present are living in the daily commission of known sin. I should "judge my brethren, and set at nought my brethren" by so doing. If we should be solemnly sincere anywhere, it should be in our confessions of sin. The fearful influence of the habit of making heartless confessions is manifest in this, that those who are most zealous about their general confessions will not allow you to admonish them in the most gentle manner for any specific sin, nor even for a common fault. "Thus saith the Lord, Be ye not mockers, lest your hands be made strong."

Section IV.—Important Misapprehension.

In his work entitled "The Higher Life," one of the most valuable publications of the class that has yet appeared, Dr Boardman makes a statement to this effect: "The brethren at Oberlin had made most important attainments in the divine life. For what they had attained, they sought a name, asking, 'Is it manna?' They at length designated these attainments by the words 'Christian perfection,' or 'entire sanctification.' In doing this," as Dr B. infers, "they greatly erred. They should have gone forward preaching Christ without giving a name to the attainments they had made." In this our brother is fully right, supposing him to have been correctly informed of the real facts of the case. Through misinformation, however, he has most essentially erred in his statement of facts. No question like this ever arose among us, namely, What shall we call this state to which we have attained?

In the term "Higher Life," Dr Boardman does not, as I understand him, merely present a name for personal attainments consciously made, but a revealed privilege to which "believers in Jesus" are authorised to expect to attain. So with us in the use of the terms above designated. In all our writings, such terms are employed exclusively to represent what we regard as revealed privileges of the sons of God, and never in any instance to represent mere personal attainments. The question, what attainments we have made, lies wholly between our consciences and our God. The question, what are our revealed privileges, is to be settled, not by an appeal to the conscious or visible attainments of any individual or class of individuals, but wholly and exclusively by reference "to the law and to the testimony." The Spirit of the Lord does know, and He only can know, what "things are possible with God" on the one hand, and what "things are possible to him that believeth" on the other. In determining the possibilities of faith, we must refer exclusively to what God, by His Spirit, has taught us on the subject.

In my endeavours to find the true revealed answer to such inquiries, I judge, that I may truly say, that I proceeded with the greatest care and circumspection. I at once perceived that if God, as many suppose He has, has absolutely revealed the fact that no believer in Christ ever has been, or ever will be, in this life, saved from all sin, that settles for ever the whole question. My first inquiry therefore, was directed to all those passages which, as I had supposed, and many do suppose, do teach the doctrine of Christian Imperfection, that is, of the continued sinfulness of all believers in Jesus. In my examinations, I determined to take each passage by itself; and, in the clear light of the known and acknowledged laws of interpretation, determine its real meaning, and then its bearing upon the inquiry before us. This I did, and, to my surprise, found that not one of these passages presented the remotest evidence in favour of the doctrine it had been supposed to teach. In the work on "Christian Perfection," all these passages are fully explained, and the explanation there given has never yet been replied to.

I then turned to the inquiry, What do the Scriptures directly and positively teach in respect to the privileges of "the sons of God" in this life? On this subject, as I found, the teachings of the Bible are of the plainest and most absolute character possible. In regard to what is revealed respecting Christ's power to save from sin, let this one passage suffice: "Wherefore He is able to save them to the uttermost that come unto God by Him." The original word rendered *uttermost* is, as I have said, and as every Greek scholar knows, one of the strongest words that can be found in the Greek or any other language, being compounded of two words, *pantos*, which means *all*, and *telos*, uniformly translated in our New Testament *perfection*. That Christ, in the most absolute sense, is *able* to save us from all sin, is undeniable. What can be the object of revealing this fact in this absolute form, but to induce us to trust Christ thus to save us? Any other supposition affirms that His grace and love are limited, while His revealed power to save is unlimited.

Equally explicit are the teachings of inspiration in respect to the provisions of grace for our present salvation from sin. "Christ loved the Church, and gave Himself for it, that He might sanctify and cleanse it with the washing of water by the Word, that He might present it to Himself a glorious Church, not having spot, or wrinkle, or any such thing, but that it should be holy and without blemish;" "who gave Himself for us, that He might redeem us from all iniquity, and purify unto Himself a peculiar people, zealous of good works." Hence we are told that "we are complete in Him," and "can do all things through Christ which strengtheneth us," and that "all things are possible to him that believeth." If such revelations do not authorise us to look to Christ to be saved from all sin, expecting to receive nothing less from Him, they do not authorise us thus to trust Him for anything at all.

But what of the promises which are given unto us for the revealed purpose that "by these we might be partakers of the divine nature, having escaped the corruption that is in the world through lust"? Take one of these as an example of the rest. "Faithful (trustworthy) is He that calleth you, who also will do it." No promise can be more explicit and positive than is this. In regard to the nature of the blessing promised, no candid inquirer after the true meaning of the Word will err in judgment. "And the very God of peace sanctify you wholly; and I pray God your whole spirit and soul and body be preserved blameless unto the coming of our Lord Jesus Christ." The original term rendered *wholly*, like that rendered *uttermost* in the passage above cited, is compounded of two words—one *olos*, meaning *all* and the other *telos*, meaning *perfection*. The promise before us presents to our faith sanctification in this utter fulness, or it authorises us to expect nothing at all.

In the remaining portion of the verse, preservation in this entirely sanctified state is also designated. Nothing less can be implied by the words, "your whole spirit and soul and body be preserved blameless unto the coming of our Lord Jesus Christ," To limit such promises is to "limit the Holy One of Israel" in a form which does peril to our immortal interests. In the midst of such revelations, which abound everywhere in the Scriptures, stands this as the crowning glory of the whole:—"Now unto Him that is able to do exceeding abundantly above all that we ask or think, according to the power that worketh in us, unto Him be glory in the Church by Christ Jesus throughout all ages, world without end, Amen." I accordingly hold and teach "Christ as the power of God and the wisdom of God unto salvation to every one that believeth," and as a Saviour from sin as fully and perfectly in the sphere of our sanctification, as in that of our justification. I dare not limit His grace in the one sphere any more than in the other. If I am asked, "Do you, as Paul did, serve God with a pure conscience?" I answer, as Paul did, "Yes." But do you never commit a sin? I answer such a question in the words of Paul, "I know nothing by myself; yet am I not hereby justified: but He that judgeth me is the Lord."

But is it not well, since people are so much prejudiced against the word *perfection* and kindred terms, to avoid, their use? To such questions my reply is ready. "I give place by subjection" to such prejudice, "no not for an hour." Since these terms are most frequent in the teachings of our Saviour and of His inspired apostles, and represent their most important and impressive truths, I should convict myself of being "ashamed of the gospel of Christ," if I should avoid presenting that gospel in "the words which the Holy Ghost teacheth." We should more than suspect our doctrines, when they induce in us prejudice against words employed under the inspiration of the Holy Ghost, as Christ and all inspired writers employ those under consideration. A prejudice which, as this undeniably does, renders wholly inoperative upon the heart and conscience large portions of the most important teachings of Christ and of His inspired apostles, is a prejudice to be repented of, and not gratified. Who does not know that, when very many ministers and members of our churches meet with a passage containing any of the words under consideration, they pass such passage by without reflecting upon it at all? Such relations to the Word of God are most perilous to our highest spiritual interests. It was by no inadvertence that the Spirit of God put such words into the New Testament, and it is no indication of veneration in us for the wisdom of that Spirit, when we become prejudiced against words and forms of language which He so frequently employs, and that to represent the most important truths of God.

Section V.—*Great and Little Faith.*

Much is said, by our Saviour especially, about great and little faith. The latter considers the difficulties to be overcome in the accomplishment of needed and required ends, and becomes appalled and doubtful in view of the same. The former thinks of the power of Christ to do all that we need, and "exceeding abundantly above all that we ask or think," and of His absolute fidelity to His promises, and consequently "rejoices in the hope of the glory of the Lord." The latter thinks of the vastness of our necessities, and of the absence of all visible means to meet them, and thus becomes "careful and troubled about many things." The former thinks of the wealth and resources of our Father in heaven, and of His omnipresent "help in trouble," and "by prayer and supplication, with thanksgiving, makes known its requests unto God," and, as a consequence, is "kept by the peace of God, which passeth all understanding." The language of the latter is, "If thou *canst* do anything, help us, and have mercy on us." The language of the former is, "Lord, if Thou wilt, Thou canst make me clean," and "Speak the word only, and my servant shall be healed." The latter takes a feeble hold of the love and promises of Christ, and with doubting expectation approaches the throne of grace." The former magnifies the love of Christ, and laying hold, with a death-grasp, upon the promised help, replies to every difficulty and seeming repulse, "Truth, Lord; yet the dogs eat of the crumbs that fall from their master's table." The latter, consequently, receives rebuke when it obtains the blessing sought, while the former receives both the blessing and the divine commendation, "O woman, great is thy faith; be it unto thee as thou wilt;" "I will; be thou clean;" and "Verily, verily, I say unto you, I have not found so great faith, no not in Israel."

Had the disciples been possessed of great faith, they would have reasoned thus amidst the terrors of that night-tempest, namely: "We are just as safe here as Christ is. The Father will not suffer Him, nor a hair of His head, to perish here, and Christ will care for us as the Father does for Him. He will live, and because He shall live, we shall live also." Thus their quietness and assurance would have been absolute under those very circumstances.

Remember this, reader, that Christ is most pleased with you and with me, when He sees in us this great faith which counts it a very small and easy thing for Him, with His infinite power and boundless love, grace, and resources, to meet all the necessities of creatures so small as we are, and which never doubts or questions His absolute fidelity to His promises. The firmer our grasp upon His plighted word, the more ineffable is His delight in us, and the more deeply is His heart moved towards us. Nothing will be impossible to us if our faith does not fail.

There is still another equally essential particular in which great and little faith differ the one from the other. The latter is not only staggered by things vast and difficult, really counting these as "too hard for God," but equally so at the minute, counting our daily and momentary cares and perplexities as of such a trifling character as to be beneath the notice of the Almighty, and thus, failing alike in respect to the vast and the minute, finds true rest and peace nowhere. Great faith counts nothing that concerns us as God's sons and daughters as above the power or beneath the notice and care of our heavenly Father, and thus in a "universal trust and confidence, and continued prayer and supplication, with thanksgiving" "in all things" alike, finds peace, quietness, assurance, and deliverance everywhere. Little faith opens its ear to "the prattle of infidelity" against the physical value of prayer," loses all confidence in regard to God's control of physical events, and in regard to all His promises in respect to our temporal concerns. Great faith, on the other hand, "looks into the perfect law of liberty, and continues therein," and rests with absolute assurance upon the testimony and promise of the Author of the universe, regarding Him as better informed in respect to His relations to His own works than creatures of yesterday can be.

We often hear about "trusting Christ in the dark" that is, counting Him faithful that hath "promised," when we have nothing but God's naked word to lean upon, and all is darkness and tempest around us. Permit me to give a single fact here in illustration of this great truth. In the early settlements in America, people are accustomed to dig their cellars beneath their rude habitations, and to enter those cellars through trap-doors in the centre of the main room of the house. As a father, without a light, was in his cellar one day, a little child looked over the brink into the palpable darkness beneath. "Do you see me, my child?" asked the father. "No, pa; it is all dark down where you are, and I can't see anything there." "Well, I see you, and my arms are right beneath you. Step right off now, and you will drop into my arms. Don't be afraid at all. I won't let you fall." Thinking a moment, the child said, "Pa, I will do as you tell me," and stepping off, found itself safe and happy in those arms. How lovingly did that father receive that trusting child to his embrace! So reader, beneath every one of "the promises" are "the everlasting arms." With God's promise to receive you, do not fear to let go every hold, and drop into those "everlasting arms," however dark all but the naked promise may appear. When you shall become thus trustful, you will "enter into rest."

Section VI.—*When the Gospel will Exert its Full Power over our Hearts and Character.*

One question more demands our special attention before closing this chapter. The question is this—When, and upon what conditions, will the gospel exert its full power upon our hearts and character? My method of attaining this high end is this:—My desire and aim is, that each truth, each precept and promise of the divine Word, shall exert its own distinct and utmost influence upon my mind. When I meet with any such truth, promise, or precept, I place myself before it, and abide in its presence until, through the Spirit, it sheds its full influence upon my mind. I read, for example, the following absolute command of Christ:— "Be ye therefore perfect, even as your Father in heaven is perfect." I do not turn away from this precept, saying obedience to it is not expected of creatures. I read the prayer, on the other hand, "Thy will be done in earth, as it is done in heaven," and I thus understand clearly the meaning of the precept.

I read still further the solemn asseveration, "Whosoever, therefore, heareth these sayings of mine, and doeth them, I will liken him unto a wise man that built his house upon a rock;" and "Whosoever heareth these sayings of mine, and doeth them not, shall be likened unto a foolish man that built his house upon the sand." I hence conclude that Christ was in earnest when He uttered this command, and expects me to heed it; to regard myself as without excuse for not rendering the obedience required, or for resting at all when consciously coming short of that obedience. I accordingly look to Christ, as the Mediator of the new covenant, to have Him put this, His own precept, "in my heart, and write it in my inward parts," and cause me to keep it.

So when I read of Christ's power to save, and of the provisions and promises of His grace, I conclude that God is in earnest in such revelations, and means what He says. Without limiting the meaning of what is written, without adding to or taking from the sacred Word of God, "counting Him faithful that hath promised," and not saying to myself, "Christ will not do this, and will not do that," I look to Him to "save me unto the uttermost," as He is able to do; to render His own provisions of grace fully effective in my experience; to render real in me, in all their fulness, every one of "the exceeding great and precious promises;" and, finally, to do in and for me "exceeding abundantly above all that I ask or think." Thus to believe, and thus to trust, I recognise my obligation as absolutely infinite, and I do thus believe and trust. In the same manner do I treat the admonitions of the gospel, such, for example, as the following:—"Fear Him who, after He hath killed the body, hath power to cast into hell;" "Be sober, be vigilant;" "Watch unto prayer;" "Hold fast till I come;" "Work out your own salvation with fear and trembling;" "We are made partakers of Christ, if we hold the beginning of our confidence steadfast even unto the end;" and "Let no man take thy crown." While, with "full assurance of faith," "full assurance of hope," and "full assurance of understanding," I sit under the canopy of God's "exceeding great and precious promises," I desire to have all such admonitions throw their full and solemn shadows over my mind. Thus trusting, thus believing, and thus heeding all that is written, we shall "walk in the light, as God is in the light," and our "feet shall never stumble." Heeding a part, and disregarding a part, of what God has written for our instruction, consolation, and admonition, we shall "walk in darkness and have no light," and shall very likely be rejected at last as "reprobate silver."

And now, reader, "I commend you to God and to the word of His grace, which is able to build you up, and to give you an inheritance among all them which are sanctified." "These things have I written unto you, that you may believe, and that believing you may have life through His name."

THE END.

THE CHARLES G. FINNEY PROJECT.
BY ALETHEA IN HEART MINISTRIES.
THE LIFE AND WORKS OF CHARLES G. FINNEY.

Volume
1. Lectures on Revivals of Religion, 1835, 1868.
2. Narrative of Revivals, or The Revival Memoirs of Charles G. Finney, 1869.
3. Skeletons of a Course of Theological Lectures, 1840.
4. *American* Lectures on Systematic Theology, 1846. Vol. I.
5. *American* Lectures on Systematic Theology, 1847. Vol. II.
6. Lectures on Systematic Theology, *Final* 1851 London edition. Vol. I.
7. Lectures on Systematic Theology, *Final* 1851 London edition. Vol. II.
8. The Character, Claims and Practical Workings of Freemasonry, 1869.
9-16. The Published Sermon Collection.
17. The Published Letters.
18. Life Work and Memories of C. G. Finney by his Associates, Students, and Friends.
19. Theological and Philosophical Lecture Notes.
20. Miscellaneous Letters, Sermon Outlines, Articles, and a Detailed Subject and Scriptural Index of the Complete Works.

Reproduction of the complete works with detailed indexes in hard and soft covers. To be available in print individually and in a complete series; on CD with full searching capabilities; also recorded on tapes, CDs, and DVDs.

Work books and multimedia helps to be created to assist in the private or classroom study of these volumes. A presentation of the influence of Finney upon the church and world to be given through the *American Reformation Project.*

www.ingramcontent.com/pod-product-compliance
Lightning Source LLC
Chambersburg PA
CBHW022106150426
43195CB00008B/284